Become GCP Cloud Digital Leader Certified in 7 Days

Getting to Know Google Cloud

Abhinav Krishna Kaiser

Apress®

Become GCP Cloud Digital Leader Certified in 7 Days: Getting to Know Google Cloud

Abhinav Krishna Kaiser
Bengaluru, Karnataka, India

ISBN-13 (pbk): 979-8-8688-0437-3
https://doi.org/10.1007/979-8-8688-0438-0

ISBN-13 (electronic): 979-8-8688-0438-0

Managing Director, Apress Media LLC: Welmoed Spahr
Acquisitions Editor: Celestin Suresh John
Development Editor: James Markham
Coordinating Editor: Gryffin Winkler
Copy Editor: Kezia Endsley

Cover designed by eStudioCalamar

Cover image by Gianni Crestani from Pixabay

Distributed to the book trade worldwide by Apress Media, LLC, 1 New York Plaza, New York, NY 10004, U.S.A. Phone 1-800-SPRINGER, fax (201) 348-4505, e-mail orders-ny@springer-sbm.com, or visit www.springeronline.com. Apress Media, LLC is a California LLC and the sole member (owner) is Springer Science + Business Media Finance Inc (SSBM Finance Inc). SSBM Finance Inc is a **Delaware** corporation.

For information on translations, please e-mail booktranslations@springernature.com; for reprint, paperback, or audio rights, please e-mail bookpermissions@springernature.com.

Apress titles may be purchased in bulk for academic, corporate, or promotional use. eBook versions and licenses are also available for most titles. For more information, reference our Print and eBook Bulk Sales web page at http://www.apress.com/bulk-sales.

Any source code or other supplementary material referenced by the author in this book is available to readers on GitHub (https://github.com/Apress). For more detailed information, please visit https://www.apress.com/gp/services/source-code.

If disposing of this product, please recycle the paper

Table of Contents

About the Author

 **Abhinav Krishna Kaiser** is a highly accomplished professional working as a partner at a prestigious consulting firm, where he plays a pivotal role in leading digital transformation programs for clients across diverse sectors. He is part of the Distinguished Member of Technical Staff (DMTS) cadre, which represents a select group of best-in-class technologists. With a proven track record in the industry, Abhinav is recognized for his expertise in guiding organizations through complex and innovative changes to stay ahead of the curve in today's dynamic business environment.

Abhinav spearheads various digital transformation initiatives, demonstrating a keen understanding of the unique challenges and opportunities presented by different industries. His leadership is characterized by a strategic and holistic approach, ensuring that clients not only adapt to current market trends but also position themselves for future success. His portfolio includes successfully steering multiple digital transformation programs, showcasing his ability to navigate and drive change in organizations of varying sizes and complexities. His hands-on experience in implementing cutting-edge technologies and methodologies has contributed to the enhanced efficiency and competitiveness of his clients.

In addition, Abhinav is a multifaceted professional with a prolific career as an accomplished writer. He boasts an impressive literary portfolio of five published books, each delving into the intricacies of digital transformation, DevOps, and ITIL. Abhinav's written works serve as authoritative guides, offering valuable insights and practical solutions to professionals navigating the complexities of modern business and technology landscapes.

Beyond his contributions in the written domain, Abhinav is a panel speaker, captivating audiences with his expertise at industry conferences and events. His commitment to knowledge-sharing extends to digital platforms, where he actively engages as a YouTuber and blogger. Through these media, he imparts knowledge, shares best practices, and explores emerging trends, reaching a wider audience eager to enhance their understanding of digital transformation, DevOps, and ITIL. As a thought leader in the digital space, Abhinav's online presence further solidifies his influence, making him a go-to resource for professionals and enthusiasts alike.

About the Technical Reviewer

 **Ravi Mishra** is a distinguished multi-cloud architect with over 15 years of rich experience in the IT industry. His journey commenced as a network engineer, where he laid the foundation for his illustrious career. Driven by an insatiable curiosity and a relentless pursuit of excellence, Ravi transitioned into the dynamic realm of cloud computing. Over time, he honed his expertise across various cloud platforms, including AWS, Azure, GCP, Ali, and Oracle, establishing himself as a seasoned authority in these fields.

A strong academic foundation complements Ravi's practical experience. He holds an electronics engineering degree and a postgraduate diploma in IT project management, providing him with a solid understanding of the technical and managerial aspects of IT projects. Throughout his career, Ravi has collaborated with various global MNCs, demonstrating his ability to adapt to diverse work environments.

Ravi's relentless quest for knowledge is evidenced by his remarkable achievement of acquiring over 43 cloud certifications, a testament to his dedication and proficiency in the domain. As a seasoned Microsoft Certified Trainer for the past eight years, he has imparted invaluable knowledge to over 1,00,000 aspiring professionals, leaving an indelible mark on the industry.

An enthusiastic advocate of emerging technologies, Ravi is a sought-after speaker at various public forums, where he shares his insights on cutting-edge technologies like Copilot, AI, DevOps, Terraform, and cloud security. Additionally, he is the esteemed author of *HashiCorp Infrastructure Automation Certification Guide*, a comprehensive resource that delves into infrastructure automation across AWS, Azure, and GCP using Terraform.

In his free time, Ravi pursues his passions for cooking, badminton, and running marathons, demonstrating a healthy balance between professional excellence and personal well-being. Connect with Ravi on LinkedIn (`inmishrar`) to learn more about his journey and insights on the ever-evolving world of technology.

Introduction

The title of this book could be misleading. Yes, it is meant to help enthusiasts earn Google Cloud Platform's Cloud Digital Leader certification. However, this book is not restricted to digital leaders. It is also a 101 course on anything to do with the field of IT, the cloud, and DevOps, among other foundational concepts that add to the foundation of digital transformation. Whether you're a seasoned IT professional, an aspiring digital leader, or an executive driving organizational change, this book is your definitive roadmap to success in the cloud. I could have very well called the book *Getting Started with IT along with the Google Cloud Platform,* because I have broken down the foundational elements of IT (databases, serverless functions, artificial intelligence, and so on) into easily consumable chunks. It's like baby food!

Dialing back, the premise of this book started with my obsession of digital transformation and Google's interface-friendly ecosystem for the cloud. I must confess that I picked up Google Cloud Platform (GCP) after I had played my hand in Amazon Web Services (AWS) and MS Azure. No disrespect to the other two major cloud service providers, but the simplicity behind GCP was awe-inspiring. It demanded a book, especially when I was in the midst of busiest time of my work life.

The beauty of digital transformation is that it has no boundaries. Its currencies are innovation and agility, and the organizations that showcase these qualities are best positioned to stay ahead of the curve and enjoy unprecedented growth. This is where the cloud comes in, by helping them with the latest innovative products that can be bent at will to meet the organization's objectives. In my previous book, *Reinventing ITIL and DevOps with Digital Transformation,* I introduced the *Battle Tank* framework. It is not prescriptive, but rather a guide for organizations to plan and embark on the digital transformation journey. If you are a digital leader or an enthusiast looking to explore the digital transformation world further, I highly recommend that book, which builds on the concepts of ITIL and DevOps to unravel digital transformation.

In the pages that follow, I dive into the core components of Google Cloud Platform, exploring everything from foundational concepts to semi-advanced use cases. You'll learn how to leverage GCP's vast array of products to drive efficiency, enhance collaboration, and unlock new opportunities for growth.

The book is structured into 13 logical chapters, and each chapter delves into an aspect of the cloud. The first four chapters focus on building the narrative on the cloud, the GCP basics, and digital transformation. Beginning with Chapter 5, GCP capabilities are bundled into chapters for ease of reading and to introduce relevance. For example, Chapter 5 covers the concept of virtual machines, including the various products that exist in GCP that support virtual machines. Chapter 6 covers containers, followed by serverless computing in Chapter 7. These three chapters introduce GCP products on infrastructure.

Chapter 8 shifts the focus to application development with the modernization products. The biggest chapter in the book is Chapter 9 and it covers data. This is followed by the exciting world of machine learning and AI, covered in Chapter 10. Financial governance and security on GCP are covered in Chapters 11 and 12, respectively. Finally, the book concludes with the topics of monitoring, observability, DevOps, and Site Reliability Engineering (SRE).

Google has partnered with Kryterion to enable users to register for this exam. You can take the exam at a physical center or remotely, which is proctored. At the time of this writing, the Google Cloud Platform: Cloud Digital Leader certification exam costs $99 USD. There are between 60-70 questions on the exam and you have 90 minutes to answer them. You are expected to choose the best answer from the options. I don't believe that you need all 90 minutes to answer the questions, but use your time wisely to revise your answers until the last minute. To pass the exam, you need to get 70 percent or more correct. Although the exam is fairly straightforward, the manner in which the questions are posed can be confusing.

I wish you happy learning as you read this book, and I hope that you reach great heights in your career. All the very best!

DAY 1

Approximate Study Time: 1 hour and 26 minutes

    Chapter 1 - 48 minutes

    Chapter 2 - 38 minutes

CHAPTER 1

Cloud Computing Overview

If I had gone into hibernation 15 years ago and woke up today, I wouldn't recognize many aspects of the world. For instance, when flying on an airplane, we no longer need to carry printed boarding passes or flight tickets. So much has gone digital. To wish a friend on their birthday, we can simply order a cake to be delivered to their house in a couple of minutes. In India as in elsewhere, everything is now entirely digital. Even many street vendors use QR codes to accept payment for purchases.

The changes, all good from the perspective of dynamism, are possible because data is available everywhere on any device—be it a smartphone or a laptop. The ecosystem of dynamism has been through its own version of evolution, which is discussed later in this chapter.

The genesis was the cloud. The cloud made it possible for new technologies to take shape. Varied use cases, ideas, and solutions shaped new user behaviors. So what do I mean by the cloud?

In principle, cloud computing refers to unlimited (or an abundance of) computing resources available on demand. Computing resources include servers, routers, storage, and containers, among others. Depending on the requirements, these computer resources can be scaled in a span of minutes if not seconds. Many people no longer worry about infrastructure constraints. Say, for example, I needed to increase the RAM on a server hosted in a datacenter. Prior to the cloud, I had to plan for a downtime,

© Abhinav Krishna Kaiser 2024
A. K. Kaiser, *Become GCP Cloud Digital Leader Certified in 7 Days*,
https://doi.org/10.1007/979-8-8688-0438-0_1

arrange for an engineer to bring the compatible RAM, coordinate with the facilities, and then manage the changes along with the post-change activities. With the cloud, it's as simple as it gets. Through a console, I can increase the RAM, and it is added without any of the pains of going through a physical set of change activities. I have the option of scaling up vertically or horizontally with the click of a few buttons, and I get the option of a load balancer and active backups. With cloud computing, managing and planning infrastructure has become seamless. Cloud computing has helped companies focus on the strategic aspects of their business rather than being bothered with operations, which has the potential to bring down the business.

Cloudification is rampant in organizations, and it continues to grow. Self-managed datacenters are becoming old fashioned and the benefits of the cloud outweigh and out-compare the rationale of owning and managing private datacenters.

Figure 1-1 shows the increase in cloud spending from 2021 to 2023 pointing towards the migration from on-premises to cloud infrastructure.

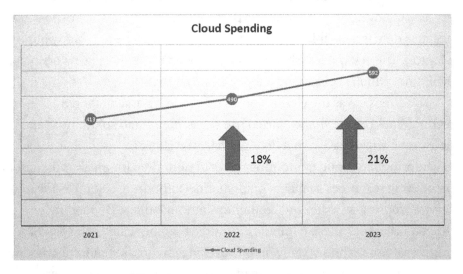

Figure 1-1. *Gartner's increase in cloud spending*

Gartner predicts (ref: https://www.gartner.com/en/newsroom/ press-releases/2022-10-31-gartner-forecasts-worldwide-public- cloud-end-user-spending-to-reach-nearly-600-billion-in-2023) that by the end of 2023, cloud spending is likely to hit 592 billion USD. This is a 21 percent increase compared to the previous year's numbers at 490 billion USD. In fact, the year 2022 saw an 18 percent jump of cloud spending compared to 2021, which clocked in at 413 billion USD. These figures provide insights to those who haven't made the change yet. It is also important that leaders become cloud savvy so they can have meaningful conversations with their clients and teams.

The Evolution of the Cloud

There was a time when major organizations housed their own datacenters. These were secure locations that were access controlled, and in some places, a guard secured the premises. It was considered a privilege to enter these rooms. Once you entered, these massive rooms consisted of stacks of racks and a whole lot of computing devices sitting inside them. Datacenters like these are now a mere memory, with the racks and servers replaced by consoles and GUI-driven controls. This journey is a stamp of evolution in infrastructure technology, and more importantly, it sets the context for future technology growth predictions.

In fact, the cloud is not just about computing infrastructure in specific. The thick red line dividing hardware and software no longer exists, and infrastructure and software have become homogenous. The evolution to cloud computing is a saga that marches from datacenters to the cloud, and the software architecture has gone from monolithic devices to microservices.

Cloud usage can be explained in three stages, as shown in Figure 1-2:

- Pre-cloud era

- Infrastructure cloud era

- Holistic cloud era

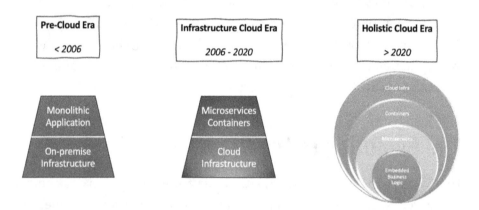

Figure 1-2. *Stages of cloud use*

Prior to 2006 (referred to as the *pre-cloud era*), there was no cloud. It was all datacenters and infrastructure hosted in datacenters. The applications were either monolithic or followed an *n*-tier architecture.

With the introduction of AWS, Azure, and GCP, organizations started to shift their infrastructure out of datacenters and into the cloud. Applications also shifted tack with the introduction of microservices, and container technology took shape. This was the transition era, with a number of organizations making the infrastructure switch to the cloud (hence, it was referred to as the infrastructure cloud era).

Today (the holistic cloud era), the cloud is a strategy for organizations to place all their eggs. There are multiple advantages to this, discussed later in this chapter. The business logic is integrated within the various cloud services, such as AI/ML, serverless, analytics, and so on, and applications no longer sit over the infrastructure. Instead, there is a harmony of various services working in tandem.

The Genesis of Networks

Before I cover computing infrastructure and software, it's important to discuss networks. The underlying technology that made cloud possible is the interconnecting network. Without the Internet, cloud computing would not have been possible. So, the evolution of cloud computing actually dates back to the 1960s, when the first networks were conceived. ARPANET (Advanced Research Projects Agency Network) was the first long-distance network developed in the United States. At the time, mainframes were expensive and mainframe users connected to them through dedicated systems connected to teletype machines. This was also during the cold war, and the thought of single points of failures if these computers were attacked was one of the main drivers for setting up remote networks.

ARPANET was implemented to connect University of California Los Angeles (UCLA) and the Stanford Research Institute (SRI). The mainframe was at SRI, while the users connected to it from UCLA. The network of systems grew through various universities and government institutions across the United States, and it spread to other parts of the world in the 1970s. ARPANET evolved and was replaced by the Internet in 1986. ARPANET was decommissioned in 1990.

Meanwhile, John McCarthy, the prominent American computer scientist, predicted during the MIT centennial in 1961 that "computing may someday be organized as a public utility just as the telephone system is a public utility." He also suggested that there would be a time when people would have to pay to use computers, which is a reality today.

Infrastructure Advancements

Accessing remote computers through networks was a major breakthrough for the evolution of computing, and the next transformation taking shape was the virtualization of infrastructure. Mainframes were expensive, and it was impractical to provision a mainframe for every user. Organizations allowed multiple users to utilize mainframes using the same access, which meant that the files and data were not compartmentalized but rather commonly accessible.

Virtualization

In the 1970s, mainframes got a major boost through the virtualization technology. Mainframe administrators could create multiple virtual machines (VM) on a single physical node. Each VM could run its own operating system, partition data, allocate CPU and memory, and set up other customizations. This VM operating system set the tone for the modern virtual machines, which have taken on a number of characteristics.

Server virtualization is a common feature that divides a physical server into multiple sub-servers. Each server created through virtualization comes with its own CPU, memory, and storage, among other computing resources. While IBM is credited for developing mainframe virtualization, VMware is the company that introduced virtualization in the 1990s to non-mainframe servers (the x86 architecture). X86 machines are typically the computers and servers that run on the Windows and Linux operating systems.

The virtualization technology leverages hypervisors that create a virtual platform on the physical node. This allows multiple instances of virtual machines to be created and used. In short, hypervisors manage the virtual machines on a physical server.

Virtualization using hypervisors flourished. Every datacenter around the globe used this technology. Hypervisor products like Microsoft's Hyper-V, VMware, and Citrix ruled the roost. Then Web 2.0 introduced a limitation.

Cloud Computing

As the digital industry grew, its users, applications, and the need for computing resources grew rapidly. The traditional virtualization was limited to a particular physical server. The maximum allocatable resources are constrained by the resources of the physical server. If a website hosted on a server demanded more RAM, the server had to be brought down, and physical RAM had to be added. With the rampant growth of digital services, this was no longer a feasible solution.

Cloud computing was the answer. It introduced scalability and reached beyond physical computing devices. The cloud technology that leveraged hypervisors could work across multiple physical nodes and pool together resources to present them as though they were coming from a single physical node. Think of it like combining all the servers in a datacenter to make it look like a single physical server. And if you want to build a server with lots of CPU power and RAM, the hypervisor can pull CPU and RAM from multiple systems to create a single powerful server. This upgraded hypervisor technology together with the spread of high-speed Internet made the cloud possible. The next level of flexibility was to access the hypervisors from a remote location that did not have dedicated lines. The only option was the Internet, and with the Internet on broadband, the cloud just eased its way in.

The idea of a cloud with a host of services was started by Amazon with their Amazon Web Services (AWS) in 2006. They started with Simple Storage Service (S3). The first remnants of the cloud were introduced by Salesforce back in 1999. They did this by providing their enterprise-grade software through a website. Users could subscribe to the services, and not really own the software. This concept is in vogue today and is called *Software as a Service* (SaaS).

Google entered the cloud space through their Google docs, which was based on their timely acquisition, Writely. Microsoft's Azure was launched in 2010, followed by IBM SmartCloud in 2011 (now called IBM Cloud).

The Software Evolution

When developers learned to code in those days, all the logic was embedded into a single application—be it how the data was transformed or how the transactions were processed. This was possibly the easiest and most straightforward way to develop an application, and this was the approach that was used in the professional software industry as well. Such applications were referred to as *monolithic applications.*

Monolithic applications are a single application with the all the logic embedded into a single process and componentized into multiple libraries. There is basically one single codebase for the business logic, the user interface, and the database calls, which is the root of all problems!

The problem is not the way the application is structured, but the ability to scale it. All the logic is embedded into a single process, so trying to make changes to one piece may break another piece. Since there is a single codebase, any change that is made, however small, requires the entire codebase to be compiled and tested. Any change risks breaking functionalities or killing performance due to the ripple effect. In other words, any change required the entire codebase to be rebuilt, tested, and deployed.

Think of this as a series of intricate wires running around a room, and you are asked to make changes to a few configurations. What is the probability that you get it right the first time? How much effort is needed to understand the layout of the wires and configure the new ones? What is the impact of wiring two wrong ends? These are the typical questions the change-management board poses whenever any changes are posted, and these questions unravel the complexity behind monolithic applications.

In short, monolithic applications are easy to build, but difficult to maintain. They are harder to scale, and reusing certain components of a monolithic application is the hardest bit.

Moving to *n*-tier

Single-tier architecture is a type of software architecture where all the components of the application are housed and run on a single platform. The software components include the presentation (the user interface), the application/business logic, and the data access/storage, and they reside on a single machine.

Single-tier architecture was predominant during the genesis of software development because it was simplistic and easy to deploy. The problem was that it was compatible with smaller applications and not preferred for applications that needed to be scaled and distributed.

As architectures evolved, the database in a single-tier was separated from the user interface and business logic. This led to a mini-revolution with multiple clients being able to access a single database and offer distributed services over the networks. This concept is called a *two-tier architecture*. Basically, the business logic and the user interface were encapsulated in a single tier, while the database was hosted on another tier.

The next step on the improvement ladder was to house the business logic and user interface into their own dedicated infrastructure. This provided further flexibility for developers to change the user interface without making changes to the business logic and vice versa. This is called a *three-tier architecture*.

The first tier is referred to as the presentation layer (the user interface). The user interface is the look and feel of a mobile application, web application, or a desktop application. This is followed by the application layer (the business logic), in which the information collected from the presentation layer is processed as per the required logic/configurations. It communicates with other layers through API calls. The application layer is developed in languages such as Python, Node.js, and Java, among others. The third layer is the data layer, where the database sits. It contains files and third-party database services. The application layer can read, modify, or delete data based on the logic and the information received from the presentation layer. The data layer typically consists of relational database such as Oracle, DB2 and MySQL, or NoSQL databases such as MongoDB and Cassandra.

Three-tier applications had a number of advantages over monolithic applications, mainly addressing the problems discussed in the previous section. As each of the tiers were physically detached from the others, development could happen on all three tiers simultaneously, which helped develop applications rapidly. Since the entire application was not compiled and deployed for every single change, the risks associated with impact to applications due to faulty changes was reduced greatly. Scaling too became simpler, as developers had to worry only about the tier in question rather than the entire application. Think of it like complexity divided by a third!

The Move to Service Oriented Architecture

The move from a monolithic to a three-tier application sparked a rush of further experimentation, and the result was the concept of building modular applications. These are not quite complete applications but rather small applications for a particular area. The concept is called *Service Oriented Architecture* (SOA) and it leverages software components called *services* that help develop business applications.

Think of a modular kitchen made of multiple cabinets, drawers, and shelves. Each of these cabinets, drawers, and shelves are independently constructed in a way so they work well together, in whatever configuration they are placed. The final outcome is a beautiful kitchen with all the customer's wants and needs taken care of. The manufacturer doesn't have to create individual elements separately, but rather they create a bulk product and retrofit it based on the customer's needs and desires. It's a win-win situation—the customer gets what they desire and at a reasonable price and the manufacturer can churn out more cabinets more quickly, leading to better profits.

Likewise, creating applications as services revolutionized the software industry. For starters, a number of common services did not have to be developed all over again, which lead to faster development.

Let's say that you are developing a new business application that has several parts, such as business logic to make transactions, a shopping cart, a payment system, and a user management system. The logging mechanism can be simplified by using a user authentication service offered by Google, Facebook, or another service provider. This would essentially allow you to focus on other parts of the application. Even for the payment system, there are a number of services available that can accept payments. All you need to do is integrate the payment service into the application. This architecture helps compartmentalize each functionality into a separate service. Making changes to a particular service is limited to that service alone. The entire application need not be deployed all over again, unless there are mitigating circumstances that make that necessary.

The other benefits of the SOA includes the ease of scalability. The application is made up of individual services, so scaling them can be as simple as hosting them on separate servers and running a load balancer. An SOA is also reliable because it does not inherit the risks that are associated with monolithic and three-tier applications. Most importantly, an SOA has changed the face of development, or rather it has provided a common face for development. It has standardized the approach to application development, and a standard way of development is necessary for easy maintenance and governance of applications.

Microservices

While the SOA was heralded as the next big thing, there were inherent weaknesses within it. Due to the nature of its development, the handshakes and validations between services rendered poor application performance. Plus, the cost of development using the SOA architecture was on the higher arc of the spectrum. The biggest disadvantage was its incompatibility with the RESTful web services, owing to real-time dependencies that ended up reducing its resiliency.

Microservices is the relatively new kid in town for web applications. Microservices do not replace the SOA, as the areas to which they apply are quite distinct. SOA is still preferred for hosting enterprise applications. The microservices architecture is the go-to architecture for web applications.

Think of microservices as smaller version of the SOA. While the SOA leverages services that were brought together, microservices goes a level deeper and is the basic application that carries out a task. Think of an SOA service as made up of multiple microservices. For example, to construct a login service, you need a microservice for authentication, a microservice for capturing information from the web, and another microservice for CAPTCHA. All three microservices work together through well-defined APIs that connect seamlessly with each other. The user who is trying to log in to the application sees a single web page, even though in the backend there are multiple microservices at work.

The organization of microservices is not around technology. When a decision is made to migrate a monolith to microservices, the basis for microservice development is not made based on technology. For example, organizations will not have all the frontend developers hooked together to create the presentation layer, and the data folks work on the database-related activities. The division or organization of development work is done around the functionality that is being developed. This would essentially mean that cross-functional teams are working together, which is essentially the idea inspired by the Agile framework and DevOps methodology.

The advantages to using microservices are several. On the top of the list is the ability to scale and make changes on a whim. Since the developers are making changes to microservices, the involved change is only to that tiny application, which is tested and deployed, and due to its small size and simplicity, this can be done rapidly. An application built on the back of microservices can potentially be developed rapidly and the changes can be brought about without going through deep planning, architectural impact, testing, and so on. Suppose a change made to a microservice goes bad. All it takes is to roll back the change involves a particular microservice. Both the deployment and the roll back can be done fairly quickly. On the upside, the customer or the business gets the functionality faster and on the downside, worst-case scenario, there could be a functionality impact for a matter of seconds to minutes. Take the example of Amazon, which has been developing their applications on microservices for a number of years. They deploy over 500 changes every hour while an average company has a quarterly release cycle with various gates defining when the scope needs to freeze, testing needs to confirm, and all other waterfall-inspired centralized governance structures. Microservices give organizations and developers the freedom to experiment. This results in an application that not only has great functionally but is also sound technically.

Why Move to the Cloud

Generally, when you compare two technologies or two products, there are pros and cons. With the cloud technology, there are advantages alone and no limitations. Of course, if your organization has invested in a datacenter and is running applications that do not necessarily have to scale, that might be a good case for sticking to a traditional infrastructure. But for every other organization, moving to the cloud will become a question of *when* rather than a question of *if*.

Cost Savings

Costs drive the majority of business decisions. The cloud offers an avenue where the user pays only for what is being used, which is a solid advantage to bank on. The cost savings from the cloud are the result of no capital expenditure. With the cloud, a company needs to only pay only for what they use.

One might argue that a company that has already invested in a datacenter might find cloud computing impractical, but there are other costs that they avoid, such as paying for datacenter engineers, power, cooling, and maintenance, among others.

The cloud also provides an avenue to save upfront and the charges that accumulate as a result of use. Therefore, it is critical that organizations enforce discipline in using the cloud to ensure that the costs don't overrun.

Scalability

A datacenter, no matter how big, is still limited. There is a point where you need to go out and procure additional resources. The cloud technology on the other hand is massive and the underlying technology can dynamically allocate computing resources and ensure that the resources are available on demand. You can add as much the computing power and resources as needed without having to worry about a new rack or physical space for the new boxes. This is perhaps the greatest advantage the cloud can offer.

Think of a use case where additional computing power and resources are needed during the year-end holidays. A traditional infrastructure shop has to procure and make the infrastructure ready for the holiday season. Once the season is past, the resources will lie dormant until the following season. Not so with the cloud—resources can be scaled up on demand, and scaled down with the same ease as well.

Security

There was a time when the cloud was perceived as risky—because data resided on a remote server. There was a good possibility of a physical server holding data from multiple customers. This supposition is untrue, of course!

Security is top notch, with every cloud service provider (CSP) investing on advanced security solutions and security SMEs to safeguard the customer's data.

Data Backup

There was a time when data backups used to happen on tape drives. In a top multi-national corporation that I worked for during the beginning of this century, the weekly backup was shipped to London from Bangalore for safekeeping. So tedious!

On the cloud, backups are as easy as they come. With datacenters around the world connected through networks, backups can be made with a click of a button and moved to physically distant locations in a matter of minutes. Storing backups is not expensive, because the CSPs have cheaper rates for data storage since they are infrequently accessed/retrieved.

Collaboration

Cloud computing provides an engine for easy collaboration. With the cloud generally accessible over the Internet, teams that spread across locations can collaborate seamlessly with the common data pool and applications that are not restricted to a particular device or region.

This ties in particularly well with the remote and hybrid working culture that we are currently experiencing, plus the onset of rapid development thanks to Agile and DevOps methodologies.

A Look at the Top Cloud Service Providers

The cloud market is getting new players on a regular basis. What started as an innovation back in 2006 by Amazon is now an accepted segment for tech players to participate in and dominate. The beauty of different cloud service providers is that they bring something new and innovative to the table.

For example, GCP's Compute Engine offers live migration of running virtual machines to another host in the same region. Other CSPs require shutting down the VM before initiating the migration. MS Azure is strong in analytics. Its employment of machine learning and artificial intelligence with Cortana Analytics and Stream Analytics has set them apart from the rest of the pack.

Likewise, there are several services that are common to all cloud service providers. Organizations do not opt for a single cloud service, but rather shift their IT load onto multiple CSPs in order to leverage the best of all worlds. This is referred to as a *hybrid cloud*, and managing multiple clouds under a single interface is picking up pace, with several solutions existing to ease the transition.

A study conducted by Synergy Research Group (`https://www.srgresearch.com/articles/q1-cloud-spending-grows-by-over-10-billion-from-2022-the-big-three-account-for-65-of-the-total`) reveals that AWS has the biggest market reach, with its infrastructure services at 32 percent in Q1'2022. It is followed by MS Azure, at 23 percent, and GCP at 10 percent. It is estimated that the enterprise spending exceeded $63 billion USD in the quarter, which is a good $10 billion USD over Q1'22.

Amazon Web Services (AWS)

Amazon Web Services was the first to dip into the cloud business, in 2006. It did not start out as a business on its own, but rather was to serve Amazon's internal IT needs. However, when presented with an opportunity to expand, Amazon jumped in to start the AWS journey.

It took a few years for the cloud service to stabilize before Amazon had enough trust in their own system to move their own website onto AWS—this was in 2010. As its popularity picked up, Amazon started their iconic annual re:Invent conference in 2012, and the following year, it launched certification schemes for individuals.

At the time of this writing, Amazon has spread globally to 31 regions with 99 availability zones. This basically shows how far spread AWS is across the globe. You learn about the regions and availability zones later in this book.

Microsoft Azure

Microsoft's idea of a cloud service was the extension of Windows NT onto the web. The development service, code-named *Project Red Dog*, was meant to be proprietary Microsoft technology on the web. They announced the arrival of their cloud, code-named Windows Cloud, in October 2008, and officially launched it in 2010 as Microsoft Azure.

With Windows as the engine, the adoption rate was slow, and it didn't attract the majority of developers who went the open-source way with AWS. Microsoft's strategy changed to incorporate Linux in their cloud system in 2014. They built partnerships with Red Hat, Canonical, SUSE, and Oracle to bring Linux to Azure. This was a roaring success and about a fourth of their VMs were running Linux as of 2017.

Microsoft Azure by far is the biggest cloud service provider in terms of geographical spread, with 60 regions and 116 availability zones at the time of this writing.

Google Cloud Platform

While AWS and MS Azure began their cloud journeys with infrastructure services (*IaaS*, which is discussed in the following chapter), Google Cloud Platform (GCP) changed tact to offer platform services (*PaaS*, which is discussed in the following chapter). The preview service, called App Engine, was opened to select developers in 2008. It offered a platform for developers to code in Python with limited CPU power, hard disk space, and network bandwidth. Over a period of time, the preview mode provided support for other programming languages as well. In 2011, the App Engine service came out of the preview mode and around this time, other infrastructure services made their way to GCP.

At the time of this writing, GCP is spread across 34 regions and 103 availability zones.

Summary

The evolution of IT services has entered the cloud phase where the traditional datacenter model has been replaced by the cloud services, and the cloud services have moved beyond the realm of infrastructure to all things IT—software, AI/ML, infrastructure, databases, and more. The shift to the cloud was systemic and natural, as the advantages that it provided far outweighed what the traditional means offered.

Amazon Web Services, Microsoft Azure, and Google Cloud Platform are the leading cloud service providers, with a trail of cloud services being offered by smaller competitors.

CHAPTER 2

Fundamental Cloud Concepts

This chapter delves a notch deeper to explain the different types of clouds and the fundamental network terminologies. The topics that are discussed in this chapter lay the foundation for the deeper topics covered in the rest of the book.

When I refer to the cloud, it isn't just the likes of AWS and GCP. Some clouds are for consumption by the general public and some clouds are sealed in a firewall. Each of these clouds serves a specific purpose, and as a cloud digital leader, it is imperative that you understand the benefits and differences between them.

Types of Cloud Environments

A cloud refers to provisioning of infrastructure and add-on application services that are available on demand, flexible to use, and easy scaled, among other aspects discussed in Chapter 1. The cloud does not necessarily have to be one of the popular ones that are ruling the market or even the less popular ones used for specific use cases (such as Oracle Cloud).

© Abhinav Krishna Kaiser 2024
A. K. Kaiser, *Become GCP Cloud Digital Leader Certified in 7 Days*,
https://doi.org/10.1007/979-8-8688-0438-0_2

A cloud implementation can be realized by procuring the services of a cloud service provider such as Microsoft Azure, which can be purchased by anybody who has the financial resources. A cloud implementation can also be created for the sole consumption of an organization. Or, an organization can opt for using certain services from a public cloud service provider and can implement certain cloud services that are in-house.

The three different types of cloud services (as shown in Figure 2-1) are as follows:

- Public cloud

- Private cloud

- Hybrid cloud

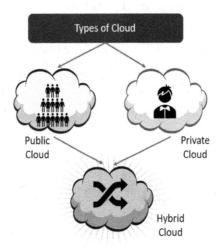

Figure 2-1. *Types of cloud services*

Public Clouds

A public cloud, as the name suggests, is available for anybody to purchase and use. It is generally available over the Internet and managed by third parties. Examples include Google Cloud Platform, Amazon Web Services, and Microsoft Azure. The services offered by these cloud service providers are often driven by a *pay-as-you-go* model.

Because the services are available commonly for the public, the underlying infrastructure is shared among multiple customers/ organizations. This concept is referred to as *multitenancy*. These clouds use high-grade security, so even though the same infrastructure is leveraged to multiple customers, a secure wall ensures that customers and users can access only the data they own. A public cloud is illustrated in Figure 2-2.

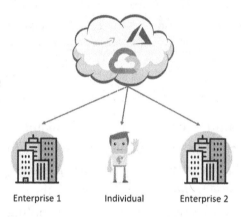

Enterprise 1   Individual   Enterprise 2

Figure 2-2. *A public cloud*

As illustrated in Figure 2-2, the public cloud can be accessed by multiple enterprises and users. Individual subscribers can also access the services offered by public cloud service providers.

Organizations and individuals opt for public clouds because:

- The public cloud service providers offer unparalleled services that cannot be made available in a private setting, due to the sheer size of investments required to develop and keep multiple services afloat.

- The public cloud services are economical. The resources are shared between multiple tenants, and the model where a company pays only for resources they use is much more affordable. This is particularly helpful for organizations just starting out.

- The services offered are scalable and offer flexibility to expand or shrink at a moment's notice (there are exceptions to some services, like long-term storage, which is based on term based contracts).

- The public cloud services are available over the Internet, which enhances the ease of accessibility of cloud services. This can also be a point of concern.

Not all is rosy with public cloud service providers. Some reasons that organizations may want to avoid them include the following:

- Some countries or industries (like banking and insurance) have implemented clauses that do not allow data to be stored out of the country or in a location that is not stored by the enterprise owning the data. This can throw a wrench in the works when opting for a public cloud service.

- The ease of accessibility over the Internet can be a problem. A credentials leak can potentially lead to data leaks and damage a company's reputation.

- The performance of cloud services may not be entirely in the hands of an organization, as the data traverses through the Internet before being consumed. There are ways to mitigate this, but generally, a lot depends on the last mile of connectivity.

- The location of the data stored, or the location of the servers, are known to an extent—such as west of the United States—but the exact location and the visibility of who is accessing the server or when they are accessing it is a black box, which can be problematic.

Private Clouds

A private cloud is when an organization has its own datacenter, and that datacenter meets the needs of the organization alone. Private clouds are built on on-premises datacenters or hosted externally by a third party, as indicated in Figure 2-3.

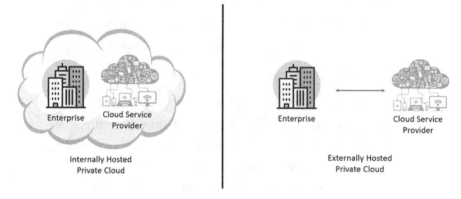

Figure 2-3. *Private cloud examples*

In an internally hosted private cloud, the organization has the option to manage the cloud on its own or can pay a third-party service provider to manage the cloud. The organization is responsible for the hardware, networks, and cloud software, such as OpenStack and Ceph. A hosted private cloud is similar to a public cloud where multitenancy is the norm. However, in a hosted private cloud, physical servers are dedicated to organizations, with no logical separation—so single tenancy is achieved. OpenMetal is an example of a hosted private cloud.

Private clouds offer the following benefits:

- They provide top-notch security, because the organization's data can potentially be stored behind a firewall, and ensuring single tenancy provides physical separation.

- Highly regulated sectors allow data to be stored on private clouds that could be sensitive in nature.

- The entire infrastructure is in the control of the organization, which allows them to implement advanced and customized services that may not readily be available on public clouds.

- Performance and availability of private clouds can potentially be high, owing to physical proximity and the ability to design one's own availability measures.

There are always downsides:

- Private clouds are definitely not economical, because the organization needs to pay for the infrastructure, the networks, and the software. In the case of a hosted private cloud, the pay-as-you-go model exists, but the costs are significantly higher than their public cloud cousins.

- When you have a private cloud, you are required to get the right people for the job and ensure that the maintenance and upkeeping of it is spotless. This can become an overhead problem when the organization's core objective is outside of IT.

- High scalability in internally hosted private cloud is still a challenge based on resource availability.

- The possibility of a private cloud being made available on private office networks can throw a wrench in the works for hybrid and remote working employees.

Hybrid Clouds

A company is said to be using a hybrid cloud if they opt to use a public *and* private cloud. For example, they might host storage services from a private cloud while leveraging servers and other computing devices from the public cloud. The servers are connected to the storage inside the private cloud, either through the Internet or through a private network. A typical implementation of a hybrid cloud is shown in Figure 2-4.

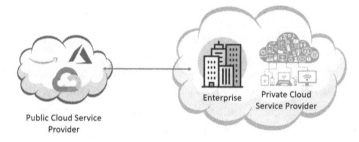

Enterprise   Private Cloud
Service Provider

Public Cloud Service
Provider

Figure 2-4. *A hybrid cloud example*

Customers opt for a hybrid cloud for a variety of reasons, but the most important are usually related to security and regulation. They want to leverage the advanced technologies and services offered by the public cloud service providers while keeping the security aspects internal by employing private clouds, probably inside an on-premises datacenter.

Another use case is when a banking organization leverages mainframes hosted in its own datacenters. While they may find it challenging to move away from mainframes, they have the opportunity to develop frontend GUI (rather than the green screens), which can be hosted on a public cloud. As long as they can make the on-premises mainframes and the public cloud hosted screens work as a single unit, they have a working setup of a hybrid cloud.

Clearly there are advantages to using hybrid clouds. They include:

- Leveraging the best of both sets of clouds. While using on-premises computing resources or a private cloud is imperative, they are making the best application of technology and integration using the hybrid cloud technology.

- Companies fare better with their regulatory agencies and have an opportunity to drive their own security measures for their data. All this can be done while still leveraging advanced services from a public cloud.

- By leveraging hybrid clouds, organizations can scale up quickly and release their software updates faster.

- Hybrid clouds provide an additional layer of flexibility for architects in their solution design. They also provide excellent coverage for backups and options for disaster recovery scenarios.

The disadvantages of hybrid clouds are as follows:

- Managing public and private clouds together is a complex task. It requires precision to be able to manage changes and a good configuration management database (CMDB) to support both structures together.

- The reliability of a hybrid cloud setup is a combination of the public and private clouds. If any one of the clouds behaves poorly, the user-facing applications can be in danger of maintaining their uptime.

Networking Concepts

The age before the cloud was dependent on company networks—between on-premises datacenters and the rest of the office. People had to plug into workstations to access the data and applications hosted on the datacenters. As companies expanded, each of the company locations were connected through underground cables, which were spruced up by undersea cables (discussed later in this chapter) for intercontinental connectivity. This kind of network connectivity helped companies expand, but it had its limits, due to point-to-point connectivity that required planning, budgeting, and execution that was time consuming.

The rocket-like expansion became possible when Internet speeds moved beyond the traditional kilobytes to multitudes of megabits. With the networking easing up with the Internet, cloud computing took shape and gave organizations wings to operate at light speed.

This section covers the basics of networking. The concepts that are covered here are general, but provide the foundation for the deeper concepts discussed later in this book. If you are comfortable with these basic networking concepts, feel free to skip to the next chapter.

IP Addresses

Every home, office, and institution across the globe has a unique IP address. Through these unique addresses, couriers, snail mail, and people can reach specific destinations. Likewise, mobile phone numbers are unique to each one of us. Any device that is connected to a network has an address, referred to as Internet Protocol (IP) address. In short, an IP address provides a gateway to communicating to your device.

IP Packets

Data flows over the network in packets. Each packet consists of two parts: the header and the payload. The *payload* is the data that is being transmitted and the *header* is similar to a postage label (to and from)—it lists the destination and origin IP addresses.

Data that is sent across a network is broken into multiple packets, with each packet having its own header and payload. The packets traverse through the networks to reach the destination and are assembled back on the destination system.

IPv4 and IPv6

There are two forms of IP addresses, the legacy IP address referred to as *IPv4* and the latest one, which is *IPv6*. Although IPv6 has been in place since the mid-2000s, IPv4 is still quite dominant.

An example of the IPv4 address is 25.543.43.111. It has four parts to it and each of the parts can range from 0 to 255 and is separated by a period. Each of the parts is a 8-bit binary number with a limit of 255–111111 converted to binary, totaling 32 bits. Therefore, there are 2^{32} IP addresses that can be accommodated. At the time when it was conceived (in early 1980), it was believed that there were plenty of addresses. But at the dawn of the century, with the boom in computing, a new system was conceived—IPv6.

IPv6 is represented as 2409:40f2:34:42de:75e9:d248:b2e7:6f1f. Instead of four parts, there is eight parts separated by a colon. The numbers are not base-10, as in IPv4, but are written in hexadecimal notation (base-16). A hexadecimal notation uses numbers 0 to 9 and letters a to f. This brings each of the individual parts to 16 bits, and together an IPv6 address is made of 128 bits. The possible range of IP addresses is 2^{128}, which is a number that has 39 digits and is called 340 *undecillion*. Compare this with IPv4, which has a possible pool of 4.3 billion IP addresses, which is 4,300,000,000.

Static and Dynamic IP Addresses

Internet service providers (ISPs) own a pool of IP addresses. When your system is connected to the Internet, the Internet service provider assigns an IP address to your machine. Due to the limited availability of IPv4 addresses, an IP address is temporarily assigned to a machine connected to the Internet, and upon its disconnection, the IP address is sent back to the pool and assigned to a different machine. This temporary assignment of IP addresses is referred to as *dynamic IP addressing,* and it helps ISPs conserve IP addresses.

Customers can also get static IPs, which means that every time they connect their laptop to the Internet, they get the same IP address. When they disconnect, the IP address does not get reassigned. Static IP addresses come at a cost, as they put additional burden on the ISP by reducing the IP address pool.

Public and Private IP Addresses

I mentioned earlier that IP addresses are unique, and that is true. However, IP addresses are unique in their respective ecosystems. For example, I have an Internet connection at home and the Internet terminates at a Wi-Fi router. I have connected five devices to the router to access the Internet. If I check the IP address (through www.whatismyip.com) on each of the five devices, I would find that they bear the same IP address, and yet IP addresses are unique to every system!

The internet service provider assigns an IP address to my location, which is terminated at my router. This public IP address is unique in the sense that none of the other systems connected directly to the Internet will bear it. My router creates an ecosystem for the devices connected to it and assigns a different set of IP addresses to each of the devices. These IP addresses are referred to as private IP addresses. None of the systems within this ecosystem will have the same IP address. Generally, home network private IP addresses begin with 192.168. Other private IP ranges include 10.x and 172.16 through 172.31.

Domain Name Servers (DNSs)

A domain name server (DNS) is like an address book. Every system that is connected to the Internet has an IP address. When people want to connect to a website that is publicly hosted, they do not type its IP address but rather a domain name—such as abhinavpmp.com. A simplistic illustration of how a DNS server is employed is shown in Figure 2-5.

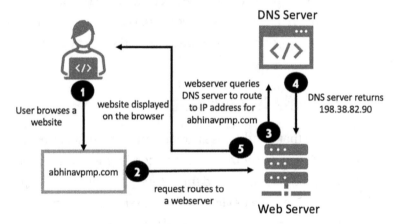

Figure 2-5. *A DNS server illustration*

When a user queries a website, the request is pointed to a webserver that hosts the domain name. The webserver looks to the DNS server, which acts as a lookup table that has a listing of IP addresses against domain names. When the domain name is queried, the DNS server returns the associated IP address. In principle, this is how a DNS works, and there are multiple parts to a DNS server, as well as various types of domains that are translated to IP addresses.

Fiber Optics and Subsea Cables

One of the key reasons that the cloud became a reality is due to the high bandwidth and low latency of networks. From an infrastructure standpoint, the backbone of the networks, which was once on copper, was fully transformed into optical fiber cables.

Fiber optic cables have largely replaced copper cables. They are made of thin glass or plastic fibers, which can enable data travel at the rate of 1 Gbps(compared to copper, which was between 50-100 Mbps). Fiber optics revolutionized the computing industry in unimaginable ways. The Internet lines to most homes use fiber optic cables, including the last mile connectivity. There was a time when people used the Internet primarily to browse websites and read content. Today, people can stream UHD movies and watch without buffering. Such is the technological advancement that fiber optics has afforded. Cloud computing has primarily benefited from the upgrade to the network infrastructure. They didn't have to specifically network with customers across locations, but rather they rode on the back of a powerful Internet to get computing done.

Submarine Cables

Fiber is the best medium for communication. We can also communicate through geostationary satellites that cover every nook and corner of the globe, but this process suffers from high latency. Speed is king when it comes to communication and an important pillar for cloud computing. Cities, counties, and continents are connected through fiber optical cables. Running the cable on the ground is a lot slower and more expensive, so the preferred method is to lay fiber optic cables on the seabed (where possible).

The practice of laying cables on the seabed is not new. It started in the 19th century between England and Ireland and Belgium and the Netherlands with telegraph cables. They used heavily insulated copper cables. Over a period of time, these telegraph cables became common and ran across the Atlantic, connecting India, Southeast Asia, and Australia.

The fiber optic-based subsea cables were laid during the 1980s by a consortium of British Telecom, France Telecom, and AT&T. Since then, subsea fiber optic cables have grown with demand. As of December 2022, there are 486 subsea fiber optic cables connecting 1306 landing stations. Figure 2-6 shows these subsea fiber optic cables.

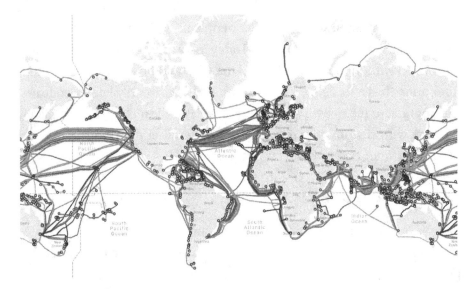

Figure 2-6. *Subsea fiber optic cable map, June 2023 (Credit:* www. submarinecablemap.com *CCL)*

Fiber optic cables are perhaps a size bigger than a common garden hose. Fiber optic cables are encapsulated in silicone gel and include a whole lot of protective layers consisting of steel, rubber, plastic, copper, and nylon. This ensures that the communication channel is well protected and is physically protected from nature, wildlife, and fishing trawlers/ vessels. There are special fiber optic-laying ships that carefully plant the cables on the seabed. Closer to the shore, where there are possibilities of human/naval intervention, subsea plows bury the cables into the seabed.

It is believed that 97 percent of our communications is carried out through fiber optic cables and subsea cables. The remaining 3 percent is through satellites.

Bandwidth and Latency

Bandwidth is commonly misunderstood to be related to network speed, but it isn't. It has nothing to do with network speed. It indicates capacity of a network; how much data can be transported at the same time. Internet services providers offer their services in various grades depending on the bandwidth—like 10 Mbps, 100 Mbps, and 1 Gbps. What they are essentially advertising is the maximum amount of data that can travel in one second. Bandwidth indicates the amount of data that can travel, in other words, the data transfer rate. Consider a water pipe as an analogy—a standard pipe can carry a certain amount of water every minute, while a bigger pipe can transport more water, proportional to its size.

What truly matters to users is not the network bandwidth. While bandwidth is important, *latency* is the true factor that provides an indication of the quality of the network. Latency is defined as the amount of time it takes for data to travel from one point to another. To avoid waiting for data to arrive, people typically expect data to be delivered in under a fraction of a second, but this is not universal. For online games, the expectation of latency can be less than a tenth of a second. This can be the case with online trading as well, when time-sensitive data is accessed. From the water pipe example, think of latency as the time it takes for the water to arrive after turning on the tap.

For cloud computing to work, it is essential that there is sufficient bandwidth available, and that latency is managed to acceptable limits. For example, say you are building a cloud infrastructure and have storage in the eastern United States and users in India. This is not the best architecture. There is bound to be latency because the data has to travel from one part of the world to another, and that takes a certain amount of time, no matter the bandwidth.

Network Edge Datacenters

We all use the likes of Netflix and Apple TV. When we select a title, it automatically starts to play with minimal to no buffer. This is possible through edge computing. Edge datacenters reside at the termination or edge of networks. They primarily exist to replicate and store cached data. This is like a datacenter, but smaller, and caters to users who access frequently accessed data. The objective is to have minimal latency. So, for example, when I start to watch a title on Netflix, the data is streaming from the edge datacenter rather than the datacenter where the content resides.

Specific to the Google Cloud Platform, the data resides on their global network, and it ensures that the data fetch and read functions are almost instantaneous, similar to their Google Search and Gmail applications. You must have noticed how quickly Google reads its indexes based on your search string and comes up with the possible results within a fraction of a second. This is purely a function of their powerful edge networks. Google's edge network liaises with ISPs to get content from outside the network and store them on its own network for quick retrieval. While long-distance communication is handled by fiber optic cables, the edge networks are responsible for the last mile delivery of data to the end users.

Summary

This chapter dug further into the concepts of the network and cloud. All clouds are not the same, and public, private, and hybrid clouds each has a specific place and a purpose in the organization's employment of a cloud infrastructure.

Networking concepts are key to understanding the rest of the book, and to becoming a *GCP: Cloud Digital Leader*. Fiber optic cables and subsea cables provide the backbone for cloud infrastructure to function. The network edge datacenters provide the necessary support for providing seamless connectivity through reduced latency to end users. The networking concepts of IP addresses, domain name servers, bandwidth, and latency were also discussed.

DAY 2

Approximate Study Time: 1 hour and 46 minutes

    Chapter 3 - 31 minutes

    Chapter 4 - 35 minutes

    Chapter 5 – 39 minutes

CHAPTER 3

Infrastructure Concepts

Although the basic infrastructure consisting of servers, routers, switches, and storage has remained intact to this day, the server infrastructure has been segmented into logical layers. This means added flexibility when it comes to infrastructure. These layers are discussed in the infrastructure models section of this chapter. With the creation of layers comes the division of responsibilities between the client's organization and the cloud service provider, or between the managed service provider and the cloud service provider. This relationship is examined under the shared responsibility model.

Cloud Computing Service Models

The world is changing rapidly. To keep up, operations must adapt to the wants and needs of the current generation. Specifically referring to infrastructures, organizations used to manage their datacenters and all the pieces of infrastructure within them. They were responsible for every part of the infrastructure setup. An organization such as a bank, for example, owned and managed their mainframes. They ran big departments to manage the IT and the underlying infrastructure. In the past, organizations

© Abhinav Krishna Kaiser 2024
A. K. Kaiser, *Become GCP Cloud Digital Leader Certified in 7 Days*,
https://doi.org/10.1007/979-8-8688-0438-0_3

had to focus much of their attention on the IT side of things. The new thinking is for organizations to focus on their core business and leave the supporting technology for others to manage. This began with the managed services model, where third-party companies were hired to manage the infrastructure and the software. While third parties managed this, the underlying accountability still lay with the business. They couldn't cut the umbilical cord completely.

With the introduction of *as-a-service* models, the accountability for managing certain infrastructure is outsourced in an abstracted way. For example, if I want to clean my car, I need to purchase car shampoo, a brush, a cloth for drying, and a hose. Using the traditional method, I clean the car myself or hire someone to clean the car with the products I provide. In the new ways of working, which I can call *cleaning as a service,* I outsource the cleaning to a third party with the expectation that the underlying products used for cleaning are also managed and provided by the third party. I am focused on the outcome, rather than the way it gets done. There is a layer of abstraction that allows me as a customer to see and expect an outcome rather than worrying about the intricate details that make it happen.

Coming back to the cloud, based on the level of abstraction, the underlying IT components are abstracted. Businesses don't have to worry about managing individual components and can focus on the big picture. The top *as-a-service* models that are employed are as follows:

- Infrastructure as a Service (IaaS)

- Platform as a Service (PaaS)

- Software as a Service (SaaS)

Figure 3-1 illustrates the various *as-a-service* models compared to the traditional on-premises way of working.

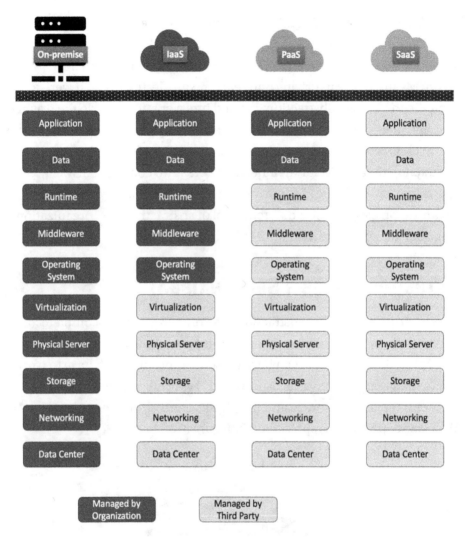

Figure 3-1. *Cloud computing models vs on-premises options*

By creating abstractions such as these, cloud service providers are necessarily removing complexities. *Why should the bank know the type of servers that are leveraged as long as the performance goals are met?*

When I drive a car, I don't need to know how the combustion engine and the transmission work. All I need to know is whether the car works as it should—whether the car is reliable, whether the brakes are effective, and so on. My interest is in driving and reaching my destination. If I were to increase the level of abstraction, I would hire a chauffeur to do the driving and my interest would only be about reaching my destination.

In cloud computing, the organization must decide what level of abstraction that is best for their needs. There is no common answer that organizations should adopt—this decision is subjective and every organization can choose a different level of abstraction. The organization must decide what level of control they require.

Infrastructure as a Service (IaaS)

IaaS is the lowest level of abstraction. The organization has complete access to their infrastructure. Think of this as a datacenter on the cloud. They get a datacenter that can be accessed online, but don't have to worry about managing the physical aspects of it. Typically, the networking elements, including storage and the physical and virtual servers, are part of the IaaS scope. This is represented in Figure 3-2.

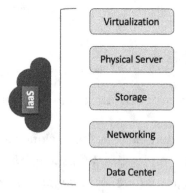

Figure 3-2. *IaaS scope*

By opting for IaaS, the organization gets complete control of their infrastructure, their data, and the applications. With more control, the responsibility to manage all the resources within the scope remain with the organization. IaaS is the best option for organizations that are looking to move out of a traditional datacenter, and IaaS provides a like-for-like solution without the responsibility of physically managing the datacenter and the infrastructure hosted in it. The migration follows the approach called *lift and shift*. With this approach, developers do not make changes to the architecture, but replicate the on-premises infrastructure on the cloud—including the virtual servers, network configurations, and databases, among other things. This will move the company quickly away from the hosted infrastructure and get them started on their cloud journey. Any further changes to the architecture can be done after the cloud implementation/migration has stabilized.

The organization is responsible for the operating system, its implementation, troubleshooting, and everything else that comes along with it. The various driver installations, software, and other platform readiness components are the organization's responsibility as well. The cloud service provider takes care of the physical security and maintaining the datacenter's temperature.

On the Google Cloud Platform, the classic example of IaaS is the Google Compute Engine, which spins up servers with specific configurations (RAM, number of CPUs, operating system, etc.) based on the requirements. A number of servers can be spun up in a short span of time. Google Cloud Storage is another GCP service representing the IaaS side of the cloud computing model; it stores and manages data. There are multiple tiers of data storage to choose from, based on the levels of access and costs.

Moving from a datacenter to the cloud is not only about outsourcing some part of the work to CSP—there are financial implications as well. On the cloud, organizations only pay for what they use, be it storage, servers, or network bandwidth. Further, the capital expenditure required to get started is zero, because the cloud model charges everything by usage and absolutely nothing upfront. This is a big plus, and a great rationale to move to the IaaS model.

While cost savings are good from a business point of view, there are often periods when the business is slow, such as during holidays, as well as busy times. The ability to scale up the infrastructure on demand is the biggest benefit of IaaS. Compare this to a traditional datacenter, where any scaling up requires planning, downtime, and capital expenditures. With IaaS, it's not only straightforward but can be automated as well.

As the cloud service provider manages the datacenters where the infrastructure is hosted, it boasts of state-of-the-art monitoring, auto-healing capabilities, and cloud engineers who work around the clock to ensure high availability of the infrastructure. This leads to IaaS being reliable, efficient, and more productive.

Platform as a Service (PaaS)

With IaaS, the organization is responsible for the underlying infrastructure—the servers, the networking, storage, and so on. If the organization decides to do away with these responsibilities and focus their efforts on the elements that sit on top of it—such as the operating system, middleware, and the applications—they would be operating in the PaaS space. This is shown in Figure 3-3.

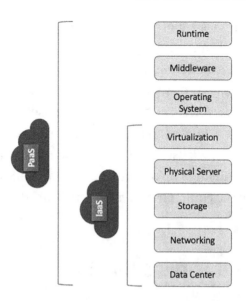

Figure 3-3. *Platform as a Service (PaaS) scope*

Consider an example of a developer's platform. A platform generally consists of an operating system, a runtime environment like JRE, development tools like Spring Boot, databases, DevOps tools like Git and Jenkins, and the other tools used by the developers. Where PaaS excels is that it gives a working environment to a developer, who simply focuses on the coding bit rather than having to build an environment for coding. This helps accelerate the rate of development, supports faster releases, and most importantly delivers value to customers at the quickest pace. SAP Hana Cloud Platform (HCP) is an excellent example of PaaS. It provides an environment where developers have access to 1,000+ applications on the cloud. An SAP developer can leverage what is already available or create something new from scratch to develop an application. Another example is AWS Lambda, which offers a serverless architecture, thus allowing developers to build services that can integrate with the outside world using APIs. The AWS Lambda platform provides everything a developer needs, like fault tolerance and auto-scalability. This means the developer does not have to create the environment in which to work.

The PaaS system also allows developers to pass on the risk of maintenance to the cloud service provider (CSP). Due to its ease of use, communities are built around platforms, which means reusable components are created. This, in turn, facilitates faster development.

On the downside, once a developer starts to use a platform or gets committed to a platform, it becomes all the more difficult to get out of it. The PaaS service can lock users in, which could restrict the direction of travel when the moment to pivot comes. Since the PaaS service generally resides outside of the company's physical structure, data privacy can be a concern as well.

Software as a Service (SaaS)

The direction of travel from IaaS to PaaS to SaaS is to give more responsibilities to a third party. While IaaS provides the basic infrastructure for the rest to build on, and PaaS provides a ready-made solution for developers to build further, Software as a Service (SaaS) offers the end product used by consumers. There is no need to develop the environment or any applications—the application generally exists on the cloud and can be used on demand. Figure 3-4 represents the various components that make up SaaS.

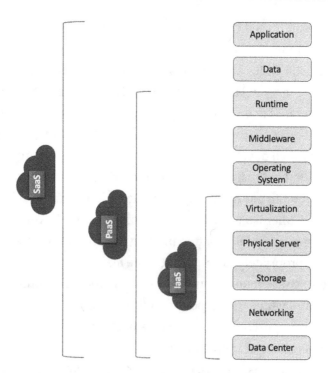

Figure 3-4. *Software as a Service (SaaS) scope*

The majority of services that people use online today are SaaS-based. Take for example Gmail, which is a complete software solution for mail management. The end user can use aspects of the service and is not responsible for the upkeep of the software, the underlying platform, or the infrastructure. The end user is expected to manage their own storage. If the user wants to scale, the email service provides an option to scale the service at an added cost. The user can enjoy the software by paying a subscription fee or, in the case of Gmail, a free service with limited features.

The majority of software manufacturers are putting their software on the web and no longer provide an option where users can purchase the software. Even when such an option exists, it comes with limitations—mainly the lack of updates after a certain period of time. Office 365 is a classic example of how Microsoft turned Office from a standard licensing model to a subscription model. At the time of this writing, the company offers the basic suite of Microsoft Office applications along with cloud storage through their OneDrive service. The Office suite receives updates as long as the user remains subscribed to the service, which necessarily means that users have the latest version at all times. It is a win-win situation in my opinion, as users do not have to shell out significant sums of money for software that will not be supported in the future. In the current economic system, whereby consumers prefer to pay in installments rather than upfront, subscription models fit well. Microsoft also has a perpetual source of revenue, which keeps their engines running better and that means they can staff their developers appropriately to churn out more features.

For the software manufacturers, the SaaS model guarantees a regular revenue stream, which over a period of time, pays a whole lot more than outright software purchases. On the flipside, there is considerable pressure on the manufacturer to keep churning out new features and to keep users glued to their products. Users can switch in an instant to a competitor in a bid to find a product that best meets their needs.

Every coin has two sides! While using the latest version might be best, not being able to choose whether or not to update can be a problem. There could be features that are better in the older version than the newer one, for example. But with SaaS, users don't have a choice.

With the subscription model, the user has the right to stop subscriptions and move elsewhere. But the cost of migration may be preventative. If they have lots of data stored on OneDrive, for example, the migration process will not be easy.

Shared Responsibility Model

I talked about the abstraction layers on the cloud and how the responsibility shifts from the consumer organization to the cloud service provider when moving from IaaS to PaaS to SaaS. It is essential that there is general understanding of who is responsible for which parts of the service, even with a model like SaaS, whereby the cloud service provider is responsible for everything.

Consider the example of Gmail again. Google provides users with a fully functional email service and ensures round the clock availability and top-notch security. The security ensures protection against unauthorized access, but users must ensure that their credentials are strong enough and are not shared with others. It's like a key to a house being handed over to a stranger. No matter how well the house is protected (the Gmail security protocols), with the possession of the key, anybody can walk in and grab everything they want (accessing emails). Secondly, the mails that are sent, received, retained, and deleted are within the purview of the users. Gmail has no control over these. If a user accidentally or unintentionally deletes an email, the responsibility for it falls on them. The shared responsibility model in this instance is simple enough. Users are responsible for the access and the content, while Gmail takes care of the underlying infrastructure, the platform, and the mail application, including security, capacity, availability, and authenticity.

The shared responsibility model is when a service being offered by one entity (CSP) and used by another (end user) is well understood and both parties understand their responsibilities and work within their limits.

Cloud service provider: Responsible for the security *of* the cloud.

Organization/user: Responsible for security *in* the cloud.

GCP's Shared Responsibility Model

Google Cloud Platform has defined the areas of shared responsibility in their cloud computing architecture for each cloud computing model. Table 3-1 shows their shared responsibility model. Anything *in* the cloud is the responsibility of the user and GCP takes charge of infrastructure and related components.

Table 3-1. *GCP's Shared Responsibility Model*

	On-Prem	IaaS	PaaS	SaaS
Content	User	User	User	User
Access policy	User	User	User	User
Usage	User	User	User	GCP
Deployment	User	User	User	GCP
Web application security	User	User	User	GCP
Identity	User	User	GCP	GCP
Operations	User	User	GCP	GCP
Access and authentication	User	User	GCP	GCP
Network security	User	User	GCP	GCP
Guest OS, data, and content	User	User	GCP	GCP
Audit logging	User	GCP	GCP	GCP
Network	User	GCP	GCP	GCP
Storage and encryption	User	GCP	GCP	GCP
Hardened kernel and IPC	User	GCP	GCP	GCP
Boot	User	GCP	GCP	GCP
Hardware	User	GCP	GCP	GCP
Physical security	User	GCP	GCP	GCP

In the on-premises model, the organization that runs the datacenter and the applications is the responsible party. They are responsible for everything that happens at any of the layers, including physical security, infrastructure (hardware), the applications, and the user content.

Moving to the next layer of abstraction, the IaaS, the organization transitions some of the responsibilities to GCP, such as the physical security to the datacenter and the infrastructure, the infrastructure, and the network, along with monitoring and logging the infrastructure and physical layers. The rest in the stack (the operating system, the applications, and the content) is still the responsibility of the organization.

With PaaS, more responsibilities are passed onto GCP. This is in addition to the responsibilities undertaken with IaaS, which includes the operating system, network security, and monitoring and logging for the platform components. The organization remains the responsible party for the deployed applications and the content.

In the highest level of abstraction, SaaS, GCP takes on even more responsibilities, including the deployment of applications, versioning, and application-level security. The organization remains responsible for the content and access policies.

Due Diligence in Understanding and Implementation

Table 3-1 shows the shared responsibility model in black and white, with no ambiguity between what is taken care on the CSP side and from the organization's end. In reality, it is not usually so straightforward. There are certain gray areas where certain security aspects may be compromised because each side believes that the responsibility is the other side's.

To ensure that maximum care is undertaken to safeguard these cracks, and to overcome the boundary responsibilities, the following activities can serve as a starting point:

1. Understand the shared responsibility model, not just from a theoretical perspective but in the GCP implementation in your organization. Understand the services leveraged, which cloud computing model it falls under, and whether GCP is managing aspects of it. If you have questions, talk to the GCP support team to confirm the understanding and to fill in the gaps where needed.

2. Based on the understanding gained of the shared responsibility model, list the various areas of responsibility. The ones under the organization's control need to be managed and monitored.

3. Define processes and procedures to control the responsibilities within the organization's control. The processes must be augmented by tools that can automatically monitor the areas of responsibility and raise alerts during breaches and other abnormalities.

4. GCP upgrades its services frequently. They introduce new services as well. Whenever there are changes to services or new services are deployed, the shared responsibility model needs to be reviewed and maintained for changes. This is a manual process, but it is a worthy exercise that all organizations must undertake.

Summary

This chapter looked at the popular cloud computing service models: Infrastructure as a Service (IaaS), Platform as a Service (PaaS), and Software as a Service (SaaS). Each of the service models were applied to specific business scenarios and use cases. The GCP shared responsibility model was also introduced in this chapter, and it identifies the responsibilities of the cloud service provider and the organization in the context of the cloud computing service models. It is not only important to understand the shared responsibility model, but you should also be able to apply it to all the cloud-related programs.

CHAPTER 4

GCP 101

The earlier chapters covered the cloud computing basics that are common across all cloud service providers. While these basics remain constant between all CSPs, each CSP provides a different offering to organizations wanting to use the cloud.

Google Cloud Platform (GCP) is powerful in the data analytics and machine learning spaces. There is a strong focus on services like BigQuery, Cloud Dataflow, and Cloud AI. Advanced machine learning capabilities and ready-to-use services like Cloud AutoML simplify the development and deployment of machine learning applications. If the applications heavily rely on advanced data processing or require sophisticated machine learning capabilities, GCP's offerings are highly attractive. There is also the possibility of Google datacenters being hosted in a geography that is in proximity of the users or other integration points, which can be beneficial in reducing latency.

This chapter goes into GCP-specific topics on account creation, explains the concept of regions and zones from a GCP context, and covers high availability and disaster recovery.

© Abhinav Krishna Kaiser 2024
A. K. Kaiser, *Become GCP Cloud Digital Leader Certified in 7 Days*,
https://doi.org/10.1007/979-8-8688-0438-0_4

Creating a GCP Account

Creating a GCP account is as easy as creating any other Google account. In fact, you can tie in your existing Google account to GCP.

1. Find the Google Cloud Platform by visiting `https://cloud.google.com`.

2. Click Get Started for Free (see Figure 4-1).

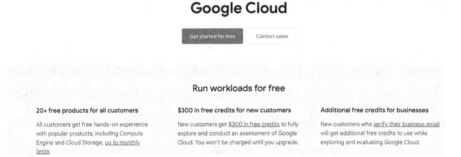

Figure 4-1. *The GCP landing page*

3. If you already have a Google account, click the Sign In button and enter your account credentials. If you don't have a Google account, click the Create Account link and follow the instructions to create a new Google account.

4. You will be taken to the GCP website, and you are required to set up a billing account to proceed (see Figure 4-2).

Step 2 of 2 Payment Information Verification

Your payment information helps us reduce fraud and abuse. If you use a credit or debit card, you won't be charged unless you turn on automatic billing.

👤   Account type ✏️

    Business

    Only Business accounts can have multiple users. You cannot change the account type after signing up. In some countries, this selection affects your tax options. If you choose Individual as your account type, you agree that use of your account is for your trade, business, craft, or profession. Learn more

📇   Business name

    GCP CDL Book

Payment method

Card details

You'll be charged automatically on the 1st of each month. If your balance reaches your payment threshold before then, you'll be charged immediately. Learn more

Access to all Cloud Platform Products

Get everything you need to build and run your apps, websites and services, including Firebase and the Google Maps API.

$300 credit for free

Put Google Cloud to work with $300 in credit to spend over the next 90 days.

No autocharge after free trial ends

We ask you for your credit card to make sure you are not a robot. If you use a credit or debit card, you won't be charged unless you manually upgrade to a paid account.

Figure 4-2. *Billing account setup on GCP*

5. You will be prompted to activate your account. The account setup process is complete after this step (see Figure 4-3).

Figure 4-3. *GCP account setup complete*

The free GCP account tier comes with a one-time credit of $300 USD or an equivalent currency in your country (₹ 24,617). The free tier is enabled for 90 days from the date of signing up. If you run a business, you can claim additional credit to be used within the stipulated 90 days.

Think of the free tier as the training ground for learning the various services of Google Cloud Platform. The free tier comes with limits, but they do not stop learners from exploring the GCP services. You can:

- Create a virtual machine (`f1-micro`) with a maximum storage of 30GB.

- Store 5GB data and perform 5000 actions every month.

- Create container orchestration using Kubernetes.

- Build web applications and mobile backend applications.

- Monitor and create alerts for your applications.

- Read facial recognition, OCR, and labels using Vision AI and more!

More than 20 services are offered in the free tier at the time of this writing. Specific services that are offered change with time and further innovation. You can find the current set of free offerings at `https://cloud.google.com/free`.

Google's Network

Google cloud is a global network. Google owns the vast majority of undersea cables and spans across 200+ countries. In terms of volume of traffic, Google's network is believed to carry about 70% of world's Internet traffic.

Figure 4-4 shows Google's world network with the current and upcoming undersea cables.

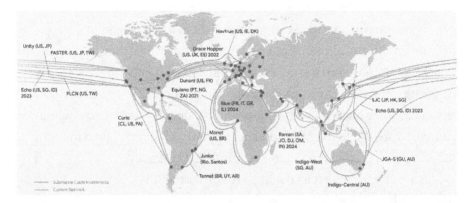

Figure 4-4. *Google's holistic network (https://cloud.google.com/ about/locations#network)*

Regions and Zones

Regions

In GCP terminology, a *region* is an independent geographical area where cloud resources are hosted; they consist of one or more zones. At the time of writing, Google owns 40 regions across the world. Depending on demand, Google has built datacenters at key geographies to ensure they provide low latency and improve the performance of applications in the demand area. Different regions are required to ensure data regulations and legal compliance. For example, Switzerland does not allow its banking data to reside outside of its borders, so a region in Switzerland is employed by Swiss banks. The pricing for GCP cloud resources is not even across regions. So, a customer can choose regions that are cheaper if latency and regulations don't impede.

A company based in Australia will prefer to have its datacenter in Sydney or Melbourne rather than tucked away somewhere in the United States. The other case could be of organizations catering to global customers—say for example YouTube. Videos stored in a single location would cause plenty of lag for users who are farther away from the datacenter. It therefore becomes necessary to replicate the data across the globe. The most commonly viewed video content is stored across various datacenters for faster access and reduced latency. Imagine having to stream a 4K video over the Internet with high latency. The constant buffering would spoil the video-streaming experience.

Also, regions can act as backups for other regions in case of unavailability.

Examples of regions are `asia-south1`, which is based in Mumbai and `europe-west2`, based in London. Figure 4-5 indicates the current and upcoming regions across the globe. Blue dots represent the current regions, and white triangles are upcoming regions.

Figure 4-5. Google's global regions (`https://cloud.google.com/about/locations#regions`)

Zones

While a region is an area that hosts multiple datacenters, a *zone* is made of one or more datacenters. Every zone is completely isolated from other zones in the area with its own power and cooling systems. The idea of creating zones is to build a backbone for strong redundancy. Zones are represented by characters (a, b, c, and so on). Figure 4-6 represents three regions—Mumbai, London, and Iowa.

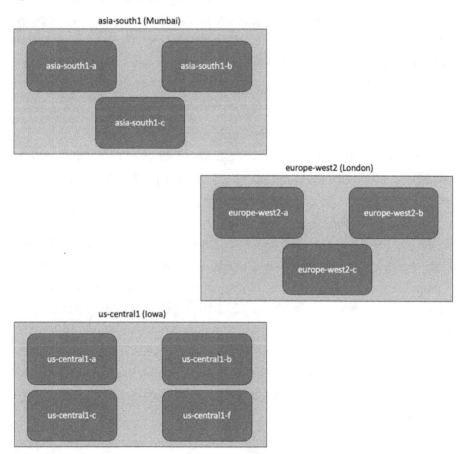

Figure 4-6. *Representation of regions and zones*

Zones are named with a suffix after the name of the region. Mumbai zones are `asia-south1-a`, `asia-south1-b`, and `asia-south1-c`. This means that in the geographical region of Mumbai, India, there are three datacenters in close proximity. Each of these datacenters operate independently.

Every product in GCP is realized in a zone, and an architect can choose to build redundancy within the same zone, within the same region, or between regions. A zone can go down due to a power or a cooling failure. It is unlikely that a region would go down altogether, unless it is struck by a disaster of epic proportions. In such an unlikely scenario, it would be wise to set up redundancy or balance the load between multiple regions to ensure that the business keeps churning no matter the fate of a zone or a region.

Exam Tip   *The number of regions and zones will not appear on the exam, as these are dynamic numbers that change frequently.*

There are 37 regions and 121 zones at the time of writing (refer to `https://cloud.google.com/about/locations` for the latest count). Not all the products are present across the zones. For example, Cloud Firestore is available in Mumbai but not in Iowa while, Bare Metal Solution is available in Iowa but not in Mumbai. There is no particular logic behind which products are available in which region. An architect needs to work with the available products at specific regions to build the solution. There are certain products that are global in nature (are available at all regions), such as Computer Engine, Google Kubernetes Engine, and Cloud Storage, among others.

> **Exam Tip**   *You are not required to remember the global and regional products, or to know which products are available/unavailable in certain regions.*

Network Edge Locations

A network edge is the entry point into a network. For the Internet, the data from your device traverses through your cloud service provider's network before entering the Internet. Google has built a massive global network that is the backbone for all their services, such as Gmail, YouTube, and others. The same network is leveraged by Google Cloud Platform.

Figure 4-4 depicts the Google global network and the gray circles across the geographies indicate the network edge locations. For the best possible performance, cost effectiveness,. and minimum latency, the architecture should consider keeping their traffic on the Google network for the majority of its journey. The longer the distance between Google's network edge to the source of data transmission, the greater chance of added latency.

Google's network that closest to the users is their Google Global Cache (GGC) nodes, which are edge nodes. Popular content that is frequently accessed by users is stored in GGCs for quick retrieval. Figure 4-7 showcases the GCCs, which are spread across 1,300 cities in more than 200 countries.

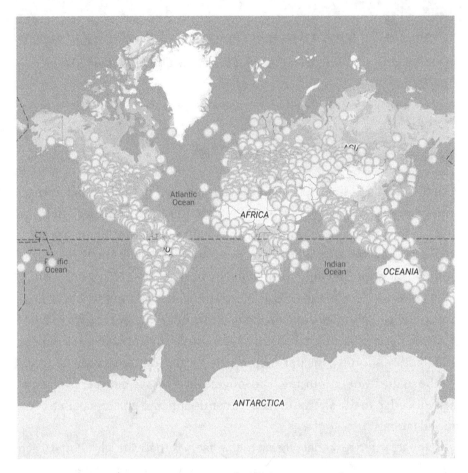

Figure 4-7. *Google Global Cache (GGC) network (`https://peering.google.com/#/infrastructure`)*

In these edge nodes, network operators and ISPs host Google supplied caches inside their network. When a common content is requested, it flows from the edge node, which may be few hundred miles away from the user rather than traversing across half the globe. These caches are temporary, and they are updated frequently.

High Availability

A company may offer the best services, but if they aren't available when users want to use them, these services will be perceived as failures. In the computing world, services must be available around the clock. Suppose a service, such as WhatsApp or Facebook, goes down. When this happens, it is big news. This is bad publicity and can lead to losing users.

Availability is an information security feature along with confidentiality and integrity. The three are referred to as the CIA triad. From the security angle, confidentiality manages access control, integrity refers to the data's trustworthiness, and availability is how reliable the data is to access.

High availability refers to systems having redundancies to allow for extended periods of uptime, which translates to minimal downtime. For cloud computing to work, it is imperative that the services have extended periods of availability and are reliable. Going back to WhatsApp and Facebook, how often have you heard about them going down? Maybe once every two years? These services are reliable because they are powered by high-availability solutions. There are multiple layers of redundancies built in to ensure that the failure of individual components do not affect the availability of the overall service.

Characteristics of High Availability

Achieving high availability is expensive. It's like having readily available backups and technology waiting to ensure seamless transition between one system and another. Let's say that you want to travel to the airport from your home and you decide to hail a taxi. What is the guarantee that the taxi will come on time? How do you know that the taxi won't break down

67

midway? What about traffic jams? All these aspects could prevent you from getting to the airport on time. Thus, to ensure that you build redundancies for your trip to the airport, you call for two taxis instead of one. While you sit in one of the taxis, the other one follows, only to be used in case the taxi you are sitting in breaks down. You also planned a circuitous route that follows the public transportation route, like the train or the bus. If there is a traffic jam, you could catch the train to the airport. As mentioned earlier, getting to the airport is not cheap. It might have been if you used a single taxi. But the redundancies you introduced (the additional taxi and the circuitous route) make your ride a lot more expensive. On the flipside, your probability of reaching the airport on time is much higher.

With cloud computing, high availability is achieved through several methods. Some of employed methods are as follows:

- *Redundancy:* Redundancy can be built at multiple levels. It can be developed to replicate datacenters, storage, network, servers, and other computing elements. The essence of redundancy is that a backup component can seamlessly take over when a component fails, ensuring that the service remains available (generally without blips).

- *Load balancing:* With redundancy, the backup component remains inactive until the primary component fails. However, with load balancing, both components are active and are routed through a load balancer that ensures uniform distribution of data traffic across the components. For example, if you are using massive Excel spreadsheets on your laptop, the data processing and computer might appear to slow down. Instead of using one laptop, you use two laptops to work on different spreadsheets, then you observe that the speeds of both the laptops is faster than using a single laptop. The intent of a load balancer is to ensure that no single resource is overloaded and becomes a bottleneck, and to optimize resource usage.

- *Auto-scaling:* The next level of maturity comes through auto-scaling. A traditional load balancer will have a set number of resources/components that are load balanced. For example, five servers may be load balanced to ensure the best possible performance. Say that the traffic exceeds the design specs for the five servers to manage. For optimal performance, seven servers are required. While traditional load balancing is static, the auto-scaling feature that cloud services offer can automatically append additional resources based on defined conditions, and it can reduce the number of resources if the traffic is below the threshold.

- *Fault tolerance:* High-availability systems are designed to be fault tolerant: detecting and responding to failures proactively. Tools monitor the health of components in real-time. If there are any abnormalities, the system is designed to reroute to healthy components or employ self-healing capabilities.

- *Geographic distribution:* This is an extension and combination of redundancy and load balancing, where none of the resources are allowed to be single points of failure. By spreading the resources across geographies, outages due to regional disasters will not bring down the entire service.

Measuring High Availability

Online services typically advertise their annual uptimes in terms of percentages. Most web hosts offer 99.9 percent uptime annually. What this means is that over a period of one year, the service will be available for 99.9 percent of the time, which roughly translates to 8 hours and 46 minutes of downtime in a year. This downtime could happen all at once, which would be more than inconvenient, or it could be spread over a period with multiple outages and downtimes, which results in questioning the reliability. Either way, a service provider will intend to deploy high-availability measures to ensure that the availability and reliability of the service remains high.

Availability is measured by the amount of time a service is available over the total service time. The formula to calculate availability is as follows:

Availability (%) = (Total Available Time/Total Time) * 100

Total Available Time is the time that the service stays up across the measurement period. A service that is operational and accessible to users is considered up.

Total Time is the total time that is available over a measurement period. It could be in days, weeks, months, or years. Do not presume that all services are available 24x7, 365 days a year. The service contract will clearly specify the service window, which should be considered the Total Time. For example, a call center may operate from 9AM to 9PM. So, in calculating percent availability, the Total Time to be considered is 12 hours.

Terms and conditions related to availability are generally stated as a percentage measured over a certain period. Table 4-1 indicates the various availability percentages and the downtimes associated with them for a year, a month, and a day.

Table 4-1. *Service Availability Chart*

Availability Percentage	Downtime Per Year	Downtime Per Month	Downtime Per Day
90%	36.5 days	3 days	2.4 hours
95%	18.25 days	1.5 days	1.2 hours
97%	10.95 days	21.6 hours	43.2 minutes
98%	7.3 days	14.4 hours	28.8 minutes
99%	3.65 days	7.2 hours	14.4 minutes
99.5%	1.83 days	3.6 hours	7.2 minutes
99.9%	8.76 hours	43.2 minutes	1.44 minutes
99.99%	52.56 minutes	4.32 minutes	8.64 seconds
99.999%	5.26 minutes	25.92 seconds	0.86 seconds

High availability is a generally referred in terms of *9s*. The higher the number of *9s*, the better the availability percentage and the uptime are. For example, two 9s (99%) represents an outage of 3.65 days over a period of one year, which generally is acceptable in the bracket of high availability. Likewise, three 9s (99.9%) reduces the downtime significantly to under nine hours in a year.

Google Cloud Platform offers varying availability terms for their individual services. Their Google Compute Engine (servers) are guaranteed 99.99 percent uptime within a specific region. Their messaging service Pub/Sub is at 99.9 percent uptime. You can refer to service availability terms and conditions on the respective service pages on the GCP documentation website (`https://cloud.google.com/docs/`).

No service provider offers 100 percent availability, as there is no guarantee that any service will be available for the total period of available time.

Disaster Recovery

Everyone knows what a disaster is. It's any untoward incident that is serious enough in nature to bring down IT services. A power blip or a server crash don't qualify as disasters, but serious outages stemming from natural calamities like floods, volcanoes, and earthquakes, and human calamities like rioting, strife, and war are regarded as disasters. Organizations cannot avoid disasters; they need to develop a plan for their eventuality. Disaster recovery in principle is about how quickly an organization can restore their services and make them available to users.

Before the COVID-19 pandemic hit, most employees worked out of their offices and used their office networks, which were generally deemed safe. But when disaster struck, overnight people had to work from their homes and use the bare Internet for all official purposes. A disaster recovery plan was put into motion to strengthen the protocols on the endpoint systems, to ensure that company data stayed within it, and anything moving out was heavily scrutinized. Most companies came out on top, although they were not ready to begin with. Generally speaking, disaster recovery (DR) plans are proactive and preemptive. All the plans are carefully laid out, and various drills are held to test the disaster recovery measures. COVID-19 was a once-in-a-lifetime disaster (we hope), and companies were totally unprepared. And yet, thanks to the cloud and the platforms powered by cloud, IT-run businesses were functioning as normal as possible pretty quickly.

Aspects of Disaster Recovery

Disaster recovery is a deep topic and is studied extensively with the support of dedicated teams. The international standard ISO-27031 dictates the minimum controls required to be worthy of dealing with natural or manmade disasters. To understand disaster recovery, there are a few aspects you must consider:

- *Disaster recovery plan:* A comprehensive plan that delves into various measures and procedures to be undertaken during the course of a disaster. This plan includes roles and responsibilities of the people involved, actions to be undertaken to bring the services back online, communication protocols, and recovery priorities.

- *Redundancy:* Developing redundancy in the architecture helps prevent service outages during disasters and is the best approach to undertake to deal with disasters.

- *Data backup:* Critical data needs to be backed up regularly, a fundamental aspect of data recovery. Data can be stored onsite (which is less secure), offsite, or on the cloud to ensure redundancy and facilitate data recovery.

- *Testing and drills:* Disasters are not a regular occurrence, so the best of plans developed for disaster recovery can fail due to lack of experience. To ensure that the weaknesses in the plan are identified, procedures are reiterated, and all stakeholders know their roles in the recovery process, it is necessary to run disaster recovery drills to test the plan and to check for readiness.

Key Terms when Planning for Disaster Recovery

A disaster recovery plan includes roles and responsibilities of stakeholders involved, actions to be undertaken to restore services, and the recovery priorities. Underlying all the best laid plans are two controls that define the swiftness of recovery and the architectural decisions to be undertaken.

- *Recovery Point Objective (RPO):* An RPO indicates the company's appetite for the maximum acceptable data loss measured in time. It indicates the amount of data the organization is willing to lose in the event of a disaster. Consider an RPO of one hour, where the organization can tolerate up to one hour of data loss. If backups are taken every hour (8AM, 9AM, 10AM etc.), then in the case of disaster recovery, the organization may lose up to an hour's worth of data.

- *Recovery Time Objective (RTO):* An RTO indicates the maximum downtime that the organization can tolerate and is measured in time. It specifies how quickly the systems and applications must be restored after a disaster—in other words, an organization must quickly leverage their backup actions to meet the RTO targets. For example, an RTO of two hours means the systems should be up and running within two hours of a disaster.

Exam Tip   *Questions that appear on the exam combine the understanding of Google's regions and zones along with disaster recovery terms.*

Summary

This chapter waded into the Google Cloud Platform (GCP) specifics. A region is a geography where Google hosts datacenters, and regions are made up of multiple zones to bolster redundancy. Network edge is the entry point into Google's network and the spread of Google's network edges is quite dense across countries.

High availability is a key characteristic that determines the success of a cloud service. There are numerous ways to achieve high availability – redundancy, load balancers and auto scaling to name a few. Disaster recovery goes hand in hand with high availability, and a disaster recovery plan is an essential exercise to predict all the things that could possibly go wrong, and the potential actions that could be undertaken.

CHAPTER 5

GCP Virtual Machines

Cloud computing basics have now been covered, so this chapter moves into the business end of the GCP Cloud Delivery Leader certification preparation. The next four chapters explore the infrastructure and application modernization topics, which account for 30 percent of the exam questions.

Virtualization is a key component of infrastructure modernization and has become the foundation for the infrastructure architecture setup. It forms the basic learning step into any cloud certification program, and this chapter looks at modernizing infrastructure through the Google Cloud computing architecture and the VMware Engine virtualization technologies. As the line between IT infrastructure and applications becomes blurred, containers represent both IT infrastructure and application modernization realms, and they are discussed in the next chapter.

There was a time when monolithic applications and hosted datacenters were the norm. We have gradually moved away from them, and into the cloud, microservices, and serverless technologies. This transformation is possible only if organizations have it in them to change their culture. This does not happen overnight and there must be sufficient push from the top to change. Unless an open, dynamic, and transformative culture is part of the organization, it will remain a dinosaur and quite possibly go extinct.

© Abhinav Krishna Kaiser 2024
A. K. Kaiser, *Become GCP Cloud Digital Leader Certified in 7 Days*,
https://doi.org/10.1007/979-8-8688-0438-0_5

This section breaks down the cultural characteristics that an organization needs to stay current. For technical advancements, it is imperative that the company mindset be based on innovation. Employees must be encouraged to find effective or efficient ways of achieving solutions. Unless and until they are allowed to experiment, an innovative culture can't exist. To encourage experimentation, organizations must allow leeway for failures and promote blamelessness.

With the market trends changing by the week, the absolute need is for all the stakeholders in the organization to become agile, where the requirements are not frozen months and years ahead of time, and development and testing is done through iterations. This should be followed up by frequent releases, which keep the product fresh in a market that measures performance based on the frequency of release and the quality of features.

Innovation, experimentation, and agility do not work unless the organization is customer focused. Keeping customers close will differentiate those who win and those who remain on the sidelines. The market today is subscription based, and customers have the power to switch to another product. Organizations must ensure that they are attentive of their customers' needs and develop what the customers want and need.

The other elements that influence digital transformation and modernization are the operating model, the team structure, and how the knowledge is managed. One of the key tenets of DevOps is to bring the development and operations teams together to reduce conflicts and increase collaboration between the build and run teams. Likewise, for modernization to work, a traditional team structure—such as having a separate Wintel team and a UNIX team—may not work. The team structure needs to be designed to create synergy and reduce friction. Organizations must also value their assets and create a system to create, store, and improvise them over time. Organizations differentiate themselves from the pack on the back of assets, accelerators, and their knowledge-management systems.

Exam Tip   *You might be asked a question about the factors that influence modernization in organizations. The theme and content in this opening section should help answer such a question.*

Google Cloud Solution Pillars

Digital transformation is the journey and the target for all companies. With the Google Cloud, the solution framework begins with seven pillars, as shown in Figure 5-1.

Google Cloud Solution Pillars

Figure 5-1. *Google Cloud solution pillars*

The seven Google Cloud solution pillars are as follows:

- Infrastructure Modernization

- Business Apps Platform Portfolio

- Application Modernization

- Database and Storage Solutions

- Smart Analytics

- Artificial Intelligence

- Security

Exam Tip   *The Google Cloud solution pillars are an important topic on the exam. You may be asked to identify the right solution pillar based on a given digital transformation scenario.*

Google has developed a framework to help organizations assess the maturity levels of their cloud adoption. This framework provides guidance on where they are and what they need to do to move up the ladder. This framework is called the Google Cloud Adoption Framework (`https://cloud.google.com/adoption-framework`).

Exam Tip   *There is a small probability of the Google Cloud Adoption Framework appearing on the exam. The question could test your understanding of the framework's objective.*

Pillar 1: Infrastructure Modernization

Typically, the journey to the cloud begins with the infrastructure. Therefore, infrastructure modernization is the first pillar. This provides flexible options for the organization to opt for virtual machines, storage, serverless computing, Anthos, or any related products.

Pillar 2: Business Applications Platform Portfolio

An organization's ecosystem consists of several applications, with a combination of those hosted on the cloud and perhaps some hosted on on-premises servers like mainframes. Working in one ecosystem or the other is straightforward, but when a combination is used, there needs to seamless connectivity between the two systems. The Business Applications Platform Portfolio pillar provides hooks and APIs to connect systems and automate the process. This involves products such as Cloud SDK, Cloud API, and Cloud CLI.

Pillar 3: Application Modernization

While modernization begins with the infrastructure, the core of transformation lies within the Application Modernization pillar. Customers and users use products that are software based, therefore it is all the more important that applications be relevant and dynamic. To make this happen, applications are expected to host features that might change often, and the rate of evolution is measured in weeks and months rather than years. Applications have evolved from the monolithic architecture to the current microservice architecture, and this transformation is one of the key elements of application modernization. Further, to support application modernization, cloud-native products such as Google's App Engine play a pivotal role.

Pillar 4: Database and Storage Solutions

While infrastructure and application modernization holds the key to their respective areas, the underlying user and system data needs to be modernized too. The Database and Storage Solutions pillar includes tools that provide assistance on the migration to the Google Cloud and the management of enterprise data. Further, this pillar guarantees security, reliability, and availability of data along with other data management services. The Cloud Storage product stores files with an assurance of 99.5 percent uptime.

Pillar 5: Smart Analytics

Storing data safely and reliably is important, but how does an organization apply the data to further business interests? The Smart Analytics pillar helps with this analysis, with products such as Looker, which is a Google-acquired data exploration tool. It provides real-time analysis and insights to help make sane decisions.

Pillar 6: Artificial Intelligence

Not long from now, artificial intelligence will be on top of every organization's priority list, and it could end becoming the first pillar in the Google Cloud Solution pillars as well. While AI has existed for a number of years, with the advent of Chat GPT and Gen AI, the world is seeing tangible benefits in using the power of cognition through artificial intelligence. On the maturity scale, AI helps with productivity and introduces innovation that can take organizations leaps and bounds ahead of their competitors. Google's Vertex AI and TensorFlow power the Artificial Intelligence pillar. Vertex AI is a unified platform for machine learning, artificial intelligence, and deep learning. TensorFlow has gone open-source and has similar capabilities.

Pillar 7: Security

The seventh and final pillar of the Google Cloud solution is security, and its core objective is to protect the business. With products going digital and online, the threat has only expounded. This makes security a key enabler. The Google Cloud has natively provided sufficient levers to secure their products. However, with configuration and customization, there is a potential for loopholes to creep in. The Security Command Center product is a security and risk management solution for discovering and managing assets against threats and hacks. With hybrid working now the norm, their BeyondCorp product has taken precedence. It's a zero-trust model framework that aims to secure individual's workstations from any remote location.

Virtual Machines

Virtual machines are servers that are logically created over a dedicated server. Physical servers are no longer preferred, as they consume space and are impractical, considering that physical servers can contain resources that are massive and cannot be fully utilized in every single context.

Virtualization started with the IBM mainframes in the 70s with a single mainframe server virtualized into LPARs (logical partitions). LPARs shared the mainframe's storage, processor, and memory and operated as an independent identities with their own operating system applications hosted on them. Likewise, physical servers are virtualized to create multiple servers, as illustrated in Figure 5-2.

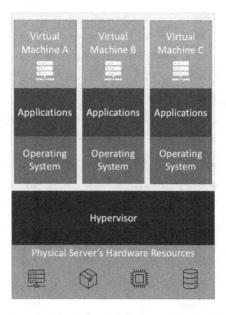

Figure 5-2. Virtual machines hosted on a physical server

Suppose a physical server has 1TB storage, 64GB memory, and 28 cores. These resources can be logically partitioned to create multiple servers using hypervisors. A *hypervisor* is (generally) software that can create and run multiple virtual machines. A hypervisor abstracts the operating system and applications from the server hardware. This abstraction allows it to create and run multiple virtual servers by sharing the physical server's resources. In this example, the 1TB storage and 64GB can be divided equally between the three virtual servers, and the processor cores can be allocated as follows: 8 cores to virtual machine A, 16 cores to virtual machine B, and 4 cores to virtual machine C. The resources can be divided in any fashion, depending on the virtual machine's requirements.

Hypervisors

The virtual machines run independently but through the hypervisor. The server's resources, network bandwidth, and other computing elements interact through the hypervisor. A hypervisor typically comes in two types—type 1 and type 2.

A type 1 hypervisor (also called a *bare metal hypervisor*) is software that is hosted directly on a physical server. These are typical for enterprise grade datacenters where blade servers are employed. Hyper-V by Microsoft and VMware's vSphere are the prevalent hypervisors in the market.

A type 2 hypervisor generally finds application on personal computers, as they are hosted on operating systems. They are called hosted hypervisors; examples include Parallels Desktop on Mac and Oracle VM VirtualBox.

Why Virtualize?

There is no dearth to enterprise computing resources. Every organization procures more than they ever need, fearing the worst. The hosted application rarely needs massive resources. So, virtualization provides a solution to optimize computing resources and helps consolidate multiple servers under a single physical server. This helps preserve physical space in datacenters and avoid situations where additional computing resources are needed.

Virtualization helps organization save on costs. First, virtualization brings about reduced capital expenditure and associated maintenance costs. Cost optimization is due to the consolidation exercise as well, as the effort needed to manage consolidated servers over disparate servers is relatively less.

Application resource usage may not remain the same throughout the year. There are use cases where application workload is much higher, such as during the holidays. During these periods, more computing resources are required compared to other times of the year. Resources can be allocated dynamically and scaled as needed to meet increased demand through the virtualization technology.

By virtualizing servers, organizations have transformed physical servers into servers that can be managed as software. This eases the workload in terms of carrying out the tasks remotely by a click of a button against running to the datacenter and keeping the lights on. Plus, new servers are spun up through a series of graphical user interface screens rather than the tedious work expected from a physical server setup.

Virtualization also provides straightforward solutions to create redundancy, and this helps in increasing uptime and reliability.

With respect to virtual machines in the Google Cloud, from the scope of the GCP Cloud Digital Leader certification, this chapter focuses on three products:

- Google Compute Engine
- VMware Engine
- Bare metal solution

Google Compute Engine

Google Compute Engine (GCE) is a product within the Google Cloud that enables users to deploy and manage virtual machines. GCE falls under the IaaS category, as it abstracts the infrastructure layer. Its competitors with other cloud ecosystems are AWS EC2, Microsoft Azure Virtual Machines, and IBM Cloud Virtual Servers.

GCE started in 2012 and it is the most commonly used product in the Google Cloud Platform. It is available across multiple regions and zones worldwide and is connected to the powerful Google network backbone. They can be managed on GCP console, a command line interface (CLI), or through RESTful APIs.

The product provides the flexibility to spin up virtual machines based on their predefined machine configurations, ranging from general purpose virtual machines to memory optimized behemoths. Their lowest configuration, an e-2 micro instance with a shared core and 1GB memory, is available free to all customers. Administrators can strategically create virtual machines in any of the regions and zones—they are typically created closer to where the users reside.

Key Characteristics

Here are the characteristics that define GCE:

- **Type of machine**: The predefined configurations range from the cheapest e-2 micro instance to the powerful m2 instance with 208 cores and 11.5TB memory. GCE provides high-performance virtual machines that work consistently around the clock. This is a good option for businesses that are looking for long periods of availability.

- **Pay as you use**: Payment for the virtual machines (VM) is based on usage. For example, if you spin up a server and use it for ten minutes before terminating it, you pay only for the time the resources were used—and the payment is charged by the second.

- **Custom and public images**: Users can run a number of operating systems (Windows server, Debian, CentOS, Ubuntu, etc.) on the virtual machines. Public images of operating systems that are optimized for GCE are made available for no extra cost. Users can get their own custom images as well. GCE supports patch management for standard images.

- **Persistent storage**: Virtual machines come attached with a persistent disk volume that hosts the operating system. To install applications, additional persistent disks can be attached and detached independently, which allows you to attach it to another VM as needed.

- **Flexible scaling**: GCE allows flexible horizontal and vertical scaling of VMs. Virtual scaling increases server resources like CPU, memory, and HDD. Horizontal scaling is adding additional VMs aided by a load balancer.

- **Creating redundancy**: Architects can define VMs to be created in different regions and balanced by a global load balancer to ensure maximum redundancy in case one of the regions goes down.

- **Spot VMs for batch jobs**: GCE can provide a significant discount (up to 91%) on standard VMs for their unused excess capacity. Customers looking for additional CPU to run batch jobs or fault-tolerant workloads without affecting their VM performance or spending for another VM can opt for Spot VMs. On the flipside, when GCE needs capacity for their standard VMs, they can reclaim the Spot VMs by giving 30 seconds notice.

Drawbacks

Some of the drawbacks are obvious. The reality is that, while GCE offers great features, there are some disadvantages (not necessarily tied to GCE but to cloud computing in general) that you need to make note of:

- **Learning curve**: The learning curve to understand and apply GCE and create and manage VMs is significant. Of course, you could hire a GCP administrator, but that comes at a steep cost, as GCP administrators and architects command a high price.

- **Management complexity**: Virtual machines by themselves are not the end-state. Storage, networking, scaling, and security (among other aspects) need to be managed in tandem with GCE, which can lead to certain levels of complexity.

- **Configuration complexity**: Configuring networking in any cloud can be complex, and the complexity increases when you need to set up virtual private clouds (VPCs), firewall rules, load balancers, and VPN connections. Incorrect network configuration could lead to security vulnerabilities or performance issues.

- **Overspend by ungoverned expenditure**: The pay-as-you-go model is good for customers to pay only for what they use, but unless there are budgets, the cost of the infrastructure can exceed if they are left turned on unnecessarily.

- **Vendor lock-in**: The biggest drawback is vendor lock-in. Once you migrate from your on-premises to GCP, you are tied to the GCP ecosystem. There are options for migrating out of GCP, or for using hybrid clouds.

Exam Tip   *You can expect to get basic questions covering the Google Compute Engine. The expectation is that you are aware of the GCE product, know what it is used for, and under what circumstances it is used.*

Provisioning VMs

You can create virtual machines on Google Compute Engine in several ways. This section demonstrates the easiest and most straightforward method for creating one, by using the GCP web console:

1. Browse to the GCP web console, found at
    `https://console.cloud.google.com/`.

2. Click the navigation menu and choose Compute
    Engine ➤ VM Instances (see Figure 5-3).

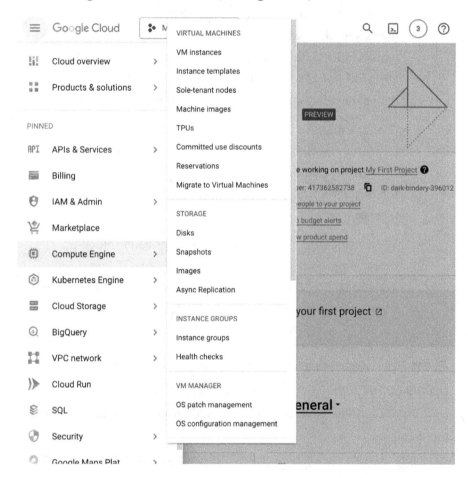

Figure 5-3. *Initiating Compute Engine on GCP*

3. If you are using GCE for the first time, you must
    enable it (see Figure 5-4).

Figure 5-4. *Enabling Compute Engine*

4. Click Create Instance.

5. In the screen that appears, provide a unique server name (gcpcdlbookvm-1 is used in this example). Select the region and zone. Asia-south1 (Mumbai) is the selected region and asia-south1-c is the selected zone in this example (see Figure 5-5).

6. The machine configuration is made (N2 in this case).

7. On the right side of the screen, the server's usage estimates are provided. For a N2 server configuration, it will cost $69.32 monthly, which is about $0.09 per hour.

Figure 5-5. *Server name, region, zone, and machine configuration*

8. There are multiple options available for the N2 machine type (see Figure 5-6).

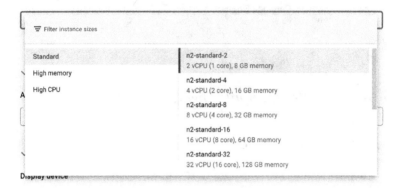

Figure 5-6. *Machine type configurations*

9. Choose the VM provisioning model and then pick Standard VM or Spot VM (see Figure 5-7).

Figure 5-7. *VM provisioning model*

10. There are other options as well—you can choose an operating system, access management, a firewall, and any monitoring agents. This example uses the defaults (see Figure 5-8).

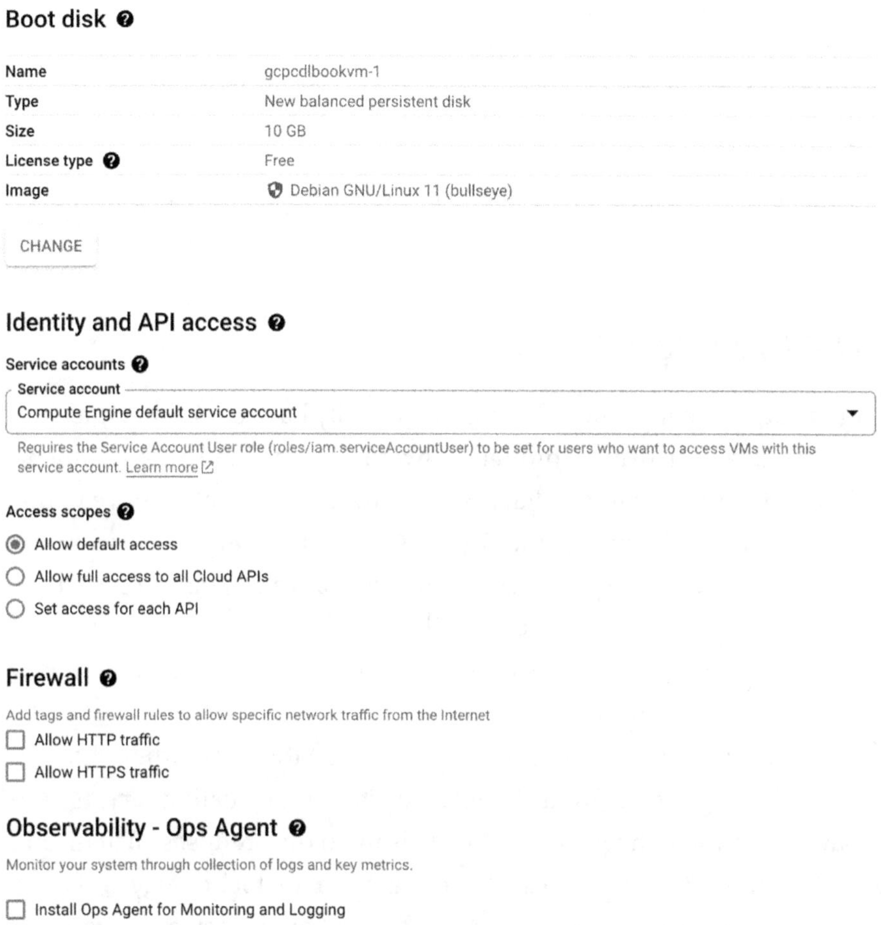

Boot disk ❷

Name	gcpcdlbookvm-1
Type	New balanced persistent disk
Size	10 GB
License type ❷	Free
Image	🛡 Debian GNU/Linux 11 (bullseye)

CHANGE

Identity and API access ❷

Service accounts ❷

┌─ Service account ───┐
│ Compute Engine default service account   ▾ │
└──┘

Requires the Service Account User role (roles/iam.serviceAccountUser) to be set for users who want to access VMs with this service account. Learn more 🗗

Access scopes ❷

◉ Allow default access

○ Allow full access to all Cloud APIs

○ Set access for each API

Firewall ❷

Add tags and firewall rules to allow specific network traffic from the Internet

☐ Allow HTTP traffic

☐ Allow HTTPS traffic

Observability - Ops Agent ❷

Monitor your system through collection of logs and key metrics.

☐ Install Ops Agent for Monitoring and Logging

Figure 5-8. *Other options in GCE*

11.   Click Create Instances. This initiates the virtual machine provisioning. This takes about 10-20 seconds for provisioning, after which you can see the virtual machine in the Compute Engine console (see Figure 5-9).

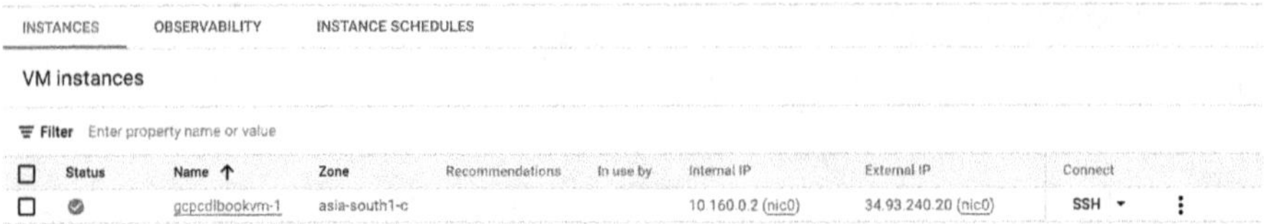

Figure 5-9. *A virtual machine provisioned on Compute Engine*

VMware Engine

Organizations that are not on the cloud usually have a hosted datacenter, with virtualization driven through VMware, Hyper-V, Citrix, or a similar solution. For organizations that are on VMware and want to move to the cloud with least disruption, the Google Cloud Platform provides a solution to migrate the VMware setup with all the virtualization intact on GCP's bare metal servers. The product is called *VMware Engine* and in this setup, it employs private physical servers that are allocated. The VMware migration is done through APIs.

Why would organizations move VMware on the cloud when the cloud offers its own solutions for virtualization and creating servers? An organization might have invested heavily in an on-premises virtualization solution, and their employees are familiar with the technology and the existing setup. Instead of shaking the tree all at once, they may choose to take an intermediate step by moving the ecosystem on to the Google Cloud using the VMware Engine.

The migration from on-premises includes the entire VMware SDDC (software-defined datacenter) into the Google Cloud along with the existing VMware licenses, servers, kernels, data, and so on.

Benefits of the VMware Engine

The VMware Engine product is available in 17 global regions at the time of the writing, and the estimated time to provision an entire VMware SDDC on the Google Cloud Platform is approximately 30 minutes. This means that the entire migration from on-premises to GCP is done in approximately 30 minutes.

VMware Engine leverages dedicated servers that are physically isolated from other customers. This is done as the entire VMware ecosystem moves from on-premises to GCP. This would necessitate sets of physical servers. Further, the product extends continuity of infrastructure and related services from on-premises to GCP bare metal. The VMware Engine product is the best of both worlds—the continuation of the existing VMware setup plus the bare metal servers hosted on Google datacenters connected to the Google backbone. These servers can also be seamlessly integrated with other Google products, like Google Storage and AI Platform. Moreover, the physical security, datacenter management, and hardware maintenance are Google's responsibility. All hardware and firmware updates are managed by Google.

Customers can extend/scale their infrastructure with more servers powered through VMware, or they can migrate the servers to GCP Compute Engine in a phased manner. This migration process can be done at the customer's own pace, ensuring minimum risk to the hosted services, and ensuring that the personnel are well versed in GCP.

Bare Metal Solution

There are complexities when implementing technologies and not all the solutions can be modularized within a cloud environment. For complex technologies that run specialized workloads in customer datacenters, the solution that the Google Cloud Platform offers is based on Infrastructure as a Service (IaaS). It's called a bare metal solution, where the cloud service provider offers managed servers to customers, who can implement specialized workloads based on their design and requirements. Running an Oracle database workload is a classic example of a bare metal solution. Oracle solutions generally have complicated licensing and hardware requirements, which may not be easily used with the Google Compute Engine.

Bare Metal at Regional Extensions

The bare metal servers are not part of the GCP's main datacenters. They are hosted in regional extensions that are connected to Google's network backbone with a low latency network fabric.

Google offers less than 2ms latency for bare metal solutions to access all of Google's cloud services.

An illustration of a bare metal solution within a regional extension and its connectivity to the Google Cloud is shown in Figure 5-10.

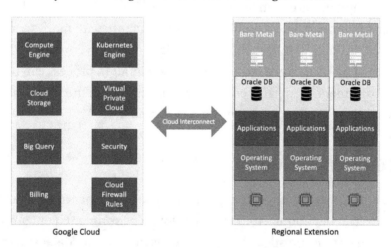

Figure 5-10. *Bare metal solution in a regional extension*

Through a bare metal solution, Google provides a core infrastructure that includes servers, server housing, power, cooling, and maintenance. Physical and network security to the servers are managed by Google, along with the network connectivity from the regional extension to Google's backbone. Plus, as in their Compute Engine and other products, the bare metal solution is supported through the various Google-provided hardware monitoring tools.

The Customer's Responsibilities

While Google manages the hardware and the associated networks, the customers are responsible for the operating system, the applications, and the ecosystem within the servers. This includes installation, upgrades, and maintenance of the operating system, the virtualization, and the applications.

Managing and maintaining the data, as well as securing it, is the customer's responsibility as well. Through identity access management (IAM), the customer has complete control over who gets access to view, modify, and delete configurations and data. Managing the database, its installation, configuration, and the various backups are all customer's responsibilities.

The bare metal solution follows the Bring-Your-Own-License (BYOL) model, which makes the customer solely responsible for all the software licensing in their solutions.

Summary

Digital transformation in the Google Cloud Platform is in principle delivered through seven solution levers, referred to as pillars. They are Infrastructure Modernization, Business Application Platform Portfolio, Application Modernization, Database and Storage Solutions, Smart Analytics, Artificial Intelligence, and Security.

This chapter discussed the elements of infrastructure modernization achieved through the Google Cloud Platform's virtualization technology. The key product that delivers the servers is the Google Compute Engine. It is used to create and manage servers.

For customers who want to move with their existing VMware-driven virtualization, Google offers the VMware Engine solution. It migrates the existing VMware ecosystem from the hosted datacenters into Google's bare metal servers.

For customers hosting specialized workloads in their datacenters, such as Oracle, the bare metal solution offers an IaaS solution with bare metal servers to host these specialized workloads. These servers are located in regional extensions connected to Google's network backbone and offers < 2ms latency to other Google's products.

DAY 3

Approximate Study Time: 1 hour and 39 minutes

    Chapter 6 - 42 minutes

    Chapter 7 - 57 minutes

CHAPTER 6

Containers

Virtual machines are the gateway to infrastructure modernization. With the need to set up the infrastructure dynamically and rapidly, the next grade of modernization is the world of containers. Containers provide modular, standardized units of infrastructure packages. Containers can also be created on-demand, which allows applications to be moved easily between environments.

This chapter focuses on the concept of containers. It explains the nuances of containers, the benefits, and their fundamental structure. Further, the chapter also looks into Google Kubernetes Engine, which is a platform that manages containers. The final topic covered in this chapter is Anthos, which is Google's product for managing Kubernetes workloads across other major clouds and on-premises.

Understanding Containers

Containers are similar to virtual machines. Virtual machines split a server's hardware resources, whereas a container is abstracted above the operating system layer. It creates an independent ecosystem that houses the application and all its dependencies.

Figure 6-1 illustrates the difference between virtual machines and containers.

© Abhinav Krishna Kaiser 2024
A. K. Kaiser, *Become GCP Cloud Digital Leader Certified in 7 Days*,
https://doi.org/10.1007/979-8-8688-0438-0_6

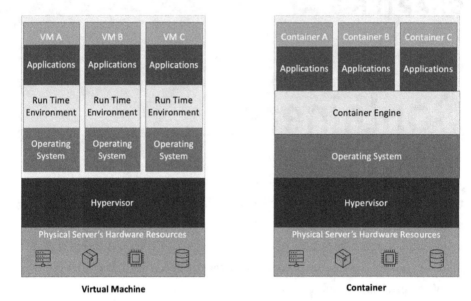

Figure 6-1. *Virtual machines and containers*

In a virtual machine, the physical server's hardware resources are sliced vertically. A certain amount of the processing power, RAM and storage are assigned to the virtual machines. So, every virtual machine operates as an independent server with its own operating system, and everything that can sit on the operating system. The hypervisor emulates a physical server and is split into multiple virtual machines. This ensures that the physical server and the virtual server are indistinguishable.

A container on the other hand is similar to a virtual machine, but its abstraction is above the operating system layer. In other words, the operating system remains common for containers that are created on top of it. Containers virtualize environments that consist of the application packages and its dependencies, which makes deploying applications more straightforward as they move from development to testing to production.

Containers vs. Virtual Machines

Containers and virtual machines both virtualize computing resources. The commonality between them ends here. Virtualization can be done at multiple layers—at the hardware layer or at the software layer. In Figure 6-1, a virtual machine abstracts at a hardware layer and creates multiple copies of a physical server, with each virtual machine having its own dedicated hardware resources. Every virtual machine needs to host its own operating system, build dependencies separately, and host applications on it.

Container virtualization is at the software layer above the operating system. Containers are lightweight compared to VMs as they do not host the operating system. The runtime environment or the kernel is common for all the containers hosted on a server. Each container will have the application hosted on it, along with its libraries and dependencies.

A container can be hosted on a physical or virtual machine. The host operating system controls the hardware resource access and usage to ensure that containers do not end up consuming all the server's resources. See Table 6-1.

Table 6-1. *Main Differences Between Virtual Machines and Containers*

Category	Virtual Machines	Containers
Virtualization	Hardware layer	Software layer
Type	Imitates dedicated hardware	Imitates platform with kernel
Weightage	Heavy with operating system	Lightweight with application libraries
Operating System	Individual operating system	Shares host operating system
Boot	Typically takes minutes to start a VM	Containers startup is swift and almost instantaneous
Memory	More memory required	Less memory
Security	More secure since the platform ecosystem is fully isolated	Less secure due to kernel dependency of host OS
Examples	Hyper-V, vSphere, and VMware	Docker, LXC, and Windows containers

Why Containerization?

Containers came into play because the virtual machines presented certain challenges that prevented organizations from rapidly developing. They represented a server that hosted an operating system and came with a set of hardware resources. Building a new server was time consuming, because the libraries, dependencies, and the application had to be built on top of the operating system, and those who have experience building it will tell you that it is no easy ask—especially when the various connections and integrations have to be established. Server restarts are not straightforward either. They consume a good portion of the time, and when fully started, the checks and balances (sanity checks) to ensure all the services are working add to the work (even though it is automated, it requires monitoring) and time. Because a virtual machine hosts the operating system, along with the libraries and the application, it is quite bulky and consumes a lot of storage. In other words, a virtual machine is a white elephant.

Containers do not try to virtualize the entire setup but only the layer above the operating system—the dependencies/libraries and the application makes it nimble, lightweight, and easy to maintain. You can start a container almost instantly, spin it up, and replicate and scale it in a matter of seconds. If a container requires a restart, it is done in a matter of seconds, as opposed to minutes with virtual machines. Most importantly, developers can create predictable environments with containers, which means faster development and deployment and more efficient maintenance. Software development today is done on the back of microservices. Containers are best suited for microservices, as the microservices can be hosted on containers with just the required libraries, making it lightweight and easy to develop, troubleshoot, and maintain. Multiple containers can be hosted on virtual machines, with each container hosting a microservice. If more containers are needed, a new virtual machine can be spun up to host the required containers.

Summarizing, containers are the preferred choice for environments because:

- They are lightweight. Fewer system resources are consumed, which leads to optimal use of hardware resources.

- Maintenance is easy. This presents an opportunity to minimize the operational costs, because containers running an application can be standardized

- They are portable. Containers can be deployed across multiple environments with ease, and with a greater chances of success.

- Scalability is easier. Containers can be horizontally scaled and load balanced at will.

- Development is rapid. This is perfect companion for leveraging the Agile lifecycle and DevOps methodologies to develop rapidly across the development, testing, deployment, and maintenance phases.

Container Use Cases

A good practice in software development is to ensure that all the lower environments represent a like-to-like copy of the production environment. Unless the production is mimicked in lower environments, there are no guarantees that the deployed software will be bug free. The problem however is creating lower environments that are exactly like the production version because of the complexities involved in creating various integrations with other systems. The other problem is that the environment-creation process involves installing the application with all the necessary libraries and dependencies. Chances are they may not always get it right. Plus, during development, if certain libraries have to be modified, the environmental changes have to be affected as well. On a behemoth like a virtual machine, this is a consuming process, and a common reason for delays in spinning up new environments.

Containers are pure gold from an environment-creation standpoint. A developer spins up a container on the development environment and installs the requisite libraries and the application. When the application works as it should, a container image is created. This image is used to create a new container on the test environment. The container is shipped with all its dependencies, so there are no surprises, and the application is likely to work as expected. This leads to rapid testing. If the testing does not reveal new bugs, the application can be deployed onto the production environment. The same container image spins up a new container on the production environment and the application is good to go, as all the dependencies are installed along with it. This is how containers support rapid software development, testing, and deployment.

Apart from software packaging and deployment, other common use cases of containers are as follows:

- Microservices architecture: Containers are a perfect fit for employing a microservices architecture. Every microservice can be packaged as a container, which allows for independent development, testing, scaling, and deployment in a larger application.

- DevOps pipelines: Containers can make DevOps pipelines dynamic by deploying applications from the build through test and production with a good probability of success.

- Infrastructure as Code: Environment creation can be codified and simplified using containers, which will aid in enabling teams to automate deployment and scale applications at will.

- Testing: Containers provide isolated environments for testing. Test environments can be spun up through CI-CD pipelines at the time of testing, and torn down once complete, which ensures that the testing is done in consistent environments.

- Infrastructure cost savings: Containers are lightweight and share the available memory across containers, so organizations can consolidate servers and hence reduce their infrastructure costs.

- Edge computing: In edge computing scenarios where the resources are constrained, containers are perfect, because they are lightweight and portable.

- Internet of Things (IoT): Containers deliver software packages in a portable manner, so they are ideal for channeling installations and updates to IoT devices.

Container Tools

Container tools come in two segments:

- The tool to create containers

- The tool to manage containers

These tools go hand-in-hand because organizations manage hundreds if not thousands of containers at any given point in time. This section highlights tools that are pivotal for creating and managing/orchestrating containers.

Docker

Docker is a de facto tool for creating containers, although it wasn't the first container tool to be developed. It has played a significant role in popularizing container technology, and it has become a principal tool in the software development lifecycle across organizations.

Docker works seamlessly on the cloud and works very well with Ansible, Puppet, and Chef (all configuration management tools). Moreover, the Docker Engine software that is responsible for creating containers is based on an open-source containerization technology and is free.

Kubernetes

Kubernetes is often abbreviated as K8s (eight letters between K and s). It is an open-source container orchestration software that manages automated deployment, scaling, and management of containerized applications. It was originally designed by Google and is now managed by the Cloud Native Computing Foundation (CNCF).

Docker is the principal tool for creating containers, and Kubernetes has donned the role of a fundamental tool for container orchestration and is widely adopted across organizations. It is known for its robustness, scalability, and extensibility.

In any environment, you would typically see a combination of Docker and Kubernetes—hundreds and thousands of Docker containers are managed by the Kubernetes platform. The platform can automate deployment into environments, scale or descale containers based on the triggers, and load balance.

LXC

LXC stands for Linux Containers, and they were the first in the market to release a tool for creating containers (in 2008). LXC is an open-source tool for creating containers on Linux hosts with process and resource isolation. Virtual machines and containers can both be created using LXC.

While the Docker project started on the back of LXC, it has moved away significantly since the release of version 1.0 in 2014. LXC is not as lightweight and portable as Docker. LXC is more comparable to a VM than a container. The tool is powerful and you can install anything on it, just like you can on a VM, and it combines the features of a container as well. Secondly, Docker is designed to host a single process in every container. LXC can host multiple processes.

Hyper-V and Windows Containers

Microsoft introduced Windows containers and Hyper-V in their Windows Server 2016 operating system.

Windows containers are similar to Docker, where lightweight containers are created with the libraries and the application. Hyper-V containers are focused on true isolation and performance, and they include the kernel, the libraries, and the application.

AWS Fargate/Cloud Run

Amazon's AWS Fargate and Google's Cloud Run are serverless container engine products. These services allow you to create containers without the need to spin up a virtual machine first. The entire process that you looked at in Chapter 5, where you chose a server type, an operating system, and other requirements, is eliminated. Serverless containerization services provide the fastest way to get development started. Developers don't have to worry about the underlying infrastructure in the software delivery lifecycle. Serverless technology is discussed in detail in Chapter 7.

AWS Fargate is like a combination of Docker and Kubernetes. You can create containers and orchestrate them using the same service. Its pay-as-you-go model allows you to create as many containers as needed, and you can create heterogenous clusters to aid in horizontal scaling. Cloud Run is covered in detail in Chapter 7.

AWS EKS/AKS/GKE

Kubernetes is by far the most popular container orchestration tool. The cloud service providers have onboarded Kubernetes into their platform, which allows users to start using them without having to configure anything.

Google, the founder of Kubernetes, was the first to onboard Kubernetes in 2014, through their Google Kubernetes Engine (GKE) product. Amazon's Elastic Kubernetes Service (EKS) and Azure Kubernetes Service (AKS) were released in June 2018.

All three cloud service providers have built automations and other features, and they all come at difference price points. If you are already invested in a particular cloud service, it makes senses to continue with their offering of Kubernetes. If you are starting out, GKE is perhaps the most mature in terms of the features offered. From a comparison of popularity, Amazon's EKS is the most popular by virtue of their cloud service having garnered the majority of the market.

Google Kubernetes Engine

Creating a Kubernetes installation typically involves creating virtual machines using the Compute Engine product. If there are hundreds of containers to be hosted, then multiple virtual machines need to be created based on the specifications and architecture. The servers need to be clustered before the containers are created using Docker and Kubernetes configured to orchestrate them. This sounds like a lot of work!

Google has simplified this process through Google Kubernetes Engine (GKE), where the underlying infrastructure (virtual machines) are managed by Google. With GKE, as a developer, you start creating containers, and the underlying infrastructure is created and clustered based on the number of containers and their configuration. In effect, you don't need an infrastructure engineer to manage the environments, and developers can (all by themselves) do what they do best. Google will fully manage the virtual machines—be it maintenance, scaling, or updating with patches and security upgrades. From a total cost of ownership, GKE should work out cheaper than the option of creating VMs through Compute Engine and maintaining containers and Kubernetes with the help of infrastructure engineers and developers.

111

Why GKE?

Some of the benefits of using GKE are as follows:

- **Faster development**: Being a managed Kubernetes product, GKE supports faster development and presents fewer dependencies.

- **Deployment**: Deploying and managing containers is simple and straightforward.

- **Scaling**: Based on the number of containers and the resource usage of the applications, GKE automatically scales up or down. Developers can configure the number of worker nodes in your cluster to accommodate changes in traffic/resource demands.

- **Performance**: GKE load balances the containerized applications to ensure optimal performance. As a next level, the Global load balancing can be leveraged as well, which distributes the traffic running on different GKE clusters across different regions.

- **Resiliency**: Self-healing and automatic failover provide high availability cover for containers hosted through GKE.

- **Integration**: Integrates seamlessly with all the Google Cloud Platform services, making it easy to build, test, and deploy applications by leveraging other products such as BigQuery and Cloud Storage.

- **Security**: GKE offers built-in security features such as VPC-native clusters, network policies, and integration with Google Cloud Identity and Access Management (IAM) for fine-grained access control.

- **Observability**: Monitoring applications for identified events and logging the events is provided. GKE notifies administrators when warnings and errors are noticed.

On the flipside, there are certain limitations that need to be considered before making the jump:

- **Cost**: The Total Cost of Ownership (TCO) may be low due to the elimination of an infrastructure engineers' support. However, if you already have one on your payroll, it may not be practical, as GKE is a fully managed service and comes at a premium cost. This may be more expensive than spinning VMs on Compute Engine and installing Kubernetes.

- **Infrastructure configuration**: You cannot choose which underlying infrastructure is created. GKE does not allow developers to specify infrastructure requirements, as they are considered a Platform as a Service (PaaS) product.

- **Lock-in**: While GKE provides a fast way in, getting out may not be straightforward. Although there is no lock-in period for the product, using a proprietary product does not make it easy to move to a different provider later.

GKE in Action

This section looks at creating a Google Kubernetes engine cluster. This product is an accelerator to create environments. For example, it took less than five minutes to set up a cluster of three servers through the GKE. The same setup can be created outside of GKE using Compute Engine, but the time and effort required is much greater compared to the five minutes that it takes GKE.

You are not expected to know how to create a Google Kubernetes cluster or the workings of the Google Kubernetes Engine. This section is optional. Feel free to skip it.

1. In the Google Cloud Platform console, search for *Kubernetes Engine.*

2. You must enable the Kubernetes Engine API if you're using it the first time (see Figure 6-2).

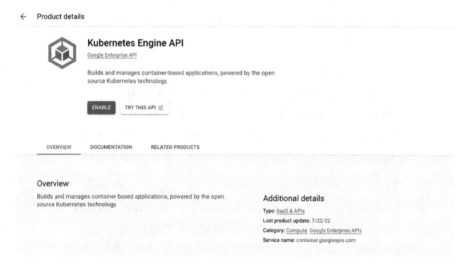

Figure 6-2. *Initiating the Kubernetes Engine on GCP*

3. Once Kubernetes is enabled, choose Clusters ➤ Create (see Figure 6-3).

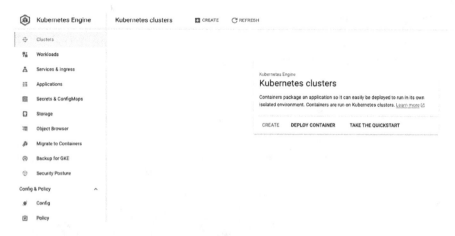

Figure 6-3. *Initiating cluster creation on GKE*

4. There are two modes to create a GKE cluster—
autopilot and standard. Autopilot gives you a sense
of serverless architecture, but underneath it isn't.
With autopilot, GKE decides how many nodes are
required, and the decision is done on the basis of
workload. When more workload is introduced,
the engine scales the cluster with more nodes
horizontally, and when the workload reduces, the
nodes are trimmed down.

In a real-world sense, think about the times of the year when people
generally buy gifts, such as holidays. Online shopping portal workloads
are typically higher during these periods than the rest of the year.
Organizations can optimize costs in such scenarios by opting for
auto-scaling through the autopilot horizontal scaling options.

You need to switch to Standard mode to run through these steps and
elements in creating a cluster.

Click Switch to Standard Cluster in the top-right corner to change the mode (see Figure 6-4). You need to confirm the selection in the subsequent dialog box (see Figure 6-5).

Figure 6-4. *Default autopilot mode and switching to standard mode*

Switch from autopilot to standard

Autopilot clusters are optimized for most production workloads and implement many Kubernetes best practices for security, scalability and cost optimization.

With standard clusters, Google still manages your control plane. But if you prefer to manage every configuration setting in your cluster and nodes, a Standard cluster may be right for you. Learn about GKE modes of operation. ☑

CANCEL   SWITCH TO STANDARD CLUSTER

Figure 6-5. *Confirmation dialog box for switching to standard mode*

5. In the cluster creation screen (see Figure 6-6):

   a. Provide a cluster name

   b. Depending on the availability requirements, you can create a cluster within a zone, within multiple zones, or across regions. There are cost implications as well depending on the decision. If you use autopilot mode, the clusters will be created with a regional location type.

c. Because this is a managed service, Google manages the Kubernetes updates. The Control Plane refers to the central Kubernetes management engine that runs the APIs, scheduler, and resource controllers. Under the Control Plane Version option, static version and release channel are the two available options. With a static version, Google automatically installs security and compatibility updates. Feature updates need to be installed manually. In the release channel option, all updates (including new features) are installed by Google. There are three channels available for updates: 1. *Rapid,* where the updates are installed several weeks after the release 2. *Regular,* where the updates are carried out two to three months after releasing in the Rapid channel. This is the default option. 3. *Stable,* where the updates are installed after two to three months after releasing in the *Regular* channel. Autopilot mode subscribes to the *Release* channel.

d. In the right pane, indicate the estimated monthly/ hourly cost of the cluster.

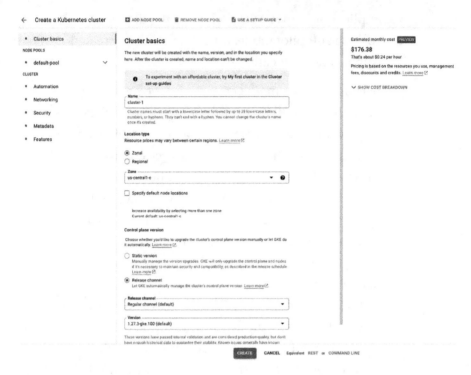

Figure 6-6. *Kubernetes cluster creation screen*

6. Creating the cluster takes about five minutes.
    Figure 6-7 indicates the completion of the cluster
    and Figure 6-8 shows the various details that makes
    up the cluster.

Figure 6-7. *Kubernetes Cluster has been created*

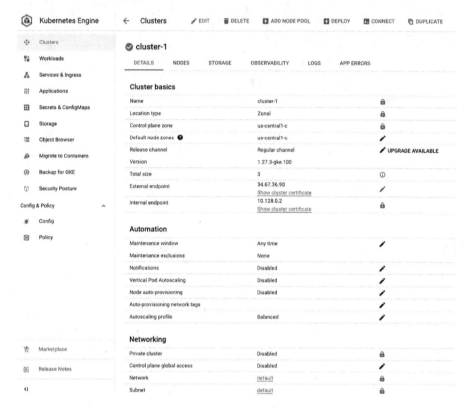

Figure 6-8. *The Kubernetes Cluster details*

7. The cluster is made up of three nodes—three servers making up the Kubernetes cluster. Individual servers/nodes are visible under the NODES tab (see Figure 6-9).

Figure 6-9. *Nodes in the Kubernetes Cluster*

8. Developers can deploy applications through
    the Workloads section (see Figure 6-10) on the
    Kubernetes Engine product. However, this is not
    the preferred approach. Applications are generally
    deployed through the DevOps pipelines.

Figure 6-10. *Deploying applications through the Workloads section*

9. The cluster and servers created through the Google
    Kubernetes Engine are also visible on the Compute
    Engine product, as indicated in Figure 6-11.

Figure 6-11. *Cluster and servers' visibility in Compute Engine*

Anthos

Anthos, initially launched as Cloud Services Platform, is a hybrid cloud management product from Google. It was introduced in 2019, and it simplifies managing Kubernetes deployments across on-premises environments and multiple public clouds. While Google Kubernetes Engine (GKE) is a core component, Anthos offers a wider set of tools for container orchestration. It also has integrations for managing virtual machines. It has partnered with companies like Hewlett Packard Enterprise, Dell EMC, Cisco, and NetApp to ensure compatibility with their infrastructure solutions.

Why Anthos

Organizations evolve with their technology over the years—starting with on-premise solutions and moving into various clouds. The trend is to diversify with clouds, and not to put all their eggs in the same basket. With that, it is possible that organizations have Kubernetes clusters hosted on their in-house datacenters and across multiple clouds. Since they are in multiple environments, managing them could end up being challenging and time-consuming. Anthos is the solution for such situations ,where the management of multiple Kubernetes cluster installations are brought under a single umbrella—making operations simple and efficient.

Anthos is aimed at enterprises who are looking for unification of their on-premises and cloud Kubernetes environments. Having Anthos on top of these installations for end-to-end visibility, standardized maintenance, and standardized monitoring will aid in rapid development involving microservices and containers.

Exam Tip   *When you are asked to identify a product that helps consistently manage infrastructure and containers, your answer should be Anthos.*

Stand-out Features of Anthos

Anthos delivers on all the boilerplate features that make up a modern product—including security, regular updates, compliance, and encryption, among others. However, there are three aspects that particularly stand out that makes Anthos a worthy addition when organizations are only dealing with Kubernetes clusters.

- **Configuration management**: Anthos provides a way to define and enforce policies consistently across all environments. This feature directly supports the DevOps ways of working with consistent environments that can be brought as close as possible to production. It accomplishes this by managing clusters as configuration files that are stored on Git repositories.

- **VM migration**: If organizations are currently hosting their applications directly on Kubernetes, Anthos helps with the modernization journey by migrating them to containers that are managed by Kubernetes. It basically simplifies the entire process of moving legacy applications to cloud native architectures.

- **Anthos service mesh**: Anthos leverages service mesh (based on Istio service mesh) to manage, monitor, and secure microservices-based applications. This provides the capability to manage the traffic on the applications, implement observability, and good security practices.

A service mesh is an infrastructure layer that is introduced in applications. It allows developers to introduce traffic management, observability, and security as microservices applications, which works alongside other applications without being part of the code. With microservices applications, there could be thousands of these applications spread across multiple Kubernetes installations. Using a service mesh, the task of monitoring, discovering, gathering metrics, and self-healing are all possible. Service meshes can also be used in canary deployments, A/B testing, end-to-end authentication, and encryption.

Anthos in Action

Anthos is an enterprise product. Therefore, you cannot use it with a free tier. However, you can try Anthos for a month before you are charged. To begin using Anthos the first time, you must enable it (see Figure 6-12).

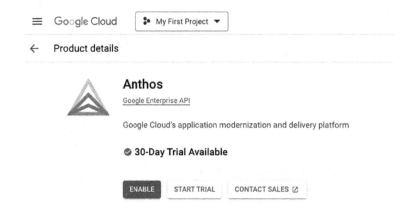

Figure 6-12. *Initiating Anthos on GCP*

You have three options for creating clusters:

1. Link the existing GKE clusters or create new clusters using GKE (see Figure 6-13).

2. Onboard the Kubernetes installations from AWS and Azure onto Google Anthos (see Figure 6-14). Existing installations on multiple clouds can be managed in a single pane, which enables organizations to choose the most appropriate environment based on factors like cost, performance, and compliance.

3. The VMware vSphere and bare metal options were covered in the previous chapters; they introduce hybrid cloud management capabilities under Google. These capabilities can be further extended to Kubernetes extensions under Anthos (see Figure 6-15).

Create a cluster
GCP
OTHER CLOUDS
ON-PREMISES
NEW
Autopilot: Google manages your cluster (Recommended)
A pay-per-Pod Kubernetes cluster where GKE manages your nodes with minimal configuration required. Learn more
CONFIGURE
Standard: You manage your cluster
A pay-per-node Kubernetes cluster where you configure and manage your nodes. Learn more
CONFIGURE
Compare cluster modes to learn more about their differences.
COMPARE

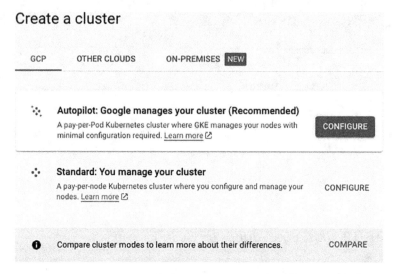

Figure 6-13. *Anthos onboarding for GKE installation/configuration*

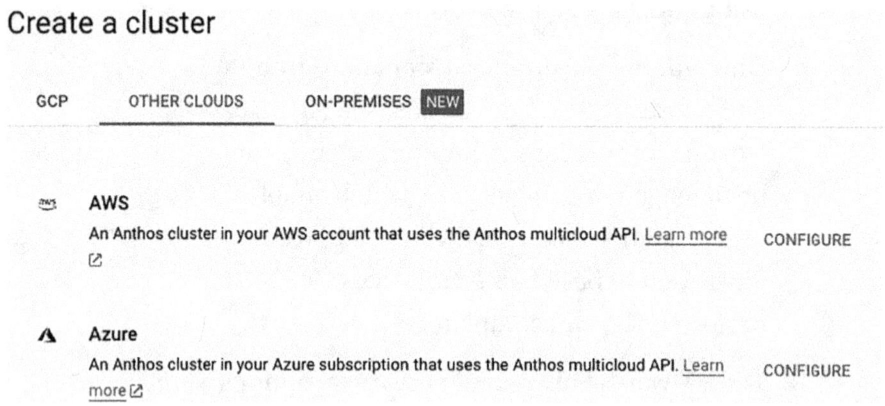

Create a cluster
GCP
OTHER CLOUDS
ON-PREMISES
NEW
AWS
An Anthos cluster in your AWS account that uses the Anthos multicloud API. Learn more
CONFIGURE
Azure
An Anthos cluster in your Azure subscription that uses the Anthos multicloud API. Learn more
CONFIGURE

Figure 6-14. *Anthos onboarding for AWS and Azure Kubernetes installations*

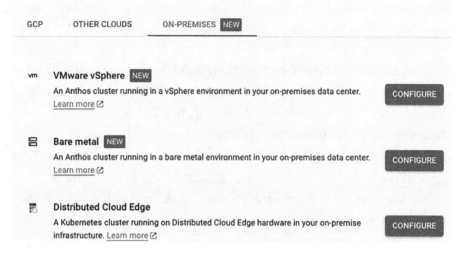

Create a cluster

GCP   · OTHER CLOUDS   ON-PREMISES NEW

vm   **VMware vSphere** NEW
An Anthos cluster running in a vSphere environment in your on-premises data center.
Learn more ☑   CONFIGURE

Bare metal NEW
An Anthos cluster running in a bare metal environment in your on-premises data center.   CONFIGURE
Learn more ☑

Distributed Cloud Edge
A Kubernetes cluster running on Distributed Cloud Edge hardware in your on-premise   CONFIGURE
infrastructure. Learn more ☑

Figure 6-15. *Anthos onboarding from on-premises Kubernetes installations*

Anthos installs an agent into the various Kubernetes clusters regardless of the environment it is hosted in. This agent obtains the necessary permissions to provide a consistent infrastructure, container management, service management, and policy enforcement.

Summary

Containers abstract at the operating system level, thus allowing developers to focus solely on the application development rather than the layer underneath it. The containers leverage the operating system's kernel and builds on top of it, with the application and its dependencies. Therefore, containers are lightweight, leading to resource utilization and cost effectiveness. Further, containers quickly spin up development and testing environments and simplify the process of deploying software from one environment to another.

The chapter looked at Google Kubernetes Engine, a container orchestration tool for managing containers on the Google Cloud Platform. The tool simplifies the process of deploying, managing, and scaling containerized applications using Kubernetes.

Further, the Google Anthos tool is a multi-cloud and hybrid cloud application that helps combine and manage the various Kubernetes installations across GCP, Azure, AWS, bare metal, and VMWare vSphere, all under a single umbrella.

CHAPTER 7

Serverless and Cloud Functions

With any software products, customers interact with the application. Everything else—including the underlying infrastructure, the connected services, and the security apparatus—support the application. While the software integrations and security are embedded into the application, the infrastructure component can be abstracted to reduce the overhead and dependencies that exist. With a serverless architecture, developers can build, test, and deploy applications without having to manage the infrastructure.

This chapter delves into the serverless architecture concepts and the products in the Google Cloud Platform that run on this architecture—Google App Engine, Google Cloud Run, and Google Cloud Functions.

Serverless Computing

Serverless computing is a misnomer. Servers are not going anywhere—in fact, the term *serverless* is from the developer's perspective. The term refers to a developer not having to worry about the intricacies and the processes around setting up and managing the infrastructure. The pans are heated, the vegetables are chopped, and all the ingredients are laid out in plain sight. All that the cook needs to do is toss the ingredients in the pan. Voila,

© Abhinav Krishna Kaiser 2024
A. K. Kaiser, *Become GCP Cloud Digital Leader Certified in 7 Days*,
https://doi.org/10.1007/979-8-8688-0438-0_7

the dish is ready in the fastest possible time. The objective of churning outcomes rapidly is perhaps the sole motivation to go serverless. The outcome in the software development industry is to rapidly develop and deploy new features. This is possible because developers don't have worry about the prerequisites (read infrastructure) and they can focus solely on the job at hand—building the software application. The developer builds the software without having to prepare and set up the environments. Servers are needed but abstracted for the developer.

The cloud service provider (GCP, AWS, Azure, etc.) takes responsibility of the underlying infrastructure. This includes ensuring the security, availability, and the capacity needs. The CSP is responsible for upgrading patches, applying updates, and observability. Developers focus on their coding bit, and the CSPs maintain the servers, including scaling the servers (horizontal and vertical) as needed. The costs for the servers are based on usage—the pay-as-you-go model ensures optimized costs.

Function as a Service (FaaS)

There is a general misconception that FaaS and serverless computing are one and the same. But they aren't. FaaS leverages serverless computing. It is a computing model in which the developers build and deploy functions. A certain event triggers a function. When the function is invoked, serverless computing creates the necessary backend infrastructure, deploys, and executes the function. Soon after execution, the backend infrastructure is dismantled. Therefore, costs of serverless computing are optimized and only charged during the deployment and execution of the function.

FaaS Use Cases

Every function is separately triggered and executed on a serverless computing product. An example could be an Internet banking website that displays data in tables that must be imported into Excel. When the user clicks the button that indicates the Excel download, it triggers a function to be deployed and executed on a container. The function ports the data into an Excel file and the container is spun down.

Some other use cases for FaaS include:

- Cron batch jobs can be executed by functions that are triggered during particular times. The application that runs the batch jobs does not need to sit on a server all the time if it is invoked a few times a day.

- APIs can be developed as FaaS products and be triggered during API calls.

- Any functionality that's used once during a session (such as logging in) can be deployed as a FaaS product.

FaaS vs. Microservices

FaaS products are short lived for the duration of the function deployment and execution. They are typically functions that carry out a particular task. A microservice is also similar in its construction as a software module that can independently carry out a single task. It is integrated through APIs. FaaS and microservices are both hosted on containers, and both can be hosted on a serverless computing product. The similarities end here.

Microservice applications are long-lived on servers that are hosted on the cloud or on-premises. They are not spun up and spun down when triggered, like the FaaS products are. The FaaS products are designed to be short lived, to be invoked when triggered, and to be dismantled soon after they produce an outcome.

It is also not uncommon for microservices software modules and FaaS products to work together. Software built on the microservice architecture can invoke a function as needed, which triggers a FaaS lifecycle.

How Does a Serverless Model Work?

Developers write code in the language of their choice (Python, Java, Node. js, .NET, etc.) as a function that produces a specific outcome. The model for development can be a FaaS computing model or based on microservices architecture.

For the FaaS product, an event triggers the function. A microservice operates through APIs.

When the microservice application is deployed, the serverless computing product automatically provisions the required infrastructure and the application is deployed in a container. When triggered, a FaaS product is also deployed and executed in a container and is spun down immediately thereafter.

Infrastructure management is managed by the cloud service provider, which dynamically allocates the necessary resources at the time of execution—the vertical and horizontal scaling and descaling based on the traffic/load.

The developer focus is completely fixated on the code and its functionality. The user gets the best possible experience that the application can offer—with the necessary capacity, availability, and security parameters. Specifically for the FaaS product, charges are levied only when the functions are triggered, thus offering efficient optimization of costs.

Pros and Cons of Serverless Computing

With the introduction of automation and the hands-off approach to infrastructure, serverless computing is the best option as architectures take shape to adapt to the world of serverless. That said, here are some of the obvious and not-so obvious benefits of serverless computing:

- **Developer productivity**: One of the key software delivery objectives is to push software to the market frequently to keep it relevant. This is dependent on the SDLC processes, which mainly involves development and testing. Getting the entire lifecycle to run faster is the goal of DevOps; serverless computing helps developers code faster. With the dependence on infrastructure no longer an issue, the development teams get more time to focus on writing code, innovating, and making quality products.

- **Cost efficiency**: The bare minimum financial, margin-led world has taught us to look for areas where costs can be optimized. As the saying goes— every penny saved is a penny earned. With serverless computing, the right-sized infrastructure resources ensure that the infrastructure spends are optimized. With FaaS, the infrastructure costs come into play only when the function is used.

- **Auto-scaling**: The concept of auto-scaling exists in IaaS as well, but the concept is more powerful with serverless computing because the scaling estimations are auto-computed by the intelligent cloud service, rather than relying on mere thresholds. This ensures optimal performance at all times of the year, with varying loads, leading to increased availability of the software and higher customer satisfaction.

- **Language compatibility**: The serverless computing architecture is a polyglot. It is compatible with a number of languages—Java, Python, node.js, and JavaScript. Since different applications are best with certain languages, developers are not constrained to specific languages when they use a serverless architecture.

- **Easy CI-CD**: As mentioned, serverless computing works seamlessly with the DevOps methodology. It catalyzes the search toward effortless execution of the build, test, and deployment activities in the pipeline. With the absence of environment management, developers can focus on building quality in the code, which helps it move quickly through production.

- **Reduced operational complexity**: With serverless computing, the cloud service provider manages the operational tasks, including server provisioning, upgrading/patching, configuration, monitoring, and maintenance. Developers can focus on the application functionality and less on managing the infrastructure.

Every coin has two sides. While the serverless architecture helps make software development seamless, there are certain drawbacks to consider before you take the plunge:

- **Vendor lock-in**: The fear of getting embedded into an ecosystem is scary, as it becomes more difficult to pivot as dependence rises. For example, consider Android and iOS users. They find it difficult to switch from one to the other, as the data transfer is not always seamless. Likewise, with serverless computing, which serverless products are delivered varies from vendor to vendor.

- **Cost unpredictability**: The right-resourcing of serverless computing provides cost optimization. This is mostly true when you can predict the workloads. For applications that have consistent or higher workloads, serverless can lead to increased costs.

- **Cold start latency**: When FaaS is employed, the infrastructure is spun up when the function is triggered. This is referred to as a cold start and it can lead to delays stemming from resource initialization. This can impact applications that rely on faster latency and immediate responsiveness.

- **Lack of control**: While developers are happy about having fewer dependencies, the double-edged sword is that this freedom means it's much more difficult to debug and monitor events. This can lead to troubleshooting ineffectiveness, which can lead to known bugs in the system, reduced performance, and security breaches that cannot be traced back to their origins.

- **Limited debugging tools**: Traditional debuggers might not work seamlessly with serverless functions due to their ephemeral execution environment.

- **Maturity**: Serverless is a relatively new technology compared to the traditional approaches. While it's rapidly evolving, it might not have the same level of maturity and established best practices as well-tested server-management tools.

Popular Serverless Products

The market is flooded with numerous serverless service providers given that the technology has existed for more than a decade. The prominent ones are as follows:

- **AWS Lambda**: Although serverless computing existed, it did not become popular until AWS Lambda was introduced in 2014. With AWS having garnered the bulk of the market at the time, it helped them penetrate the market with ease. Lambda supports multiple languages, including Python, Java, Ruby, .NE, and Node.js, among others. As with other AWS products, integrating Lambda is seamless, and if you are already on the AWS truck, it makes complete sense to move to AWS Lambda. One of the criticisms of Lambda is the cost unpredictability. The overall cost deduction is based on several factors, including the type of server architecture, concurrency usage, deployment location, and more.

- **Microsoft Azure Functions**: Microsoft followed AWS' footsteps in setting up their serverless computing product. The Microsoft Azure Functions product was launched in 2016. It supports PowerShell, Bash, C#, .NET, Java, JavaScript, Python, and TypeScript, among other languages. Integrating with other Azure products is seamless. The criticism around this product is that it has been trying to follow Lambda's footsteps by matching features. From a cost perspective, Azure Functions is relatively simpler and follows a tiered model to support different types of use.

- **Google Cloud Functions**: Google Cloud Functions released in 2016; it's not GCP's first serverless product. Their Google App Engine was released in 2008. I discuss both Google serverless products in detail in the upcoming parts of this chapter.

- **IBM Cloud Functions**: IBM's answer to serverless computing was called IBM Cloud Functions. It was launched in 2017. It is based on Apache Open Whisk—which is an open source FaaS product. IBM Cloud Functions, which is part of the IBM ecosystem, supports Go, Java, NodeJS, Python, Scala, Swift, and .NET, among others.

- **CloudFlare Workers**: While the rest of the serverless computing products that were discussed in this section were from the stable of cloud service providers, CloudFlare Workers, which was released in 2018, is from a company that specializes in web tools. The differentiation lies in their focus toward improving performance and reducing latency. This is achieved by deploying the products close to the client site when possible. CloudFlare Workers is economical compared to the big players.

Google App Engine

Google App Engine (GAE) is a Platform as a Service (PaaS) product that provides a scalable runtime environment for web applications. It offers the quickest way for developers to get started on a secure environment and provides access to a wide array of APIs/integrations. It is a serverless computing environment that lets developers focus on writing code on a fully managed infrastructure set up by Google.

The programming languages compatible with GAE are Node.js, Java, C#, Go, Ruby, Python, and PHP. The product is capable of hosting web applications and mobile backend applications—as the infrastructure leveraged is the same as the ones that power Google applications like Gmail, Google Drive, and so on.

Google Cloud Software Delivery Kit (SDK)

Google provides an SDK called Google Cloud SDK. It allows users to emulate the runtime environment on their own local machines. It includes the necessary tools and libraries for developing, testing, and deploying applications on the Google Cloud Platform, including Google App Engine.

The Google Cloud SDK provides a collection of command-line tools for interacting with and managing Google Cloud services, such as Google App Engine, Google Compute Engine, Google Kubernetes Engine, and Google Cloud Functions.

Developers can use the SDK to develop and test applications on their local machines, and upon satisfaction, deploy them to Google App Engine or other Google Cloud products.

The SDK provides functionalities for deploying applications, managing resources, configuring authentication, and accessing various Google Cloud services. It also includes tools for managing authentication, viewing logs, and monitoring the performance of applications deployed on the Google Cloud Platform.

GAE Key Features

The following are some of the key features of Google App Engine:

- **Security**: Inarguably GAE offers the best infrastructure security, as the application is hosted on the same backend that hosts other prominent Google applications. It also provides a built-in application scanner that identifies any security vulnerabilities.

- **Scaling**: Provides a managed infrastructure that can scale horizontally and vertically to provide the best performance to users during any given load.

- **Integration**: GAE provides various built-in services and APIs, including data storage with Google Cloud Datastore, user authentication and authorization, task queues, and more. These services help developers easily integrate different functionalities into their applications.

- **Observability**: Tools for monitoring and observability of applications are available on GAE.

- **IDE support**: Integrated development and deployment tools with Google Cloud SDK that allow seamless application development, testing, and deployment.

- **Pay as you use**: GAE offers a flexible pricing model, which allows users to pay only for the resources consumed by the application. There are free tier and pay-as-you-go pricing models, which depends on the resource/service consumption.

- **Versioning**: The product maintains different versions/instances of the software. Each version can be tested separately by routing traffic to it, which is a classic use case of A/B testing.

GAE in Action

Google App Engine is part of GCP's free tier and provides certain resources for free: CPU, storage, application programming interfaces (APIs), and concurrent requests. For example, hosting an F type server comes with nine instance hours daily. Users are charged for usage beyond the free limit.

You are not expected to have hands-on experience with Google App Engine. This section is optional. Feel free to skip it.

This section looks at GAE and investigates some of the options in the suite.

1. In the Google Cloud Platform console, search for App Engine.

2. The dashboard/entry page is shown in Figure 7-1.

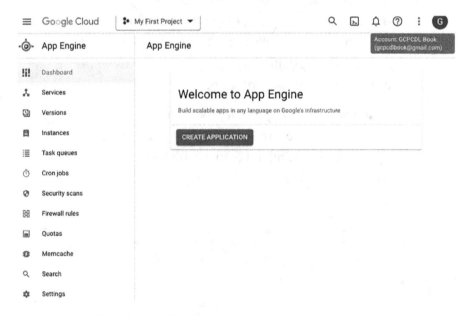

Figure 7-1. *Google App Engine*

You can maintain versions of the application directly in the GAE product, as well as deploy and recall versions as needed.

Multiple instances of the application can be maintained simultaneously. This is a handy feature that supports A/B testing.

Tasks and cron job scheduling can be directly through GAE or you can leverage another product such as Cloud Scheduler to run a job based on cron or on triggers.

The security apparatus in the GAE is quite solid (see Figure 7-2). You can run application security scans and vulnerability scans through Web Security Scanner. It crawls through your application looking for weaknesses and vulnerabilities—by looking through the links and providing various permutations of inputs and event handlers.

Figure 7-2. *Security scans in GAE*

Further, you can place your application hosted on GAE behind a firewall, secure it with SSL, manage the applications with nameservers pointing to custom domains, provide SMTP functionality for mailing, and enable/disable the application (see Figure 7-3).

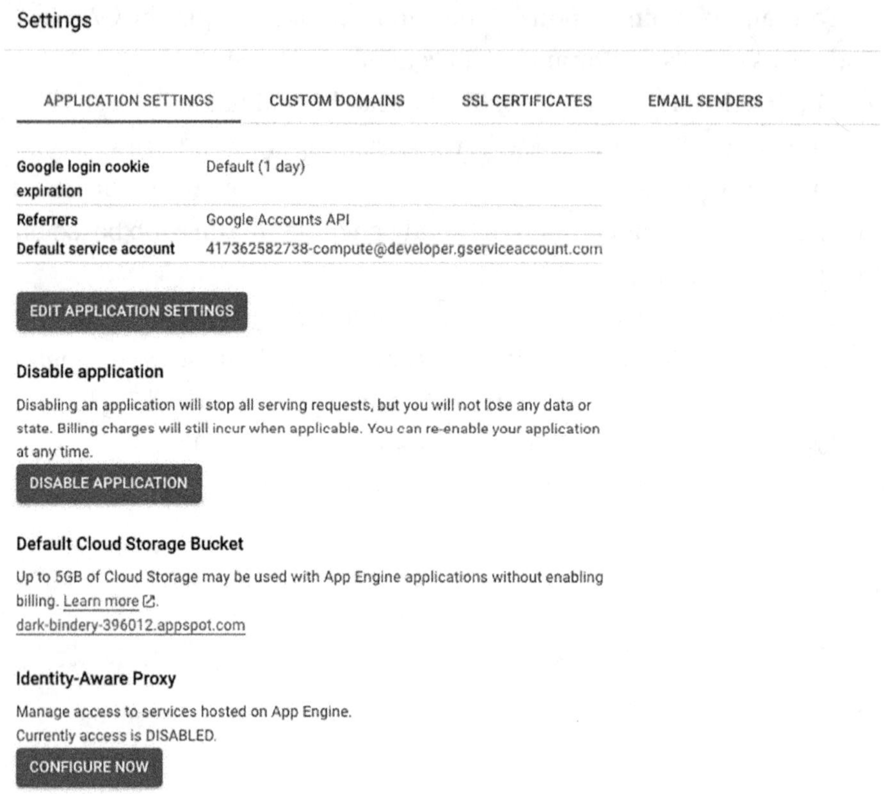

Settings

APPLICATION SETTINGS	CUSTOM DOMAINS	SSL CERTIFICATES	EMAIL SENDERS

Google login cookie expiration	Default (1 day)
Referrers	Google Accounts API
Default service account	417362582738-compute@developer.gserviceaccount.com

EDIT APPLICATION SETTINGS

Disable application

Disabling an application will stop all serving requests, but you will not lose any data or state. Billing charges will still incur when applicable. You can re-enable your application at any time.

DISABLE APPLICATION

Default Cloud Storage Bucket

Up to 5GB of Cloud Storage may be used with App Engine applications without enabling billing. Learn more ☑.
dark-bindery-396012.appspot.com

Identity-Aware Proxy

Manage access to services hosted on App Engine.
Currently access is DISABLED.

CONFIGURE NOW

Figure 7-3. *Application settings in GAE*

3.   As a developer, you can select the region where you want the application to be hosted (see Figure 7-4).

Create app

① **Configure application** — ② Get started

Region

Select a region for your App Engine application. Please remember, once selected the region is permanently tied to the project.

Select a region *
us-central

Identity and API access

Select a service account
Compute Engine default service account

If no service account is selected the default App Engine service account will be used.

NEXT

Figure 7-4. *Create an app on GAE: choosing the region*

Applications are generally created by development teams. Managing access to an application is through the service accounts that help map the access to authorized developers, as shown under Identity and API Access. The service account where the team members are mapped needs to be selected accordingly.

4. In the next screen, you are asked to select the programming language and environment (see Figure 7-5).

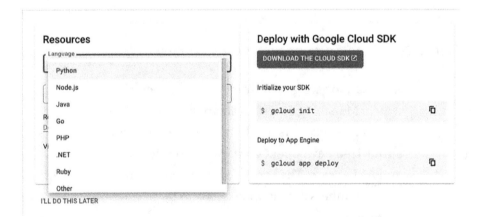

Figure 7-5. *Programming language and environment selection on GAE*

The various languages supported by Google App Engine are shown in Figure 7-6. *Other* refers to languages that are supported through custom runtime in Docker containers.

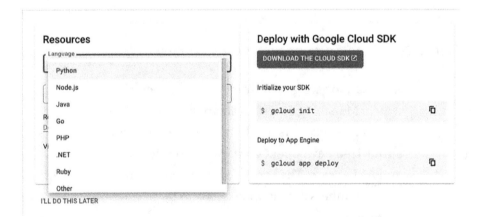

Figure 7-6. *Programming languages supported in GAE*

144

Google App Engine offers two types of environments—standard and flexible. Standard is meant for applications that are lightweight and can be written in one of the languages listed in Figure 7-6. The standard environment manages scaling efficiently, getting down to zero instances if there is absolutely no traffic and quickly spin up thousands of servers to cater to spikes and holiday demand. A flexible environment manages Docker containers and allows the developer to choose the configurations from the Compute Engine. Unlike standard environment, at least a single instance needs to be active at all times. So, it can turn out to be more expensive. If you have an application that needs to be online persistently, or it requires powerful computing power, the Flexible environment is a good option.

Exam Tip   *You might be given a scenario where an application that is running in a sandbox environment needs to scale to spikes within a matter of seconds. For such a scenario, the correct option is App Engine on a Standard environment.*

---

5. If the developer chooses to develop on a standard environment, the Google Cloud SDK needs to be downloaded (see Figure 7-7) and configured on the local system to gain access to Google libraries and interact with Google Command Line Interface (CLI).

Figure 7-7. *Google Cloud SDK*

Google Cloud SDK not only supports Google App Engine but supports across the Google Cloud Platform (GCP). It accelerates various tasks like creating servers, deploying code, and more, by passing the commands in a terminal rather than using the GUI.

Google Cloud Run

The world of serverless environments has changed the game with respect to resource management and cost optimization. Google App Engine delivered the first-generation serverless product, with its own set of limitations: namely the compatibility with the programming languages discussed it in the last section. Although the flexible environment tried to mitigate this limitation with a containerized version, the solution called for a specialized product of its own. Enter Cloud Run.

Google Cloud Run (GCR) brings together the serverless computing technology with the world of containers. This is a great alternative for applications that run in a containerized environment. Developers are free to code in the language of choice, and more importantly, they are not forced to change the underlying technology to fit the serverless platform. Portability of applications is another plus with Cloud Run.

GCR Key Features

Google Cloud Run is based on the open-source project Knative, which adds serverless computing and portability to applications. The product allows developers to run stateless HTTP driven containers without managing the underlying infrastructure (see Figure 7-8).

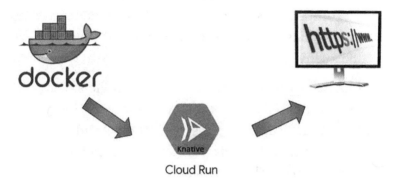

Cloud Run

Figure 7-8. *Google Cloud Run Construct*

Some of the key features that make GCR a popular product are as follows:

1. Google Cloud Run is a fully managed serverless platform that abstracts the infrastructure management. This allows developers to focus on their core development activities and build applications on containers.

2. Developers can use any programming language, library, or framework that can run inside a container. It's an ideal product for developing web applications, APIs, and background jobs.

3. GCR is a good option for web applications and backend jobs, because it allows developers to set up container execution on the back of HTTP requests or events.

4. The GCR workloads are fully portable and are managed by Google, and it can also be deployed into on-premises or Google Cloud-hosted Anthos installations, or even on any platform supported by the Knative framework.

5. Cloud Run can automatically scale the number of instances based on the incoming traffic load. This helps with resource and cost optimization, and more importantly, it ensures that the application's performance is always at or above par.

6. As with other Google Cloud Platform products, GCR provides seamless integration with other Google services like the Google Cloud Storage, Cloud SQL, and Cloud Firestore. This accelerates the application development and enhances the application's feature portfolio.

7. The fully managed GCR product is a complete product with its own monitoring and logging capability provided through Stackdriver, which is in turn integrated with Cloud Console. Cloud Run can be accessed through Google Cloud SDK using CLI.

8. Customers are billed only for the resources consumed, based on the number of vCPUs and the memory consumed during the execution. In today's cost-centric world where organizations look to pinch every penny, GCR is a great addition.

Google Cloud Run vs. Google Kubernetes Engine

One of the key capabilities of the Google Cloud Platform is that it offers a wide range of products that can alternatively cater to certain uses. For example, if a developer wants to develop an application, several options are available. In other words, architectural discretion comes into play.

Google Compute Engine (GCE) can be employed to spin VMs and applications can be developed directly on it. Or, a Docker container can be leveraged on GCE. Additionally, Kubernetes can be used to manage the Docker containers on this existing setup. Google Kubernetes Engine (GKE) can be used to create managed Kubernetes clusters. All these options consider infrastructure as a part of the design. The options that abstract away the infrastructure include Google App Engine (GAE) with standard and flexible options. Or, you could move completely into containers with Google Cloud Run (GCR). As I mentioned, there are several options and there are no wrong choices. Every circumstance and every application calls for a specific use case and one of the products is typically better suited than the others.

Specifically talking about GCR and GKE (considering that the rest do not support containers natively or have limitations), running applications on GCR is straightforward, because the service involving containerization is completely managed by Google. And with GKE, although the clusters are managed by Kubernetes, they are not necessarily doing away with it. That adds a certain level of complexity to the architecture.

GKE does not abstract the infrastructure layer. Therefore, an additional dependency is introduced—even with the auto-pilot mode, the application's configuration needs to be scripted considering the Kubernetes cluster. Secondly, if the application is small enough to be deployed on a single container or is a set of microservices that can be deployed into multiple containers, GKE may be too much.

149

GCR has its strengths, mainly that it is stateless and is the quickest way to set up applications on containers. There is no beating around a fully managed container service. It is particularly called for if the application gets triggered by HTTP, cron jobs, Cloud Scheduler, web sockets, or equivalent events.

GCR or GKE is not a question that deserves a binary answer. The answer is—it depends.

Exam Tip   *You might be given a scenario where an application is required to respond to events and cater to spikes by scaling. The correct option is Cloud Run or Google Cloud Run.*

GCR in Action

This section looks at creating a new Cloud Run service and installing a Docker image.

You are not expected to have hands-on experience with Google Cloud Run. This section is optional. Feel free to skip it.

---

1. On the Google Cloud Platform console, search for Cloud Run. The entry page is shown in Figure 7-9.

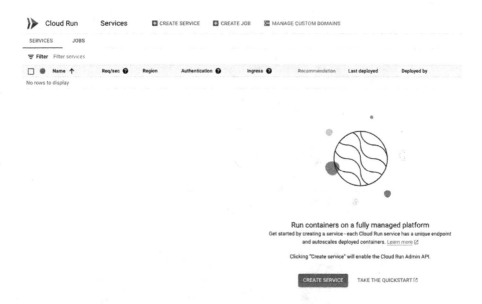

Figure 7-9. *Google Cloud Run*

2. Click CREATE SERVICE to create a new Cloud Run service/containerized application. Alternatively, you can click CREATE JOB to create a backend job hosted on a container.

3. The new service creation page is shown in Figure 7-10.

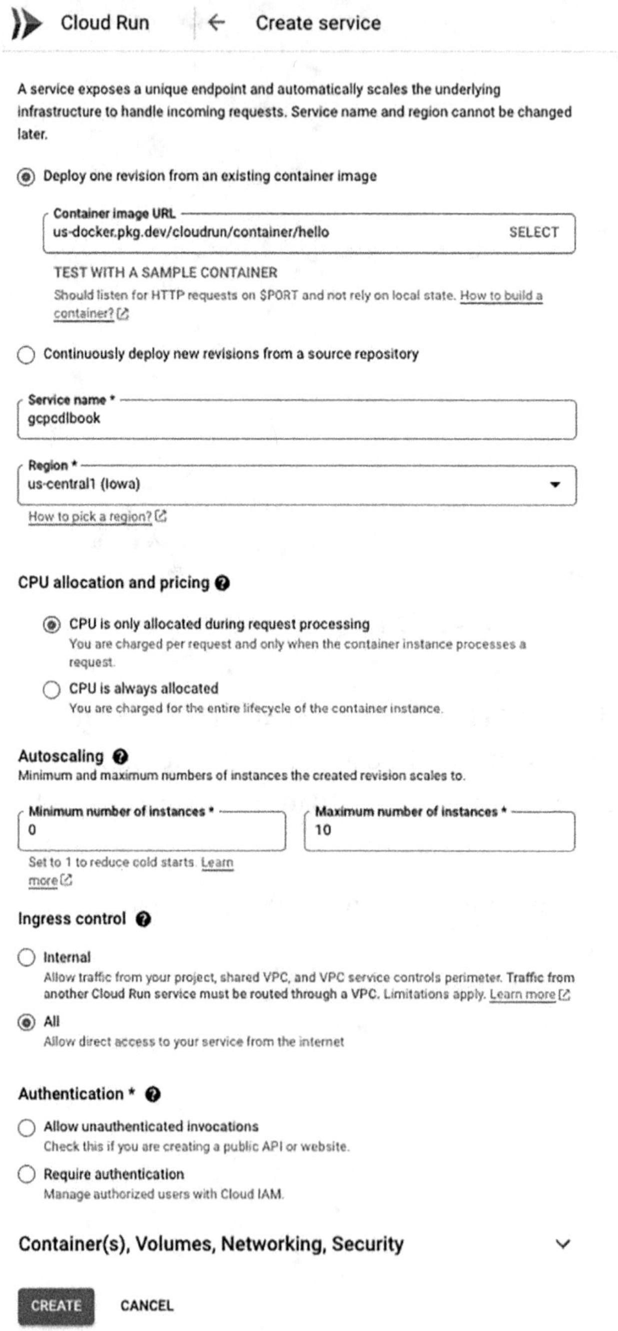

》》 Cloud Run   ← Create service

A service exposes a unique endpoint and automatically scales the underlying infrastructure to handle incoming requests. Service name and region cannot be changed later.

◉ Deploy one revision from an existing container image

┌─ Container image URL ─────────────────────────────────┐
│ us-docker.pkg.dev/cloudrun/container/hello   SELECT │
└───┘

TEST WITH A SAMPLE CONTAINER

Should listen for HTTP requests on $PORT and not rely on local state. How to build a container? ☑

○ Continuously deploy new revisions from a source repository

┌─ Service name * ──────────────────────────────────────┐
│ gcpcdlbook   │
└───┘

┌─ Region * ──┐
│ us-central1 (Iowa)   ▼ │
└───┘

How to pick a region? ☑

CPU allocation and pricing ❷

◉ CPU is only allocated during request processing
You are charged per request and only when the container instance processes a request.

○ CPU is always allocated
You are charged for the entire lifecycle of the container instance.

Autoscaling ❷
Minimum and maximum numbers of instances the created revision scales to.

┌─ Minimum number of instances * ─┐ ┌─ Maximum number of instances * ─┐
│ 0   │ │ 10   │
└─────────────────────────────────┘ └─────────────────────────────────┘

Set to 1 to reduce cold starts. Learn more ☑

Ingress control ❷

○ Internal
Allow traffic from your project, shared VPC, and VPC service controls perimeter. Traffic from another Cloud Run service must be routed through a VPC. Limitations apply. Learn more ☑

◉ All
Allow direct access to your service from the internet

Authentication * ❷

○ Allow unauthenticated invocations
Check this if you are creating a public API or website.

○ Require authentication
Manage authorized users with Cloud IAM.

Container(s), Volumes, Networking, Security   ⌄

[CREATE]   CANCEL

Figure 7-10. *Service creation on Cloud Run*

4. The first input is a Docker image. It can be pointed to an URL or to a source code repository. In this demonstration, I pointed it to a Docker image on Docker Hub (Test with a Sample Container option).

Docker Hub is a container image repository. It has public repositories where developers can host Docker images made available to the general public. A paid version of Docker Hub offers private repositories along with other features like building a team and vulnerability scanning, among others.

---

5. Specify a service name (gcpcdlbook in this example) and a region (us-central1 in this example).

6. CPU allocation options: The first option is for FaaS, where the CPU is allocated, and where the application is triggered. The second option is if the application in online all the time.

7. Ingress control refers to the incoming traffic— whether the traffic is coming from the Internet or through a proxy server, etc.

8. Users can be authenticated before accessing the web application.

9. Service creation takes about five minutes. Figure 7-11 indicates the page when the service is created.

Figure 7-11. *Service created on Cloud Run*

A green checkmark next to the service name indicates that the stateless container has been created successfully. An URL appears next to the service name so you can access the web application.

10. The web application can be accessed through the URL. In this example, it's a simple hello page, as seen in Figure 7-12.

Figure 7-12. *Web application output*

11. Coming back to the Cloud Run console, there are several management options available:

    a. Figure 7-13: The metrics for the web application are provided through Stackdriver.

    b. Figure 7-14: All the logs—including informational, warnings, and errors—are recorded in the logs tab.

    c. Figure 7-15: Triggers for the web application can be added through the Triggers tab.

Figure 7-13. *Metrics on Cloud Run*

Figure 7-14. *Logs on Cloud Run*

Figure 7-15. *Triggers on Cloud Run*

Google Cloud Functions

Google Cloud Functions (GCF) is a serverless product for hosting functions or small pieces of logic that work independently. It is built in the mold of the Function as a service (FaaS) offering, which is both cost effective (as it directly relates to the consumed memory, CPU, events, and load) and scalable. GCF does not leverage containers, and being a serverless product, the infrastructure setup and mobilization is taken care in the background by Google.

Cloud Functions is meant to be used for small logic alone. The logic built on the serverless instance is initiated when triggered by an event. Upon delivering the intended output, the instance is spun down. Google will charge for the product only during its execution—starting with when the event was received until the intended delivery of the logic.

To use this product, developers write a piece of logic in one of the compatible programming languages: Node.js, Python, Go, Java, Ruby, PHP, or .NET Core. The functions are triggered through events from the cloud like adding a file on a storage bucket, pub/sub triggers like notifying downstream applications, and Eventarc triggers. The triggers can also come from the HTTP—say, for example a new video uploaded on YouTube can trigger a function that notifies all its subscribers.

Pub/sub is a publisher subscriber messaging pattern that provides the architecture for asynchronous communication. It allows for the exchange of information between components of a system in a decoupled manner. For example, a publisher service delivers a message to the message broker. Subscribers interact with the message broker to pick up messages they are interested in.

Some typical use cases of GCF include batch programs, ETL, webhooks, and chatbots.

GCF Key Features

Google Cloud Functions is based on the Function as a Service computing model that allows customers to execute code on the back of triggers. The code execution is typically short lived, and the nature of this serverless product ensures that the necessary resources—like the infrastructure, platform, and runtime—are created when the event is triggered.

Exam Tip   *If you are asked on the exam to identify the best product to choose when a small piece of code needs to be executed based on an event or HTTP trigger, choose Google Cloud Functions or Cloud Functions from the list of possible options.*

The following are the key features of the GCF product.

1. Google Cloud Functions (GCF) is a fully managed serverless platform that abstracts the infrastructure management. This allows developers to write the piece of logic and forget about the underlying infrastructure, platform, and runtime.

2. The functionality can be triggered by HTTP requests and cloud events. This allows developers to build logic that responds to events, where use cases that move through a workflow make an ideal setting.

3. Cloud Functions supports multiple programming languages—Node.js, Python, Go, Java, Ruby, PHP, and .NET Core. This flexibility enables developers to choose the best programming language for the requirements.

4. As with other Google serverless computing products, the underlying infrastructure layer automatically scales to meet the load and performance requirements. In the normal state, zero instances exist. When triggered, depending on the traffic/load, a number of instances are created to cater to the demand. When the traffic is processed, the instances are spun down, bringing it back to the normal state of zero instances.

5. Cloud Functions is cost effective because customers are charged only when the instances are created and executed. Depending on the CPU, memory, storage, and other resource usage, customers are proportionally charged. The pay as you go model

is ideal for use cases when the instances do not have to live long, and when there is a possibility of unpredictable workloads.

6. Google Cloud Functions can be seamlessly integrated with other GCP services, including Cloud Storage, Cloud Pub/Sub, and Cloud Firestore, among others. The integration accelerates development and standardizes the ways of working in the cloud platform.

7. Google by default provides a number of developer, monitoring, and logging tools that help monitor execution and quickly diagnose issues in the event of abnormal execution.

GCF in Action

This section looks at Google Cloud Functions.

You are not expected to have hands-on experience with Google Cloud Functions. This section is optional. Feel free to skip it.

---

1. On the Google Cloud Platform console, search for Cloud Functions. The entry page is shown in Figure 7-16.

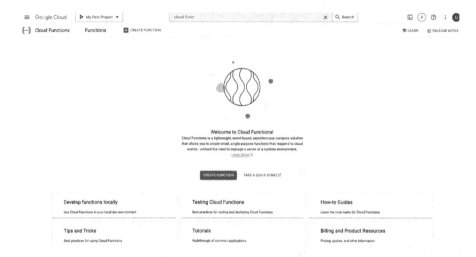

Figure 7-16. *Google Cloud Functions*

2. To create a function, you must enable all the related
    product APIs (see Figure 7-17):

    a. Cloud Build API

    b. Cloud Functions API

    c. Cloud Logging API

    d. Cloud Pub/Sub API

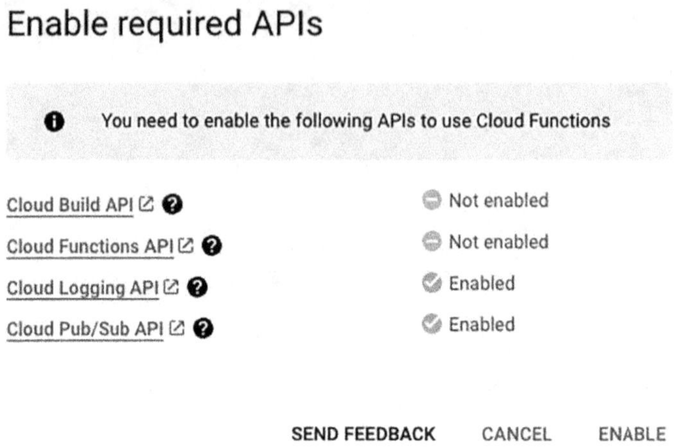

Enable required APIs

> ℹ   You need to enable the following APIs to use Cloud Functions

Cloud Build API ☑ ❓   ⬤ Not enabled

Cloud Functions API ☑ ❓   ⬤ Not enabled

Cloud Logging API ☑ ❓   ✅ Enabled

Cloud Pub/Sub API ☑ ❓   ✅ Enabled

SEND FEEDBACK   CANCEL   ENABLE

Figure 7-17. *Related APIs for GCF*

3. Figure 7-18 shows the GCF configuration screen:

a. GCF is currently in its second avatar (second gen) that is built on Cloud Run. The original version has limited comparatively. The second-gen GCF can intake Eventarc supported events ,which is currently at 90+ distinct cloud events. Plus, the new version supports request concurrency and offers better infra specifications. For more details, see: `https://cloud.google.com/functions/docs/concepts/version-comparison`

b. Specify a unique function name and the region where the FaaS needs to be hosted (`us-central1` in this example).

c. You can choose to allow only authenticated requests to be accepted by the function. This example is using unauthenticated invocations.

d. The URL for the function that is getting created on GCF can be changed through a DNS system.

e. Triggers can be added by clicking the + sign.

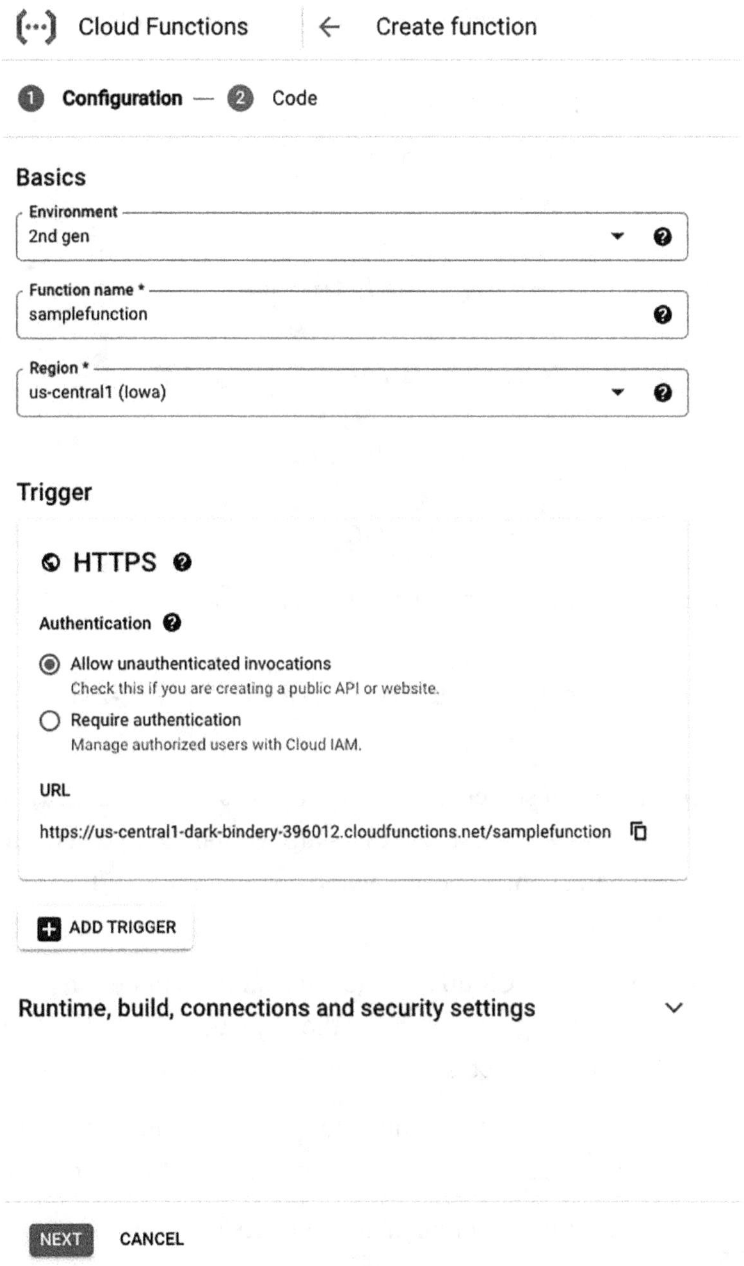

{···} Cloud Functions   ←   Create function

1 **Configuration** — 2 Code

Basics

Environment
2nd gen   ▼   ❷

Function name *
samplefunction   ❷

Region *
us-central1 (Iowa)   ▼   ❷

Trigger

⊙ **HTTPS** ❷

Authentication ❷

◉ Allow unauthenticated invocations
   Check this if you are creating a public API or website.

○ Require authentication
   Manage authorized users with Cloud IAM.

URL

https://us-central1-dark-bindery-396012.cloudfunctions.net/samplefunction ▢

➕ ADD TRIGGER

Runtime, build, connections and security settings   ⌄

[NEXT]   CANCEL

Figure 7-18. *GCF configuration screen*

4. You can add a number of event types to trigger the
    function, as shown in Figure 7-19. This example
    uses the Cloud Storage trigger.

+ ADD TRIGGER

⁂ Pub/Sub trigger

☰ Cloud Storage trigger

⮜ Firestore trigger

▦ Other trigger

Figure 7-19. *Adding trigger events in GCF*

5. See the event configuration screen (see Figure 7-20)
    for Cloud Storage:

    a. The event selected in this example is google.cloud.storage.
        object.v1.deleted. This is an Eventarc supported trigger
        and an event is created whenever an object is deleted on the
        Cloud Storage.

    b. The Google Cloud Storage bucket needs to be selected. This
        is the storage space where the object deletions are monitored.
        When an object is deleted in this bucket, an event is triggered.

    c. Certain permissions need to be provided for the events to talk
        to the message broker in order to invoke the event.

    d. Save the event when all the permissions are granted.

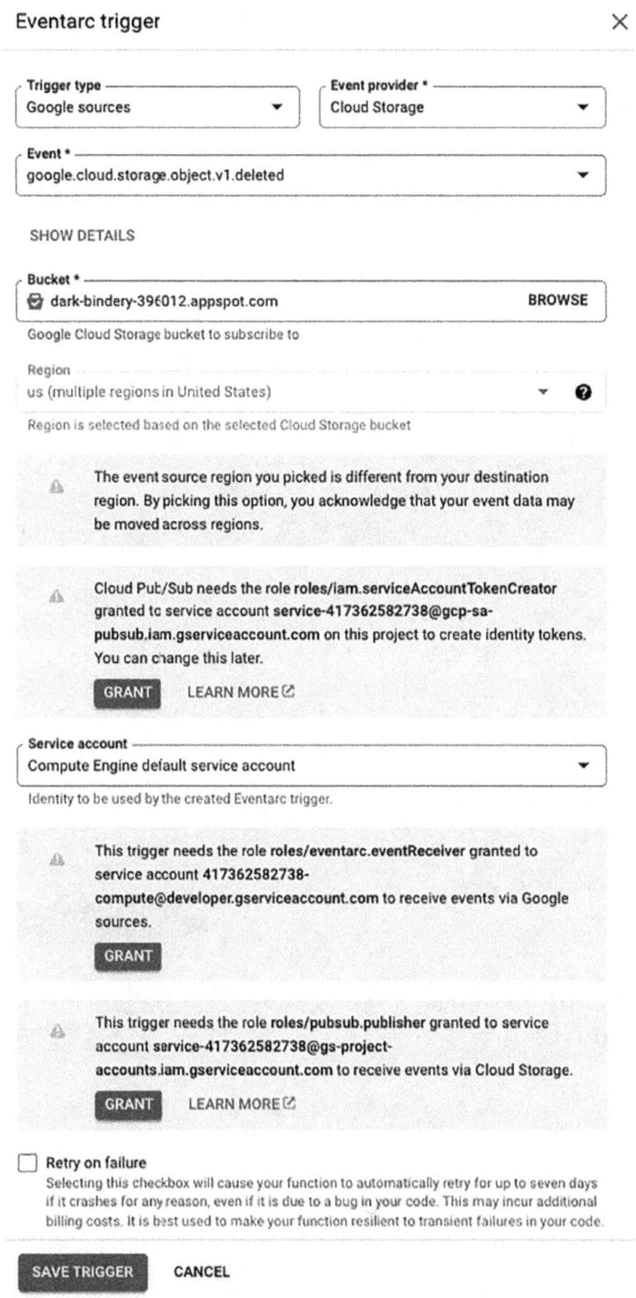

Eventarc trigger   ✕

Trigger type
Google sources   ▼   Event provider *
                                                   Cloud Storage   ▼

Event *
google.cloud.storage.object.v1.deleted   ▼

SHOW DETAILS

Bucket *
🗑 dark-bindery-39€012.appspot.com   BROWSE

Google Cloud Storage bucket to subscribe to

Region
us (multiple regions in United States)   ▼   ❓

Region is selected based on the selected Cloud Storage bucket

> ⚠ The event source region you picked is different from your destination
>   region. By picking this option, you acknowledge that your event data may
>   be moved across regions.

> ⚠ Cloud Pub/Sub needs the role **roles/iam.serviceAccountTokenCreator**
>   granted to service account **service-417362582738@gcp-sa-**
>   **pubsub.iam.gserviceaccount.com** on this project to create identity tokens.
>   You can change this later.
>   [GRANT]   LEARN MORE ⬈

Service account
Compute Engine default service account   ▼

Identity to be used by the created Eventarc trigger.

> ⚠ This trigger needs the role **roles/eventarc.eventReceiver** granted to
>   service account 417362582738-
>   compute@developer.gserviceaccount.com to receive events via Google
>   sources.
>   [GRANT]

> ⚠ This trigger needs the role **roles/pubsub.publisher** granted to service
>   account **service-417362582738@gs-project-**
>   **accounts.iam.gserviceaccount.com** to receive events via Cloud Storage.
>   [GRANT]   LEARN MORE ⬈

☐ Retry on failure
  Selecting this checkbox will cause your function to automatically retry for up to seven days
  if it crashes for any reason, even if it is due to a bug in your code. This may incur additional
  billing costs. It is best used to make your function resilient to transient failures in your code.

[SAVE TRIGGER]   CANCEL

Figure 7-20. *Event configuration screen in GCF*

6. When the event trigger is created, click Next to move to the second configuration page on GCF, as shown in Figure 7-21.

Figure 7-21. *An event is created and the first configuration page is populated on GCF*

7. In the second configuration screen, you can
    choose the runtime (programming language) for
    your function. Depending on the programming
    language, the code construct and the defined events
    are prepopulated, as shown in Figure 7-22. This
    example uses Node.js 20. When this changes the
    runtime to Java 17, you will notice (see Figure 7-23)
    that the codebase on the right has changed as well.

    a. Developers can construct their function from the inline editor
       to develop further functionalities.

    b. Predeployment tests can be carried out in GCF. This is
       supported for Node.js and Python runtimes. Pretesting
       sets up a testing environment, installs the necessary
       dependencies, and executes the function in the Cloud Shell
       environment. The resources leveraged for the testing process
       are not charged.

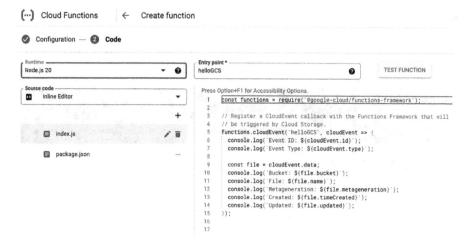

Figure 7-22. *Runtime selection and functionality*
development in GCF

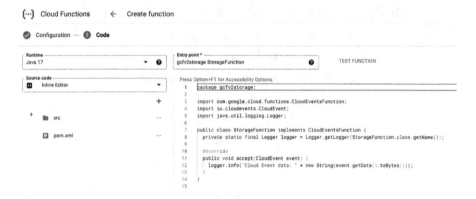

Figure 7-23. *Runtime Java 17 selection*

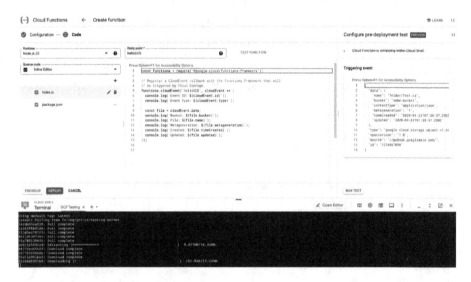

Figure 7-24. *Predeployment testing in GCF*

Summary

Serverless computing abstracts the infrastructure layer, providing an ideal platform for developers to focus on their trade rather than expending time on infrastructure and environment setup activities. Google's serverless products can spin up necessary environments automatically and scale them to meet specifications and performance requirements. They support a number of languages, and more importantly, they charge for the resources used based on the uptime, which is generally during code execution.

This chapter looked at three Google serverless products:

- Google App Engine for developing web applications

- Google Cloud Run for running containers on serverless technologies

- Google Cloud Functions for executing short-lived functions triggered through events

DAY 4

Approximate Study Time: 58 minutes

Chapter 8 - 58 minutes

CHAPTER 8

Application Modernization

It's rather impossible for an organization that is not digitally strong to remain a leader for extended periods of time. With technology and business needs changing regularly, businesses have to build digital backbones that leverage modern technological constructs and flourish through constant changes to align with market needs. In essence, for businesses to adapt to changes and release product/feature updates in a timely manner while exercising cost controls, it's critical to modernize their portfolio of applications.

Application modernization is a broad term that has several meanings in varied contexts. It's very much like the DevOps elephant that has a vast scope. Carrying out any of these activities could be labelled as doing modernization.

This chapter covers the why, what, and how parts of application modernization. There are several techniques and recommendations for modernizing applications, and this chapter covers Google's pattern for modernization. Finally, the chapter touches on application programming interfaces (API).

© Abhinav Krishna Kaiser 2024
A. K. Kaiser, *Become GCP Cloud Digital Leader Certified in 7 Days*,
https://doi.org/10.1007/979-8-8688-0438-0_8

Challenges with Legacy Applications

Cellphones are a classic example of a technology that quickly goes from state-of-the-art to obsolete. The shiny phones that we purchase today become slow and sluggish in a couple of years, and in the next couple of years, they are unusable. This is partly by design but mostly due to the advancements in technology, integrations with other systems, and new features that become ubiquitous. Over a period of about five years, a cellphone becomes a liability, leading to a new purchase.

Likewise, applications have a shelf life. Their look and feel ages, as well as the underlying technology. Mom-and-pop stores managed all their transactions using cash registers decades ago. To be able to track multiple sources of purchase, most stores upgraded to simplistic billing and account software programs. With increasing digital transactions, they are now looking at a new piece of software that can integrate directly with banks, wallets, and buy-now-pay-later accounts. When they do make a decision to purchase this software, it will definitely not be their last. In the next five years, the paradigm of purchasing could change, leading to upgrades of the existing software or new software altogether. This is a never-ending cycle which is true for a mom-and-pop store and also for multi-billion dollar enterprises. Applications become obsolete over time, and they need to be modernized.

Reasons to Leave Legacy Applications Behind

Organizations that can make good decisions to move out of legacy applications have the best possible opportunity to become business leaders. They get the early-mover advantage, which leads to associated benefits. While the good things that lie at the end of the legacy tunnel and modernization program are discussed in detail in the next section, here are some top reasons why organizations should leave legacy applications behind.

1. In the cost-sensitive economy, running and
    maintaining legacy applications is expensive.
    Using legacy technology leads to conventional
    infrastructure setups, on-premise datacenters, and
    procuring resources that may not be fully used.
    Organizations that buy infrastructure systems put
    a depreciation cost on them year on year, and this
    can be as much as 40 percent. With infrastructure
    heavily depreciating every year, they need to
    consider buying or renting this infrastructure.

    With the cloud, we have experienced the power
    behind paying for only what we use, and not buying
    infrastructure but rather renting it. Depending on
    the service leveraged (IaaS vs PaaS vs SaaS), the
    maintenance is outsourced to the cloud service
    provider.

2. The other problem with legacy applications is lack of
    support. For COTS products, there is a shelf life that
    comes with a support end date and organizations are
    then arm-twisted to upgrade to the latest version. As
    the support period and warranties end, the cost of
    maintaining such software becomes expensive.

    With bespoke applications, there are no such
    controls, which possibly leads to support issues. The
    knowledge of the software fades over time, leading
    to additional time needed to fix issues.

3. Legacy applications are built on monolithic
    technologies of the past, where all the logic is
    embedded under a single hood. This worked
    well when systems were not necessarily meant to

integrate with other systems, or did so minimally. But as we move into the connected world, legacy applications find it challenging to adapt to the new ways of working. Especially legacy applications that work on-premises find it challenging to connect to the outside world.

The way we consume data has also changed. We no longer develop data silos, which was the established method during legacy days. This leads to manual retrieval of data that is not error-free.

We interact with applications mainly on our mobile phones. With legacy applications, that may be challenging or impossible—making it (literally) immobile.

4. Since the legacy technology is antiquated, it may not withstand the rigors of the security hacks and may become susceptible to various attacks. In most cases, legacy applications may have a target on their backs for hackers who want to penetrate the weakest entry points in solutions and data systems.

5. Legacy applications are slow and take longer to respond to requests. This is due to the absence of advanced features and technologies that optimize performance. The lack of dynamic scaling can leave legacy applications wanting during periods of heavy load.

Bad performance will lead to poor customer experience, which can possibly turn current and potential customers away. Customers want to have a pleasant experience without lags. Plus, customers want to see progress, which translates to new features that make the software easy to use and create value to users. For example, I moved to a new trading platform, because the portfolio dashboard provided the profit/loss percentages for all my scripts that I held in the same view. While on my old trading platform, I had to go back to the purchase records to calculate the profits/losses manually. The new platform made my life easy, which helped me make quicker decisions. With customers seeking better experiences, legacy applications can potentially turn customers away. All the more reason to modernize!

6. Legacy applications work on legacy technologies. Most developers who worked on legacy technologies have either switched to newer technologies or have retired. Therefore, finding a pool of developers who can work on legacy technologies is becoming more difficult. To rub salt on the wound, legacy applications have a history of poor documentation maintenance, which leads to increased maintenance.

Why Do Organizations Still Swear by Legacy Applications?

There are a number of compelling reasons to move away from legacy applications. I provided the top reasons why legacy applications are bad for business. Yet, many organizations continue to run their businesses on the back of legacy applications. For example, a number of banks are still on mainframes, and for a reason—they do the job well. While banking and mainframes might be an exception, let's take a look at other factors:

1. Legacy applications still deliver value to organizations. There is no reason for them to discontinue using them. Case in point—mainframes. It is believed that two thirds of the fortune 100 companies continue to use mainframes for their critical processing—especially the banks. The reasoning is that there is no technology that can overpower mainframes in high-speed transaction processing, in terms of speed, volume, and the costs incurred. They argue that unless the technology is not hindering their business, there is absolutely no reason to switch to modern technologies. At the end of the day, a modernized application costs a lot of money and unless businesses find a decent return on investment, they are not going to switch.

2. The legacy applications are not at par with the latest security measures. However, their current levels are acceptable, and organizations are able to accept the associated risks. For example, an organization using a legacy application to run a non-critical batch job may find the legacy application to be sufficient. A failed batch job may not have major implications.

3. Organizations that are on the verge of getting acquired by another company or are planning to change their strategy, which could involve sunsetting their current processes and developing a set of new ones, might choose to continue using legacy applications for the time being. This may be a temporary phase but with major changes on the horizon, there is no telling how long the legacy applications may be used.

Application Modernization

Application modernization is a technical exercise that results in changes to the technical wirings of an application. Merely reforming the application technically (on its own) does not serve any purpose. The business should be an equal participant in any modernization program, because the essence of modernization is to align to changing market needs, and to create applications that cater to current problems with an eye on future changes.

Application modernization can be defined as *the process of making updates or transforming legacy applications to enrich the functionality, performance, and user experience, and most importantly, to align with the current and future business needs.*

Application modernization involves upgrading the software. The upgrades are carried out within the confines of the cloud ecosystem. This may be further broken down into these steps:

1. Moving out of traditional datacenters into the cloud.

2. Adopting the cloud-native architecture that reimagines an application through the components natively available on the cloud, such as serverless technologies, automated scaling, and seamless integration with other cloud services.

3. Developing applications with technologies that are fit for the cloud, including using containers, building microservices, using management frameworks such as Agile to align with the business, and adopting the DevOps methodology to accelerate the development process.

179

Cloud-Native Architecture

The basis for application modernization is carried out on the back of a cloud-native architecture. This means leveraging cloud services such as Google Kubernetes Engine and Google App Engine to act as catalysts for rapid development and reduce costs. It is an architectural construct that relies on building scalable applications, resilience, flexibility, and offering regular releases. Figure 8-1 provides an overview of the prominent cloud-native architecture elements.

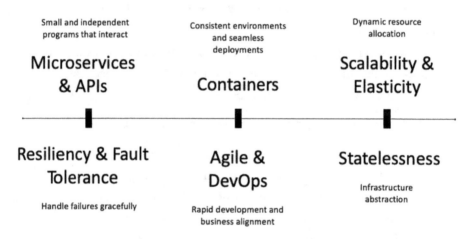

Figure 8-1. *Cloud-native architecture elements*

Cloud-native applications are nimble and allow for rapid development. This is possible through the microservices architecture, which is composed of small and independent programs. Microservices talk to each other through APIs (discussed later in this chapter). The architecture emphasizes developing an API-first design approach, which means that products and services can be easily integrated.

Cloud-native architectures work better with containers as they reduce the dependency on developers to manage the underlying platform. The encapsulated application, along with its dependencies, provides consistency across environments, which allows for seamless deployment into lower and higher environments. Developers find it easier to work with containers rather than directly on a virtual machine. Managing containers using an orchestration platform such as Kubernetes, or better still, working with a service like GKE, reduces the overhead on developers. Having container orchestration managed by the cloud service provider ensures smooth deployments, scaling appropriately, and high availability.

You may have the best architecture, one that's dynamic, flexible, and scalable. And yet, as the market shifts (which happens fairly often) and the products don't change with it, the game of conquering the market is lost. Therefore, a cloud-native architecture needs to be supported with Agile and DevOps practices that allow for the business to be involved in day to day product development. DevOps practices provide an ecosystem for increased experimentation, the highest possible quality, and quick deployments.

Consider any of the business areas that you interact with today. They all have competition, which is growing by the day. As the world gets more competitive, businesses are forced to work with smaller margins, which means reducing costs wherever possible. A cloud-native architecture provides flexibility through its elastic technology and allows for resources to scale as needs grow, as well as reduce dynamically when needs shrink.

While scalability and elasticity infuse cost optimization, it is equally important, or more so, for the systems and applications to be available with sufficient capacity and security. If paying customers encounter a shopping website that is down, they will move to the next site that is available. Components fail but that should not be a single point of failure for the entire system. Resiliency and fault tolerance are inherent parts of the cloud-native architecture and provide more uptime and better performance.

181

Statelessness reduces the overhead on developers, so they can focus their effort on developing applications. Stateless design also allows for independent functions/programs to exist that are scalable and fault-tolerant.

Business Alignment

Application modernization is a massive transformation program. Therefore, it requires the business and the C-suite to stand firmly behind the program and be sponsors. This exercise is not about breaking down a monolithic application into microservices while retaining all the application features.

Instead, it must be viewed as an opportunity to reimagine the application to meet the strategic goals of the business and contribute toward business needs, such as entering new markets, increased customer participation and satisfaction, and reduced operational expenditure.

There are benefits to staying in close alignment with the business. On one end, a close collaboration with the business stakeholders ensures that the modernization program builds products that the business needs. On the other end, the required budget and other resources flow through as needed.

High cost are associated with this program, and the objective therefore should be to extract the return on investment (ROI) and fuel business growth. By prioritizing modernization and tying costs to business value, business can make informed decisions on where to invest their resources for the greatest impact on the bottom line.

A close alignment with the business ensures that the associated risks are well managed, and the corrective, preventive, and other mitigative actions are identified and plans are put in place. This includes the potential risk to data integrity, system reliability, and changes to product features.

Benefits of Application Modernization

Application modernization has several benefits, enabling companies to transform their applications, increase efficiency, and stay competitive in a rapidly evolving business landscape. The key benefits of application modernization include the following:

1. **Cloud-native architecture**: Every organization charts a path for their business to grow, and the necessary applications and features are developed. Somewhere along the way, the goals lead to pivoting to a different direction or picking up adjacent areas of interest. In this situation, an application built on a cloud-native architecture is the perfect tool.

2. **Development efficiency**: The faster you get your product to the market, the better the chances of success. Application modernization has a direct effect on business agility, which correlates to releasing features faster to market. Plus, the decoupled nature of modernized applications provides developer efficiency and is a solid ground on which to experiment.

3. **User experience**: The proof of an application pudding is in its application—the experience users have when using it. Modernized applications can help improve user experience, which has a direct impact on customer satisfaction. Increased satisfaction in using an application can potentially lead to increased sales. Intuitive interfaces, responsive design, and other user-centric features contribute to higher customer satisfaction and engagement.

4. **Reduced costs**: The cost benefits derived from application modernization are immense. By optimizing code and infrastructure, organizations can reduce resource consumption, benefit from cloud-based cost models, and avoid the expenses associated with maintaining outdated technologies.

5. **Agile and DevOps**: In the modern world, outcomes are a byproduct of moving at a rapid pace, which is possible by working in parallel or removing hurdles. Application modernization leverages Agile and DevOps, which aims to do both. This has a direct effect on how quickly features can be released to production.

6. **Developer population**: The problem with legacy applications is multi-fold. The number of developers qualified to work on legacy technologies is shrinking, because some of them are upgrading to modern technologies and others are retiring.

7. **Security**: Legacy applications can have security vulnerabilities that pose risks to organizations. One of the key reasons to modernize is to stay ahead of the vulnerabilities by transferring the security risks to the cloud service provider. With modernization, the latest technologies adopt modern security practices and ensure compliance with industry standards and regulations.

The 5 Rs of Application Modernization

Organizations with legacy applications want to move to the cloud in the least disruptive way. There are various strategies that are commonly employed to bring applications to the cloud. The Gartner group calls them the five Rs of application modernization. The strategies to modernize legacy applications are listed in Figure 8-2.

5 Rs of Application Modernization

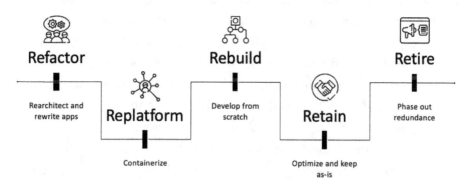

Figure 8-2. *The five Rs of application modernization*

Refactor

Refactor refers to rewriting the code to improve the non-functional aspects of an application. You don't necessarily change the underlying functionalities, but you do change the code. This is required to move an application into a cloud environment from an on-premises environment.

Some examples of refactoring include removing technical debt, which will make the application more efficient due to better logic wiring inside the application. For instance, perhaps the legacy application code had multiple instances of redundancies and duplicates. When these are removed, the binaries, and hence the application, turns out to be efficient and in theory will provide better performance.

Refactoring can also include changing the architecture—say from three-tier to microservices. This necessarily changes the construct of an application, which involves breaking down a monolithic application into a modular architecture or into microservices. The change in architecture is at times referred to as the sixth R—rearchitect.

Replatform

Replatforming is generally referred to as "lift and shift" and is the most popular approach used to migrate from on-premises to the cloud. This approach is also referred to as *rehosting*. There are major advantages to this approach, as the cost effectiveness offered by public clouds can quickly be enjoyed. Because the functionality does not change, nor does it warrant significant code changes, it does not present resistance from stakeholders. We looked at Anthos for Kubernetes and bare metal for Oracle. These are some specific use cases for replatforming.

When replatforming, the entire application is migrated to a cloud environment without making significant changes to the code. Some code changes may need to be carried out to make the application compatible with the cloud services, but there is little to no effort to change the functionality or refactor the code.

An uncommon example of replatforming could include moving an application from one cloud host to another—say for example from AWS to GCP. This may be done to lower costs and utilize better functionalities. In this use case, some code changes may be required to integrate it into the new cloud.

Rebuild

Rebuild refers to developing a new version of the application from scratch while preserving its core functionalities and features. This approach often involves using modern development tools, frameworks, and best practices. Under refactor, the code base does not change, and if it did, it was for some parts alone.

Under rebuild, all the applications are rebuilt to suit the cloud-native architecture. While the best of frameworks and practices are leveraged, this is the most expensive form of application modernization.

Retain

This can be confusing. *Retain* means that you don't migrate to the cloud but keep rooted in the on-premises environment. Yet, it is a part of the application modernization approach, as retain presents a classic case of hybrid environment usage.

While some applications in an organization's portfolio could be moved, this may not be feasible in some cases. Say for example there is high volumes of data or there are complex applications running on mainframe computers. A common use case for retain could be legal and regulatory norms that may not allow data to be moved to a public cloud. It might be better to keep them on-premises while moving the rest of the portfolio to the cloud.

Retire

Retire refers to phasing out outdated or redundant applications that no longer serve a purpose in the organization's ecosystem. Retiring products takes great courage and can lead to organizations affecting cost savings and focusing their efforts on priority items rather than on redundancy.

Often, the retire approach is combined with the *replace* approach, where a redundant application makes way for a better application that is preferably built on cloud-native architecture.

Another variation of retire is *repurchase*, where existing licenses expire, and a new license is procured. An example of this is going to traditional on-premises Salesforce to the Salesforce cloud, an SaaS product. It is not necessary to move with the same vendor—an example could be moving from Citrix to the Google Compute Engine.

The Roadmap to Modernization

Application modernization is the end state, where legacy applications are modified to fit the current technological ecosystem and they are migrated onto the cloud. While we know where we want to end up, the path may not be clear. The type of applications, the kind of market they cater to, the technologies involved, and the journeys they take differ from one organization to another. Therefore, a cookie cutter approach doesn't normally work for application modernization use cases. That said, there are a few established patterns of application modernization that are commonly used with a fair amount of success.

Steps to Modernize

Before undertaking a modernization journey, you need to take these key steps to prepare for modernization:

1. Understand the reasons behind the modernization journey. If things are working well, there may not be a case for changing. Getting ahead of the competition due to exemplary customer experience is a good reason to modernize. Determine the *why* before embarking on the journey.

2. To understand the current state, conduct a discovery exercise. Analyze the findings to identify the aspects that are working and those that aren't. The analysis provides intelligence and insights into the aspects of which technology/application to change, which further uncovers the downstream impacts and associated costs. Most importantly, this step helps build a business case for application modernization.

3. Unless the senior-leadership stands behind the application modernization program, it is not going to succeed. For starters, any application modernization program is expensive and has the potential to shake up internal stakeholders and the customer community. Get the leadership support—uncover the existing problem areas and the business values that can potentially come out of the modernization program, aided by the total return on investment.

4. Expect a major cultural shift within and outside the organization. New technologies and processes are bound to cause disruption and pull people out of their comfort zones. Prepare the organization to begin with the upcoming changes. Share the vision and the direction that you are headed, as well as how the modernization will improve things.

5. Plan thoroughly for the changes—from a technology, people, and process perspective. Identify the various risks and mitigation actions. Even the best plans fail sometimes, so remain nimble and ready to pivot as needed. Remember

that the objectives and plans are centered around the customers. Make sure they meet customer expectations and requirements, and not just internal expectations.

6. Identify the right technology and tools to invest in early in the process. Since this is a critical step of the journey, spend as much time as you need assessing the tools and technologies, getting advice from experts, and running proof of concepts.

7. Build a system for the future that can scale dynamically and could integrate seamlessly through application programming interfaces (API). Design a robust configuration management system that maps out the applications to their integration and relationships to upstream (infrastructure) and downstream segments.

8. Select an optimal pattern to modernization (discussed in detail in the next section).

9. Involve customers in the application modernization journey. Work with them from the early stages, and let them be part of the pods that build the application.

10. Execute the program and measure its progress against the goals. It is important to measure at every step to avoid developing an application that works and delivers like legacy applications.

11. Plan for deployment in the least disruptive way. Mull over approaches, such as canary deployments, to test with select customer base before releasing to the rest of the customer community.

Modernization Patterns

This section looks at some of the common patterns of application modernization. The patterns discussed here may not be comprehensive, but they cover the majority of cases.

Replatform and Change

Replatforming was explained earlier as a strategy that employs moving the application as is from on-premises to a cloud environment.

This approach can work depending on the complexity of the application, its dependencies, and the data it hosts. This approach is also referred to as lift and shift or rehost. After replatforming the application on the cloud, the application is modernized with the necessary modifications.

This is a common pattern of application modernization used by organizations. However, organizations were not able to take complete advantage of the cloud—as in dynamic scaling, the cost efficiencies and using other cloud-native applications. In 2022, Forrester predicted (https://www.forrester.com/blogs/predictions-2022-cloud-computing-reloaded/) that organizations would move away from this approach and embrace cloud-native technologies.

Change and Replatform

The next pattern is a rehash of the previous one. Instead of changing the application after moving to the cloud, the modernization exercise is carried out on-premises with the changes that make it compatible with the cloud. When the changes are completed, the application is then rehosted to cloud. This is an aggressive move as the intent is for organizations to enjoy all the benefits of what the cloud has to offer upon landing. This is not a commonly employed pattern of modernization.

Greenfield Modernization

Starting with a clean slate is perfect for building anything. There are no hindrances, hangovers, and adjustments to consider. A *greenfield modernization* refers to a development program where an application is developed from scratch—all the code is written afresh. Organizations can build a utopian product by opting for this modernization approach. Once the application is built in a cloud environment, the data and connections from the legacy applications can be moved over during a weekend, and out goes the legacy to a completely new application.

Although this sounds great, this almost never happens. Organizations with legacy applications have pockets of assets within the legacy application that they want to bring over to the new application. This not only accelerates development but it can also save on costs, as greenfield development is the most expensive modernization pattern.

Brownfield Development

Greenfield and brownfield are the terms borrowed from the construction industry. Greenfield refers to constructing buildings on land that previously had no construction and Brownfield refers to building an annex or making major modifications to an existing building.

Brownfield development considers building an application on the cloud by incorporating parts of the legacy application or improving on the existing legacy application. The depth of change can vary from simple changes to an architectural overhaul. Examples are an addition of features, integrating new applications, and enhancing existing functionalities.

This pattern provides the fastest path to modernization, as developers have the best of the legacy and the cloud ecosystems. To embark on a brownfield development, you must have thorough knowledge and documentation of the legacy application. This can be tricky, as you are reengineering the ecosystem to meet the current modernization requirements, and existing bugs can sneak into the modern system.

Application Programming Interface (API)

Application Programming Interfaces (APIs) are classes/pieces of code that connect two applications so they can communicate. APIs are potent weapons for planning and executing application modernization because legacy applications must be able to talk to modern applications or legacy applications are replaced with microservices that talk to each other through APIs. Before digging deeper into the modernization use case, it's important to understand how APIs work and why they are so helpful.

Consider a news portal's home page. You might see news snippets from multiple sources, the current weather reading, a stock market ticker, and of course advertisements. The news snippets (data) do not essentially reside on the portal's system; they are pulled from various sources. The interface through which the data is pulled are the APIs. The source sites where the news items are published use APIs at their end to publish their newsfeed. The news portal uses API calls to pull the newsfeeds. Of course, there is authentication and validation of the APIs that call the data.

APIs are like tiny middleware systems and are more powerful than a single interface. They can be programmed to publish data only to authenticated services and record audit logs. APIs written in a particular programming language can interact with software written in the same language. However, language-agnostic APIs do exist as well—web APIs or more specifically APIs that rely on protocols and not on programming languages. For example, HTTP API and WebSocket API.

Commonly, developers use two architectures for developing APIs—Representational State Transfer (REST) and Simple Object Access Protocol (SOAP). REST APIs are most commonly used, and they are simple to build, easy to deploy, and scalable. Web applications leverage these APIs. SOAP is based on Extensible Markup Language (XML).

The Role of APIs in Application Modernization

Application modernization involves either adding more features/modules to a legacy application or creating a new application with microservices. In both of these cases, there is a need to communicate between multiple systems and APIs have therefore become an integral part of an application modernization program.

Extending the API prominence, there is another architectural approach called API-first design, where the APIs are developed first, and then the piece of software is developed. This concept is somewhat similar to TDD, where unit test cases are developed before the application code.

Earlier, the enterprise architecture was dependent on middleware and the purpose/objective was to make the applications compatible with it, and eventually to connect to it. APIs have made communication straightforward, simple to develop, and secure to use. APIs can work with various types of applications, data lakes/warehouses, and Internet of Things (IoT) devices, as indicated in Figure 8-3.

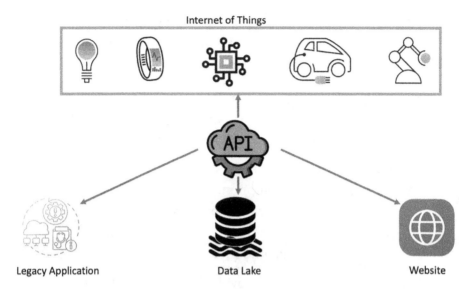

Figure 8-3. *Representation of APIs connecting legacy applications, data lakes, websites, and IoTs*

Further, APIs are secure and create compartments. They allow controlled access to data stored in legacy systems. Rather than directly interacting with databases, applications can use APIs to request and receive specific data, promoting a more secure and modular approach to data management.

Apigee

Apigee is a Google Cloud Platform product that specializes in managing APIs comprehensively. The product can be used to build, effectively manage, and secure APIs under a single roof. It is designed to streamline the process of developing, managing, and analyzing APIs, making it easier for businesses to create and maintain their digital ecosystems.

Sonoa Systems founded the Apigee Enterprise API Platform product in 2008. The product became so popular that the founding company decided to rebrand itself after the product called Apigee. Google acquired

195

Apigee in 2016 and brought it under the GCP ecosystem. Since then, the product has become a leader in the API management space and has been consecutively featured on Gartner's magic quadrant as a leader.

Key Features of Apigee

Some of the key features of Apigee include the following:

1. **Unified platform**: Enterprises generally have a mix of SaaS, hybrid, and on-premise applications, and Apigee is compatible with them. This means it is a single API management platform that can be used to manage an organization's APIs.

2. **Best practices**: Apigee provides tools that accelerate API design and development. These tools help create a well-defined structure to the APIs and ensure that the best practices are followed, including defining the API's structure, endpoints, data models, and security policies.

3. **Unified gateway**: Apigee doubles up as an API gateway, which is the entry point for all API requests. When requests hit Apigee, it handles tasks such as request routing, security enforcement, traffic management, and protocol translation. With Apigee managing the gateway, it can centrally manage the security and control the data flow between the publisher and caller of the APIs.

4. **Security**: Apigee Advanced API Security is robust and comprehensively secures APIs and data. It supports authentication, authorization, encryption, and other security measures to ensure that only authorized services can access protected resources.

5. **Governance**: The organizations are in complete control of the API traffic and its management through Apigee. The product can limit the rate of data transfer, introduce a quota for each service to leverage, optimize performance with caching, and ensure that APIs operate within specified limits.

6. **Analytics and monitoring**: One of the standout features of Apigee is its strong analytics and monitoring capabilities. Organizations can gain insights into API usage/misuse, the users' preferences/behavior, and performance. This business intelligence can potentially help organizations reprioritize and restructure their businesses based on user interests.

7. **Scalability**: Apigee is scalable depending on the number of API requests it receives. This feature helps maintain a minimum performance parameter for APIs. Additionally, API performance is bolstered with load balancing, caching, and throttling, which ensures reliable and efficient APIs that work as expected, even during high traffic.

8. **External support**: The developer portal in Apigee helps on-board external developers who want to discover and consume APIs. The self-service environment allows developers to collaborate and provides a pathway to accessing, discovering, and testing APIs.

9. **Integration with Google products**: Apigee seamlessly integrates with other Google products, enabling organizations to leverage additional cloud capabilities as part of their API strategy.

10. **Multi-cloud capability**: Apigee doesn't just work with Google Cloud Platform; it can be deployed across multiple cloud services, such as Amazon Web Services and Microsoft Azure. Its compatibility with other clouds means no vendor lock-in.

Summary

Except for startups, all organizations are burdened with legacy applications. These applications are embedded into the organization's processes and replacing them can be a major hassle. This process often includes behavioral changes from the internal and external stakeholders. Application modernization looks into the aspects of modernizing legacy applications by considering the latest technological constructs and leveraging the power of the cloud.

APIs are an inherent element of an application modernization program, because they form the connectedness between applications, including legacy and microservice applications. The Google Apigee product simplifies API management and acts as an accelerator in creating and managing APIs.

DAY 5

Approximate Study Time: 1 hour and 36 minutes

Chapter 9 – 1 hour and 36 minutes

CHAPTER 9

Data Driven Transformation

Data by itself is not useful. Adding context to data and analyzing it reveals valuable insights. Using this knowledge and combining it with the wisdom of experience helps organizations achieve new heights.

The beauty of data is that it comes from different sources and holds multiple meanings when placed in context. An organization typically needs to balance and deal with internal organizational, customer, and industry/sector data.

Internal data can be financial data like revenue, margins, and costs. This is data from production that deals with the health and well-being of products and services. Quality control data is yet another critical internal data that organizations swear by.

Organizations manage customer data as well, which could include personal details, user behavior, and feedback. As in the EU's General Data Protection Regulation (GDPR), it is likely that organizations have several guidelines for managing data they collect.

Every industry mandates several controls pertinent to their standards and benchmarks. For example, certain countries impose restrictions that the customer data should be stored within their borders. Likewise, industry-specific data clauses call for data to be treated and stored in a particular fashion. For example, how data is retained once accounts are closed.

© Abhinav Krishna Kaiser 2024
A. K. Kaiser, *Become GCP Cloud Digital Leader Certified in 7 Days*,
https://doi.org/10.1007/979-8-8688-0438-0_9

This chapter jumps with both feet into the world of data, exploring and revealing the importance of data for organizations on their journey to the cloud and transformation. Databases, data lakes, and data warehouses are discussed. Finally, the chapter briefly covers Google Cloud's data products—Looker, BigQuery, Cloud Spanner, Cloud SQL, and Cloud Storage.

Why Data Matters

It wouldn't be wrong to state that we are in the age of transformation. With the changes happening around us at such a rapid pace, we do not have an option but to keep the transformation train running. Organizations need to reinvent themselves frequently in order to stay relevant. We are in a state of ever-changing flux and the only path to survival is to transform over and over again. A caterpillar turning into a butterfly isn't sufficient; the butterfly needs to transform into something else, and then the transformed being into something else—all this to survive and stay relevant.

How does one transform? What is the basis for transformation? What do they turn toward? There is no single path to transformation that leads organizations to glory. Every organization, in every industry, in every sector needs to chart its own path. To embark on their respective journeys, they need data from the ground. They need to understand the pulse of the market; they need to know how things are currently progressing; they need to collaborate with customers to understand what they need rather than what they want. The lifeblood of any transformation in any field is through data.

Data is merely discrete facts. Reading data on its own does not tell us anything. Say I told you that the movie *Avatar* made $2.9 billion worldwide. So what? Does this indicate that movie did well in the box office or about average? The data (revenue made from movie) doesn't reveal anything along. But if I told you that the movie is currently the all-time highest grossing film in the box office, you would understand the meaning! Giving context to data makes it usable.

Think of making a movie as a transformation exercise—there is constant data and feedback awaiting to be collected and analyzed. On the back of the data, follow-up transformations can be planned, and with sound analysis and accurate reading of the market, these transformations are bound to take a company to new heights, just like *Avatar* did to its makers. Let's look at the some of the key reasons why organizations must embrace data and invest in sound analysis.

Informed Decision Making

An organization can survive and thrive if the leadership takes appropriate decisions to move the organization along the right path. By analyzing historical and real-time data, they can get insights into market trends, customer behavior, and operational performance. Organizations will have the requisite data to decide how to conquer the market in near and long term. Data provides the basis for setting up goals, objectives, strategies, and measurement techniques. Analyzing data continuously helps them adapt to changing circumstances, leading them to pivot as the market shifts.

Decision making doesn't only apply to leadership but to all levels of an organization's structure. For example, a developer can change the style of coding based on the feedback received from a tool such as SonarQube.

Pulse of the Customer

Understanding the true needs of the customers is considered a skill. It's a skill that relies on getting feedback from customers. The information is valuable for getting the feel of what the customer is truly thinking, and to deliver what the customer actually needs.

Some of the data points that come in handy with respect to customers are their preferences, buying preferences, and feedback about products and services.

Staying Ahead of the Competition

We are in particularly difficult times as far as the market goes—for organizations that sell products and services. In the age of subscriptions, there is no lock-in, so customer behavior needs to be monitored every day. With several competitors in the market, customers can easily be swayed to the next shiny thing. In this scenario, staying ahead of the competition requires plenty of data points in every nook and corner.

Organizations can effectively collect, analyze, and act on the data to identify new opportunities, improve products and services, optimize processes, and enhance offerings to stay ahead of the competition in this rapidly changing business landscape.

Operational Efficiency

Operations in an organization do not add any value to their products and services. They do not directly contribute to customer's value proposition, but yet no organization can function without an able operations engine. Therefore, it is the interest of the organization to make the operations efficient so they spend less on operations and more on their product/ service development.

In operations, there is plenty of data to be collected, and organizations need to leverage it to build efficient operations. Operational efficiency mainly boils down to improving and optimizing processes, including scrapping redundant activities and introducing checks and balances.

Performance data analysis provides insights into bottlenecks that slow down an effective mitigation. This can potentially save on costs and increase customer satisfaction.

Managing Risks

This is an uncertain world and especially a turbulent market. No plans go by the book. While there are plans to mitigate risks, measuring the right set of data points provide insights into any risks that materialize.

There are multiple types of risk—financial, market, and operational. They all need to be assessed and managed. This is generally done on the back of historical data, real-time data, and advice from analysts.

Innovation

It is no secret that organizations that do well are good innovators. They bring products, services, and features to the market that customers want.

For innovation to excel, data is a key driver. Organizations uncover patterns, market trends, and discover new opportunities by collecting and analyzing data. The outcome of data-driven innovation leads to great products and services that sell well and consistently climb the market ladder.

Data on Cloud Technology

The cloud has changed the way we work. We are no longer constrained by the physical. The cloud is an all-encompassing, omnipresent technology that has given us flexibility.

Data is the result of all the computing we do, and whatever the cloud does, it impacts the way we consume and process data. This section focuses on the positive changes brought about by cloud technology to the world of data.

Limitations of the Traditional Ways of Working with Data

When I started using computers, I remember sharing data with friends on 5.25-inch floppy disks. The floppy disk technology improved over time, and with it the storage. Then, we got an exponential raise with compact discs. And then DVDs came along. All this while, data was treated as a physical commodity which necessarily needed a physical medium. Emails were not a great option, as the Internet speeds at that time were dial-up at 33.6 Kbps. They were metered and expensive.

The emergence of the cloud changed the paradigm of computing. The data that we labored for, was not something that necessarily stayed on a physical hard drive on a desktop. It was anywhere and everywhere. To meet the demands of the cloud, the Internet had to give in. While Internet speeds increased, the cost of accessing the Internet reduced. Without the Internet playing ball, the cloud would have become an elite technology and beyond the reach of the common folks.

Even after the Internet opened up, most investment was carried out on on-premises infrastructure. There were monthly maintenance activities to clean up the unnecessary data and make space for new data. Data was limited at that time, and it was a precious commodity. During my initial working days, my email inbox had a limit of 100MB. We were required to create local PST copies of the email files on a regular basis. If a server required a hard drive upgrade, this was considered a major change, and the plans started at least a quarter earlier. After several meetings and a dozen approvals, an entire weekend change window would be required to carry out the change. Several engineers were involved in the process. The traditional infrastructure did not scale on demand. The scaling was a major project in itself. Imagine having to do this over hundreds and thousands of servers!

Suppose you had to store, download, and analyze huge amounts of data. There were restrictions on when you could do that. By processing data in high volumes, the resource utilization of CPU, hard drive, and RAM would be high, which would impact other processes running on the servers. Due to these resource limitations, we could not carry out long-running queries during the daytime. These activities were done at night when we had minimal load on the servers. This limitation put hurdles in the way of developing quickly, making rapid decisions, or being able to act on pressing matters.

The resource constraints further limited the progress that we could make technologically. For example, using ratification intelligence and machine learning requires enormous amounts of data processing in order to make accurate predictions. With the traditional infrastructure, this was nearly impossible unless there was a dedicated infrastructure setup for this business case.

Data can be in any format. It can be part of a structured database or images and videos (unstructured). The traditional infrastructure did just fine for structured datasets, but it could not handle unstructured data. The technological advancements that we see today coming from copyright detection on YouTube or face recognition on Google Photos are the result of the processing of unstructured data. Such activities were not possible on traditional infrastructure.

Effects of the Cloud on Data

The proof of the computing pudding is in the data. With the cloud, data has enhanced several times, and has lifted our innovation limits to new heights as we discover it every single day. The volumes of data, extensive accessibility, and the speed at which data analysis and generation is being done is simply mind boggling. Let's look at some of the ways the cloud is contributing to the application of data.

- The ability to scale computing resources at a moment's notice has changed our perception of infrastructure upgrades, and it has reeled in infrastructure upgrades as an administrative task. For data especially, the resources required for data storage and processing are available as and when required, which is a key differentiator between the traditional method and the cloud. This has been the catalyst for digital transformations to take shape.

  The ability to scale on-demand enables developers to work with varying workloads. This has contributed to optimizing costs and to processing huge amounts of data efficiently.

- Resources used to be limited because of underlying costs. Higher resource requirements were necessary during certain times of the year, month, or day, but may not be all the time. In such a scenario, scaling up to higher resource specifications was expensive. The cloud helped optimize such costs through dynamic scaling, and the pay-as-you-go model reduced operational expenditure. The cloud itself has minimized capital expenditure.

- The ability to store large volumes of data with a zero capital expenditure is a massive benefit, considering that data is generated daily, and it is only going to grow further.

  Moreover, the ability of users to access data from anywhere, using any device, and whenever they want has changed the nature of our computing behavior, and birthed the innovation that followed.

- As mentioned, data processing and analytics consume considerable amounts of computing power, which was not generally available earlier. With cloud service providers offerings tools to analyze huge datasets, organizations can derive insights from their data. Examples of cloud analytics products include Google BigQuery, Amazon Redshift, and Azure Synapse.

  The analysis being performed is not restricted to structured data alone, but can include a whole range of unstructured and semi-structured data, including emails, images, and videos. The cloud provides enables organizations to dynamically read data from federated sources, create structure from unstructured data, and perform data analysis.

- One of the modern applications of data analysis is in the area of artificial intelligence and machine learning. The tools provided by the cloud service providers make it easier for organizations to apply advanced analytics to their data. These services provide pre-built models, tools for training custom models, and scalable infrastructure for running machine learning workloads.

- With hybrid and remote working becoming the norm, collaboration between team members is driven by technology. One of the key applications is real-time co-authoring of documents, which has changed the meaning of sharing documents in shared spaces.

  There was a time when documents were checked out, modifications done, and documents checked back in by the user. Only when the document was checked back in could the next user make changes. The power of the cloud means that such sequential- and dependency-based processes are no longer necessary; instead multiple users can simply jump in and make changes as needed. No check-ins and check-outs. All changes performed are in real time and visible to all other users who are using and modifying the document. This cloud technology has changed the depth of collaboration and has made remote working feasible.

- Early in my career, I worked as a process consultant for a multinational corporation. The data retention process was quite elaborate—one such control was that a complete backup was loaded weekly on tape drives and shipped to London as a secure backup, and this data was meant to be retained for seven years. This arduous backup maintenance job kept a handful of engineers occupied. Today, cloud service providers are responsible for backing up client data, and organizations too regularly back up their data—in some ways, it is the joint responsibility of the cloud service provider and the organization. More importantly, the backups are not on a tape drive but are transferred over the network to another storage drive sitting in the other part of the world. All these backups are automated, so there is no human intervention or manual triggers. With backups happening like clockwork, this releases precious human capital to work on important/cognitive activities that matter.

Types of Data

This section explains the fundamentals of data, especially the different types of data.

Data can be segregated into three types: structured, semi-structured, and unstructured. Data that is organized in a specific format is referred to as structured data, such as a database. Data that does not reside in a database, yet is organized due to inherent properties, is referred to as semi-structured data, such as email. Data that has no semblance of organization is unstructured data, such as an image gallery. Figure 9-1 illustrates the differences between these three types of data.

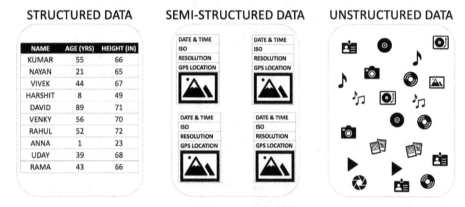

Figure 9-1. *Structured, semi-structured, and unstructured data examples*

In Figure 9-1, structured data is represented by a simple table with names along with ages and heights. The unstructured data is a folder or a gallery containing media—music, movies, and pictures. The semi-structured data is represented by an image which by itself is unstructured, but every image contains technical metadata, such as date and time, ISO, resolution, location, and so on, which is structured.

Structured Data

Structured data is organized into a defined format. That defined format could be a database or a simple Excel spreadsheet (typically in the form of rows and columns). Because the data follows a particular pattern, it's easy for machines to analyze and process it, and that data is also searchable.

Figure 9-2 shows the database schema for WordPress. The MySQL database tables are created when the software is installed.

Table ▲	Action							ROWS	Type	Collation	Size
☐ wpt7_commentmeta	★	▥ Browse	⚡ Structure	✱ Search	⥅ Insert	▤ Empty	⊝ Drop	0	MyISAM	utf8mb4_unicode_ci	4.0 KiB
☐ wpt7_comments	★	▥ Browse	⚡ Structure	✱ Search	⥅ Insert	▤ Empty	⊝ Drop	1	MyISAM	utf8mb4_unicode_ci	7.3 KiB
☐ wpt7_links	★	▥ Browse	⚡ Structure	✱ Search	⥅ Insert	▤ Empty	⊝ Drop	0	MyISAM	utf8mb4_unicode_ci	1.0 KiB
☐ wpt7_options	★	▥ Browse	⚡ Structure	✱ Search	⥅ Insert	▤ Empty	⊝ Drop	194	MyISAM	utf8mb4_unicode_ci	488.8 KiB
☐ wpt7_postmeta	★	▥ Browse	⚡ Structure	✱ Search	⥅ Insert	▤ Empty	⊝ Drop	5	MyISAM	utf8mb4_unicode_ci	10.3 KiB
☐ wpt7_posts	★	▥ Browse	⚡ Structure	✱ Search	⥅ Insert	▤ Empty	⊝ Drop	5	MyISAM	utf8mb4_unicode_ci	18.5 KiB
☐ wpt7_termmeta	★	▥ Browse	⚡ Structure	✱ Search	⥅ Insert	▤ Empty	⊝ Drop	0	MyISAM	utf8mb4_unicode_ci	4.0 KiB
☐ wpt7_terms	★	▥ Browse	⚡ Structure	✱ Search	⥅ Insert	▤ Empty	⊝ Drop	1	MyISAM	utf8mb4_unicode_ci	13.0 KiB
☐ wpt7_term_relationships	★	▥ Browse	⚡ Structure	✱ Search	⥅ Insert	▤ Empty	⊝ Drop	1	MyISAM	utf8mb4_unicode_ci	3.0 KiB
☐ wpt7_term_taxonomy	★	▥ Browse	⚡ Structure	✱ Search	⥅ Insert	▤ Empty	⊝ Drop	1	MyISAM	utf8mb4_unicode_ci	4.0 KiB
☐ wpt7_usermeta	★	▥ Browse	⚡ Structure	✱ Search	⥅ Insert	▤ Empty	⊝ Drop	20	MyISAM	utf8mb4_unicode_ci	11.6 KiB
☐ wpt7_users	★	▥ Browse	⚡ Structure	✱ Search	⥅ Insert	▤ Empty	⊝ Drop	1	MyISAM	utf8mb4_unicode_ci	8.1 KiB
12 tables	Sum							229	MyISAM	utf8mb4_unicode_ci	573.7 KiB

Figure 9-2. *WordPress schema*

This WordPress database is an example of structured data. The data that goes onto the website is stored in the database in the form of tables. Every table has its own set of predefined columns. Figure 9-3 shows the columns within the wpt7_users table.

ID	user_login	user_pass	user_nicename	user_email	user_url	user_registered	user_activation_key	user_status	display_name
1						2019-08-23 20:10:37		0	

Figure 9-3. *Columns within the wpt7_users table*

The predefined columns in this example include ID, user login, user password (which is encrypted), user email, and so on. Multiple sets of data can be keyed in, and in some cases the structure of the data can be enforced. For example, the user_email column mandates keying in an email address (something@something.com). Data that does not resemble this format is rejected.

The data in a database or a structured dataset is defined based on the schema and the set constraints. It's written into the defined slots only. Every dataset is considered discrete and can be called uniquely, either by itself or with a combination of other datasets. For example, you can create a query to pull all the users who have posted at least ten articles on the website—this queries the wpt7_users and wpt7_posts tables to identify the relevant data.

Structured data is an ideal foil for conducting data analysis and, based on it, sane decisions can be made. Consistent data makes it easier to organize and store, and since the constraints can be introduced, securing this kind of data is easier compared to other the data types.

On the downside, fitting the data in a particular schema is like losing the intelligence that could be gathered outside of such a structure. There could be data that is unstructured that could potentially help in decision making.

Semi-Structured Data

There is a method to the madness with semi-structured data. It is a type of data that does not fit perfectly into a traditional relational database schema, but it isn't unstructured either. Recall the example I provided earlier—an image is unstructured but contains metadata that is structured.

There is flexibility in the type of data that can be stored, and yet the advantage with structured data where analysis and search are quite efficient is passed over to the semi-structured data for the structured part of its data.

Semi-structured data does not have a schema like structured data, but it can have a loosely formed style that allows variations in the structure of individual records. Configuration file scripting like XML (eXtensible Markup Language) and JSON (JavaScript Object Notation) are classic applications of this data type.

The following project object model (popularly known as pom.xml) is a configuration file used in Maven to define project, module, and other configuration details required to build code. When Maven is asked to build a binary, it refers to the pom.xml file for various parameters.

```
1.    <project>
2.    <modelVersion>4.0.0</modelVersion>
3.
4.    <parent>
5.    <groupId>com.gcpcdl.app</groupId>
6.    <artifactId>my-book</artifactId>
7.    <version>1</version>
8.    </parent>
9.
10.   <groupId>com.gcpcdl.app</groupId>
11.   <artifactId>my-module</artifactId>
12.   <version>1</version>
13.   </project>
```

pom.xml is an example of semi-structured data. While there is structure to the XML file, there are no limits. Any number of dependencies can be called out, plugins can be executed, and other metadata can be added. Note also that the XML file includes nested elements. This means the data can be organized in a hierarchical fashion, with parent-child relationships. One element can contain other elements.

NoSQL (Not Only SQL) databases and data lakes are capable of storing semi-structured data.

Unstructured Data

Most companies don't store all their data in MS Excel spreadsheets, in XML, or over emails (well, some actually do). The majority of data that is generated is unstructured. All the photos and videos that people shoot on a whim are adding to this. There is no structure to unstructured data—try finding a particular photograph that you took on your wedding day, among the thousands of pics that were taken that day.

Unlike structured data, which is consistent and organized in a well-defined manner with a fixed schema, unstructured data lacks a clear structure and is inconsistent. It's often more challenging to analyze unstructured data using traditional data-processing methods.

It is no secret that big data is a result of unstructured data like images, videos, social media posts, emails, and texts. There is so much intelligence in unstructured data that requires special attention to analyze. The problem is partly solved through the emergence of natural language processing (NLP) and artificial intelligence (AI). NLP and AI techniques are often used to analyze and extract information from unstructured text data. These techniques enable the understanding of human language, sentiment analysis, and the extraction of relevant information from text documents. Consider search engines, for example. To deal with the vast amounts of unstructured data, its crawlers create indexes from effective algorithms, which can help retrieve information from websites, documents, and other sources in under a second.

GCP Data Products

Google, Amazon, and Microsoft offer a host of data-related products catering to a broad spectrum of businesses. Each brings its expertise to the fore. Within the data segment, the Google Cloud Platform, with its quiver of data products, is a leader, especially due to Google's prowess in the data analytics and artificial intelligence/machine learning areas. Their tools are capable of handling huge amounts of data effectively, transforming the lives of data engineers and scientists.

The upcoming sections focus on the key GCP data products, as presented in Figure 9-4.

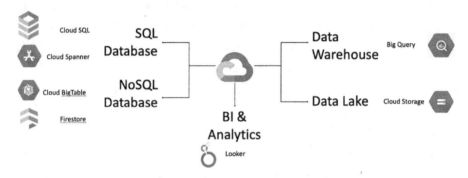

Figure 9-4. *GCP data products*

SQL Database Products

A structured query language (SQL) or a relational database is a highly structured database. This topic was briefly discussed in the "Structured Data" section with the example of a WordPress database, which is a SQL database. These databases are widely used for various applications, from small-scale projects to large enterprise systems. They provide a reliable and structured way to store, manage, and retrieve data, making them a fundamental component of many software systems and applications.

In a database, columns specify the information to be stored and rows represent the data. Several such tables can be nested together in a single database.

To work with relational databases, developers use SQL commands to create tables, and insert, modify, delete, and retrieve data from the database. MySQL (which is used in WordPress), PostgreSQL, SQLite, and Oracle are popular SQL databases.

The Google Cloud Platform ecosystem includes the Cloud SQL and Cloud Spanner services, which are relational database products.

Cloud SQL

Cloud SQL is a fully managed relational database product from the Google Cloud Platform stable. It allows for creation of MySQL, PostgreSQL, or SQL Server databases. Similar to other fully managed products on GCP, users can run and manage relational databases without worrying about the underlying infrastructure.

Cloud SQL Key Features

In the past, organizations would hire database administrators (DBA) to install, maintain, and manage on-premises databases. With the cloud, the role of a DBA has evolved and been diluted—the new role is referred to in some organizations as cloud DBAs. Fully managed database services on the cloud reduce the dependence on DBAs, and with the emergence of DevOps and automation, their role has transformed. The changed role looks at the DBAs to help integrate databases with CI-CD pipelines for automated database deployments, testing and integration with other systems. The other challenge that cloud DBAs face is concerning cost. With on-premises, costs are embedded in the capital costs, but with the cloud pay-as-you-go model, cost controls are necessary.

Here is an overview of the key features of Cloud SQL:

1. Cloud SQL is a fully managed database product that translates to administrative tasks—such as patch management, backups, and failover—being managed by Google. This allows users to focus on application development and data management.

2. The product supports multiple database engines: mySQL, PostgreSQL, and SQL Server. At the time of instance creation, users can select the type of database.

3. Google supports menu-driven migration of databases from on-premises and other cloud service providers.

4. Cloud SQL guarantees high availability of database with an SLA of 99.95 percent uptime. The databases are automatically at a different region of Google's choosing, and the DBs are monitored periodically. At the time of failure, the traffic is automatically routed to the backup DB.

5. The pay-as-you-go model ensures that organizations are charged based on use, which can help protect the capital and avoid unnecessary costs.

6. Cloud SQL instances can be scaled vertically (up to 30TB) by adjusting the resources (CPU and RAM) allocated to them. Additionally, horizontal scaling is achieved by using read replicas to distribute read traffic across multiple database instances.

7. Cloud SQL integrates seamlessly with other GCP products like Computer Engine, GKE, and Cloud Functions. This that allows end-to-end solutions to be built.

8. Cloud SQL ensures data encryption at rest and in transit. SSL/TLS for secure connections can be enforced as needed, and this provides options for network isolation through Virtual Private Cloud (VPC) peering and Private IP.

9. A free tool called Cloud SQL Insights allows developers to diagnose database issues for faster and smoother performance.

10. On the downside, databases can be created at a particular region only. So, organizations catering to worldwide customers might find it inadequate. Cloud Spanner alleviates this shortcoming.

Cloud SQL in Action

This section looks at creating a new database instance on Cloud SQL.

You are not expected to have hands-on experience with Cloud SQL. This section is optional. Feel free to skip it.

---

1. On the Google Cloud Platform console, search for Cloud SQL. The entry page is shown in Figure 9-5.

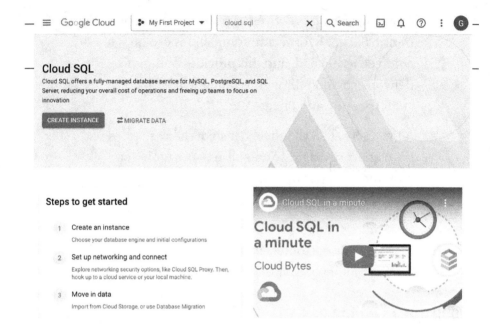

Figure 9-5. *The Cloud SQL product*

2. There is an option to either create a new instance or to
    migrate data from on-premises or from the cloud. In this
    example, you learn how to create a new instance.

3. Depending on the use case, choose a database
    engine—mySQL, PostgreSQL ,or SQL Server (see
    Figure 9-6). MySQL is selected for this example.

Figure 9-6. *Choosing a database engine*

4. On the next screen (see Figure 9-7), you provide the instance details, including an ID and password. You can set the password policy on complexity, reuse, and other parameters, or you can proceed without a password.

Instance info

Instance ID *
gcpcdl

Use lowercase letters, numbers, and hyphens. Start with a letter.

Password *
••••••••••••••••   ▣ ⟳   ⊗ GENERATE

Set a password for the root user. Learn more ⬀

☐ No password

∨ PASSWORD POLICY

Database version *
MySQL 8.0   ▼

∨ SHOW MINOR VERSIONS

Choose a Cloud SQL edition

A Cloud SQL edition determines foundational characteristics of your instance and cannot be changed later. Choose based on your price and performance needs. Learn more ⬀

◉ **Enterprise Plus**
- 99.99% availability SLA for eligible instances
- High-performance machines, up to 128 vCPUs
- Up to 35 days point-in-time recovery
- Data cache (optional)

○ **Enterprise**
- 99.95% availability SLA for eligible instances
- General purpose machines, up to 96 vCPUs
- Up to 7 days point-in-time recovery

Pricing estimate

$2.30 per hour (estimated, without discounts)

That's about $55.32 per day.

Feature usage and traffic costs aren't included in estimate

∨ SHOW COST BREAKDOWN

Summary

Cloud SQL Edition ❷	Enterprise Plus
Region	us-central1 (Iowa)
DB Version	MySQL 8.0
vCPUs	8 vCPU
Memory	64 GB
Data Cache	Enabled (375 GB)
Storage	250 GB
Connections	Public IP
Backup	Automated
Availability	Multiple zones (Highly available)
Point-in-time recovery	Enabled
Network throughput (MB/s) ❷	2,000 of 2,000
Disk throughput (MB/s) ❷	Read: 120.0 of 800.0
	Write: 120.0 of 800.0
IOPS ❷	Read: 7,500 of 15,000
	Write: 7,500 of 15,000

Figure 9-7. *Database instance configuration (1/2)*

5. Based on the database version and edition, the costs are calculated. You can specify the instance's application—development or production (see Figure 9-8). A lower configuration server is used for a development instance and a higher one is used for a production instance.

221

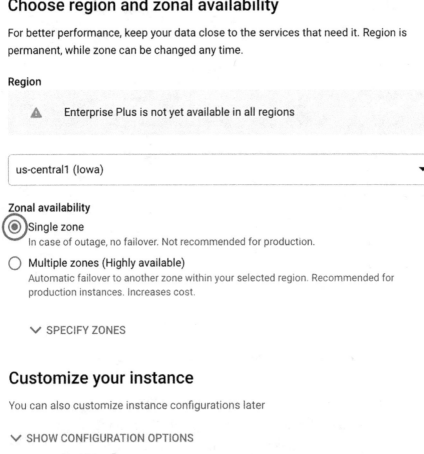

Choose a preset for this edition. Presets can be customized later as needed.

Production ▼

COMPARE EDITION PRESETS

Choose region and zonal availability

For better performance, keep your data close to the services that need it. Region is permanent, while zone can be changed any time.

Region

⚠   Enterprise Plus is not yet available in all regions

us-central1 (Iowa) ▼

Zonal availability

◉ Single zone
In case of outage, no failover. Not recommended for production.

◯ Multiple zones (Highly available)
Automatic failover to another zone within your selected region. Recommended for production instances. Increases cost.

⌄ SPECIFY ZONES

Customize your instance

You can also customize instance configurations later

⌄ SHOW CONFIGURATION OPTIONS

CREATE INSTANCE   CANCEL

Figure 9-8. *Database instance configuration (2/2)*

6. While Cloud SQL can be created in a single region
    (us-central1 in this example), you can choose to
    install it over a single zone or over multiple zones for
    higher availability.

7. You can further customize the database instance
    (see Figure 9-9) with the preferred server type,
    storage size, public/private IP, backup window,
    point in time recovery, and maintenance window
    for applying upgrades and patches.

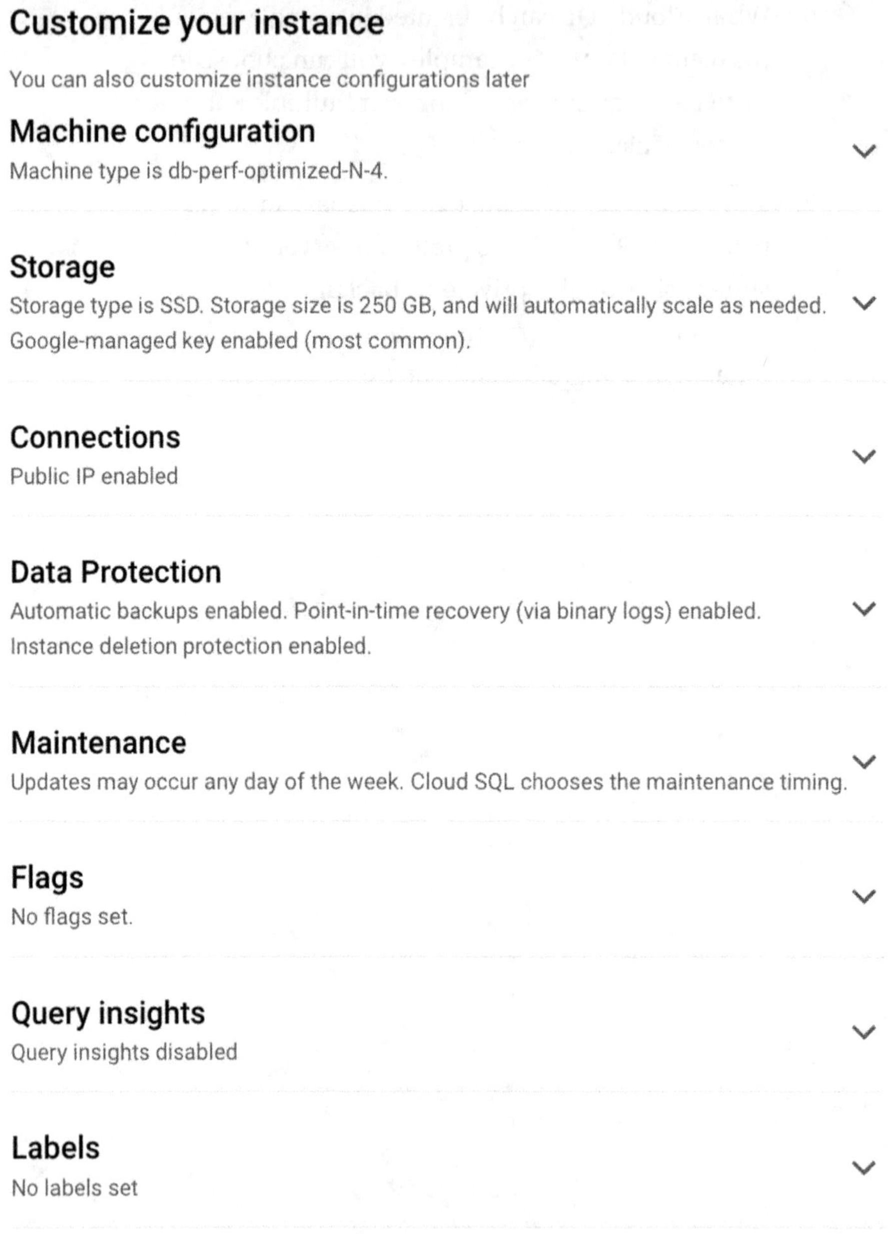

Customize your instance

You can also customize instance configurations later

Machine configuration
⌄

Machine type is db-perf-optimized-N-4.

Storage
⌄

Storage type is SSD. Storage size is 250 GB, and will automatically scale as needed. Google-managed key enabled (most common).

Connections
⌄

Public IP enabled

Data Protection
⌄

Automatic backups enabled. Point-in-time recovery (via binary logs) enabled. Instance deletion protection enabled.

Maintenance
⌄

Updates may occur any day of the week. Cloud SQL chooses the maintenance timing.

Flags
⌄

No flags set.

Query insights
⌄

Query insights disabled

Labels
⌄

No labels set

Figure 9-9. *Database instance customization*

8. Instance creation takes about five to ten minutes depending on the customizations and other selected options. You can monitor the database for its CPU utilization, memory utilization, and other parameters (see Figure 9-10).

Figure 9-10. *Instance Creation and Monitoring Window*

9. You can perform other database-related activities like creating external connections, users, database tables, and schemas, directly from the console (see Figure 9-10, left sidebar).

Cloud Spanner

Cloud Spanner is metaphorically Cloud SQL 2.0. It does everything that Cloud SQL can do and more.

Cloud Spanner is a fully managed relational database product that is globally distributed, strongly consistent, and can scale horizontally. In effect, it has the consistent behavior of structured data along with the advantages of cloud-native NoSQL databases.

It overcomes the limitation of Cloud SQL by meeting the demands of globally distributed and mission-critical applications that require strong consistency and high availability. When a database is created in one region, based on the preferred criteria, a database replica is created in other regions (horizontal scaling) as well. When a user retrieves information, Cloud Spanner pulls the data from the closest database. This allows it to handle large amounts of data and high transactional workloads while maintaining low-latency performance. From a performance standpoint, Cloud Spanner can process up to 1 billion requests per second.

The product offers strong consistency guarantees across global distributed data by ensuring the integrity of data across geographic regions. For example, when a user writes data into a database in a particular region, this new data is replicated instantaneously across its replica in real time, following strict consistency requirements.

Since the databases are spread across multiple regions, and with automatic failover being made available, Google can promise an uptime of 99.999 percent.

Exam Tip   *You can expect at least one question on either Cloud SQL or Cloud Spanner or a question relating to the two products. If you are asked to identify a product that has high availability, global scale, multiple regions, and higher configuration, you can safely select Cloud Spanner.*

NoSQL Database Products

The SQL database had a set structure—a schema that defined how the data was stored. With the cloud and other advancements in technology, people expect flexibility and dynamism with resources. A SQL database that is constraint-ridden is not going to work. There was a need for a database that could take data of any kind, scale it as needed, and be distributed. Enter the NoSQL database.

A NoSQL database is a non-relational database that is flexible, scalable, and distributed. It is designed to handle large volumes of structured and semi-structured data and provides flexibility in terms of data models and schema. While SQL databases are tabular in nature with data fields as columns and data as rows, NoSQL databases support various data models, including document-oriented, key-value, wide-column store, and graph formats. Popular NoSQL databases include MongoDB, Redis, Apache Cassandra, and Couchbase, among others.

NoSQL stands for Not Only SQL. It is not a rejection of SQL or relational databases but highlights the expansion to include certain scenarios as well. NoSQL databases are chosen for specific applications and in a real world, they coexist with SQL databases to create polyglot persistence architectures.

NoSQL databases don't have a set schema, which means the data does not have to adhere to a schema. This flexibility allows for the storage of diverse and evolving data structures. The data models supported by NoSQL are as follows:

- *Document oriented:* The data is stored as documents without adhering to a schema. It is stored in a JSON-like document. Popular applications include content-management systems and e-commerce applications. An example is MongoDB.

- *Key-value:* The data is stored as key-value pairs, where a unique key is paired with an associated value. This is used to manage sessions for web and gaming applications. An example is Redis and DynamoDB.

- *Column family:* The data is organized into columns rather than into rows. It finds use in fraud-detection algorithms, recommendation engines, and catalog management. An example is Apache Cassandra.

- *Graph:* The data is stored and processed as a graph structure. The structure resembles a configuration management database (CMDB) where the data is stored as a node and there are relationships built between the nodes. It finds application in social media (connections and friends) and customer relationship management. An example is Neo4j.

The Google Cloud Platform includes Cloud Bigtable (a column family) and Firestore (which is document oriented) NoSQL databases, which are discussed in upcoming sections.

Cloud Bigtable

Cloud Bigtable is a fully managed distributed column family-based NoSQL database product in the GCP ecosystem. It is scalable and highly available, and it is designed to handle large-scale, analytical, and operational workloads.

It is well-suited for applications that require low latency—like real-time analytics and high-throughput data access. Cloud Bigtable is based on the open-source Bigtable distributed storage system developed by Google, which is also the underlying technology for several Google services, including Google Search and Google Maps.

Cloud Bigtable supports big data and is capable of handling petabytes (1 petabyte = 1024 terabytes) of data. It is designed to be implemented in a distributed model, supporting the polyglot persistent architectures.

Exam Tip   *If you are asked to identify a GCP product that supports big data, Cloud Bigtable should be your obvious choice.*

The product leverages Google's coverage across the globe to provide a single digit millisecond latency. Google search and other real-time analytics functions rely on low latency read and write and high throughput capabilities. The database scales horizontally, which enforces faster throughput—a result of adding/removing nodes. Each node is capable of running 10,000 operations per second. So, if a higher throughput is required, additional nodes can be added on demand.

Cloud Bigtable is behind the popular Google services like Google Search, Google Analytics, Gmail, and Google Maps. It integrates with other Google Cloud services, including BigQuery for analytics and Dataproc for processing and analyzing large datasets using Apache Hadoop and Apache Spark. Bigtable supports the open-source HBase API standard and can integrate seamlessly with the Apache ecosystem, including HBase, Beam, Hadoop, and Spark.

Cloud Bigtable is suitable for a variety of use cases, including gaming, AdTech, FinTech, time-series data, IoT (Internet of Things) data, and applications requiring real-time data analytics. For example, when you are checking your emails on Gmail, the ads that appear are based on your browsing pattern and your interests. The intelligence required for the contextual ads is read, processed, and the closest matched advertisement is displayed in a matter of milliseconds. All this is possible because of Cloud Bigtable.

Firestore

Firestore is a fully managed serverless NoSQL database product. It is designed for building web, mobile, and server applications that require real-time data synchronization and offline support. The database is accessed directly through the native SDK by iOS, Android, and web applications. It is also available in native Node.js, Java, Python, and Go SDKs apart from REST and RPC APIs. Firestore is part of the Firebase suite, which is a mobile and web application development platform owned by Google.

Some of the key features of Firestore are as follows:

- Firestore is part of the Google Firebase application development platform. The platform provides a wide range of tools and services to help developers build, improve, and enhance their applications. The platform offers solutions for various aspects of application development, including backend services, real-time data synchronization, authentication, hosting, and others.

- Since it is a serverless product, developers do not have to manage the database like server provisioning, scaling, monitoring and maintenance. Cloud Bigtable is a serverful database, where the underlying server continues to run and accrue charges even if no queries are executed. On Firestore, it is a serverless product and the database is spun up from zero to global scale in a matter of milliseconds, offering no downtime.

- Firestore is a document-oriented database. It stores data in a flexible, JSON-like format called a document. Each document is a set of key-value pairs, and collections of documents make up the database.

- Its built-in offline support for web and mobile applications is noteworthy. Even without the Internet, the mobile applications on your mobile phone work. Any data that you save is uploaded once there is an active Internet connection. This feature is powered by Firestore.

- Scalability is one of cloud's salient features and Firestore fully adheres to it. Depending on the load and user demand, the product is capable of scaling to meet performance requirements. It is designed to scale horizontally to handle large amounts of data and high read and write throughput.

- Firestore is a part of both Firebase and Google Cloud Platform. The dual residency of the product allows it to seamlessly integrate with Firebase services such as Firebase Authentication, Firebase Cloud Functions, and Firebase Hosting, along with other GCP products like BigQuery and Cloud Functions. This integration simplifies the development of end-to-end solutions.

- To improve performance and latency, Firestore leverages multi-region and global distribution services, which allow developers to deploy databases across multiple regions.

- A feature that goes hand in hand with distribution and horizontal scaling is the need to synchronize data in real time. There are wide variety of cases where users may need to wait the entire day for data to be replicated across systems and regions, which defeats the purpose. Firestore provides real-time data synchronization, which allows the distributed database to reflect changes to data to be automatically reflected in connected clients.

- Firestore is a serverless product and is active when there are queries to be executed. So, organizations do not have to shell out money for it during zero transaction period, which can potentially save costs due to its pay-as-you-go model.

Data Warehouse Products

A warehouse is a (typically huge) place where either the raw or manufactured goods are stored before distributing or processing them further. A data warehouse is similar to a warehouse. It houses huge amounts of data from several heterogenous sources. It is used for collating and analyzing the data, which eventually leads to making good business decisions and preparing and publishing various reports.

Let's take a step back and revisit databases. Databases are repositories that store the current data of an application. This data churns depending on the number of transactions carried out. This data is in real-time. This transactional data source is not used for analytics for obvious reasons— to avoid hogging database resources. There is also a possibility that conducting analysis could lead to sub-par performance of the application or could lead to down time. Therefore, the data from the database is moved to a data warehouse product for preparing and conducting analytics.

A data warehouse collates data from multiple sources—be it relational or non-relational databases, or it could even be from documents. This data is put through a cycle of ETL (extract, transform, and load) to normalize it. The data warehouse operates on standardizing data in a structured dataset, which would be processed through an online analytical processing (OLAP) engine along with other analytical tools, defined by data scientists.

While a database contains current data, a data warehouse is significantly larger and contains historical data, which is useful in deriving trends through data modeling and analysis. A typical use case may be a batch job that's run during off-business hours to extract data from databases and transform it into the required schema before migrating to a data warehouse. In this use case, the data on a data warehouse will be behind the current data by a day at most.

The popular data warehouse products in the market are Google BigQuery, which is discussed in the next section, Snowflake, IBM DB2 Warehouse, and Amazon Redshift.

BigQuery

BigQuery is Google Cloud Platform's answer to data warehousing solution. It is a fully managed, serverless, and scalable, powered with a built-in query engine warehouse product. As per Google's own admission, it is capable of analyzing terabytes of data within seconds and petabytes of data in minutes.

Since BigQuery is a serverless product, developers do not have to worry about maintaining the underlying infrastructure or setting up the data warehouse. It is built on the powerful column, family-based structure and can ingest petabytes of data. BigQuery can scale on demand. It uses a distributed architecture to parallelize query execution, and to provide rapid response even for complex queries on massive datasets.

The data in BigQuery is stored in a structured format, so standard SQL queries can be used to carry out required transactions and subsequent analysis.

Google has enhanced its data warehouse product by enabling it with real-time analytics as well, which was uncommon at the time of its release. BigQuery can integrate with pub/sub for real-time data streaming and running it through DataFlow (a Google product that transforms the data). The data is transformed from unstructured to semi-structured and can then by analyzed using standard SQL queries.

BigQuery integrates seamlessly with other Google products, such as Cloud Storage, Cloud Dataprep, DataFlow, and others, and it supports multiple data formats such as JSON, Parquet, Avro, and ORC. An inherent feature called BigQuery ML allows users to build and deploy machine learning models using SQL queries, which allows data scientists to perform machine learning tasks directly from the data warehouse product.

Data Lake Products

Data warehouses are limited by their structure. The data has to be transformed into a structured dataset in order to be useful. With data being embedded into images and videos, crucial data elements for analysis were being missed. The upgrade: data lakes. A *data lake* is a central repository that holds massive amounts of data in its native format. The data can reside in its original format and does not need to go through cycles of ETL to get into the repository. There were multiple cycles of processing, and with the proprietary technology, managing and operating a data warehouse became an expensive affair.

A data lake is capable of storing structured and unstructured data like text, documents, images, and videos at any scale. Alongside, it can hold structured data from relational databases as well.

While a data warehouse stores data in a structured or semi-structured format, data lakes employ flat architecture and object storage for storing data. Data is stored with metatags and unique identifiers, which leads to faster retrieval of data that's spread across geographies. This happens in a matter of seconds or minutes depending on the size of the data. More importantly, since the data does not go through transformation, data lakes enable organizations to leverage the data as a reasonable cost and build integrations with applications as they see fit.

In a data lake, the schema is applied when the data is read rather than when it is consumed. This makes it flexible to handle evolving data structures and makes it easier to accommodate new types of data.

The inherent design of data lakes to scale horizontally allows them to handle massive loads of data by progressively adding storage and processing power.

Amazon S3, Databricks, and Google Cloud Storage are the leading data lake products in the market today. The next section discusses Google Cloud Storage.

Cloud Storage

Cloud Storage is Google Cloud Platform's data lake product. It is a fully managed and scalable product that allows organizations to store and retrieve any amount of data, and it provides highly durable and available storage solutions for a wide range of use cases.

Google Cloud Storage is often confused with Google Drive. They are completely different. Google Drive is a personal storage solution and not enterprise class. Cloud Storage is an enterprise grade, data lake storage solution. Developers can integrate with other Google services as well as with third-party applications through APIs, and scale storage based on demand, among a host of other features, which are discussed in this section.

Key Features of Cloud Storage

Google Cloud Storage was launched in 2010 as a competitor to Amazon S3. The product has grown leaps and bounds over the years, and it is now considered the top product in the market today. The following are the key features of Google Cloud Storage:

- **High scalability**: Cloud Storage is highly scalable and is capable of handling data of any size.

- **Auto versioning**: The product supports automatic object versioning, which allows users to maintain multiple versions of an object. It mitigates against risk of accidental deletion and unwanted unforced modifications. The previous versions can be recalled seamlessly.

- **Lifecycle management**: With versioning, the question that comes to the fore is how long do we maintain objects? Object lifecycle management allows users to define rules for automatically transitioning or deleting objects based on criteria such as age or storage class. This helps optimize storage costs and manage data retention.

- **Performance enhancement**: Cloud Storage is available with Multi-Region storage support. Maintaining data across geographies helps reduce latency and enhances performance.

- **Access control**: Cloud Storage controls access to objects and buckets. This is handled through Identity and Access Management (IAM) policies. Users can define detailed access controls, and the product supports encryption at rest and in transit.

- **Google product integration**: Cloud Storage seamlessly integrates with other Google Cloud Platform products such as BigQuery, Cloud Functions, Cloud Pub/Sub, and others.

- **Strong data consistency**: Strong data consistency is available with Cloud Storage for all upload, delete, and modification operations. This refers to immediately accessing a file after uploading it, and once an object is deleted, users can access it immediately thereafter.

Storage Classes

One of the key benefits of moving to the cloud is the savings that organizations can achieve through the pay-as-you-go model. Applying the principle of paying for what they use, and digging deep with storage, organizations can further segregate types of storage based on the kind of data that is stored. Organizations generate large amounts of data, and only a small portion of it is read and modified on a regular basis. The network usage for that data is larger than the data that is infrequently or never accessed. For example, an incremental backup may not be accessed unless the need arises.

Based on the frequency of access and retrieval of data, Google Cloud Storage has the following storage classes:

- Standard, for frequent access

- Nearline, for accessing data perhaps once a month

- Coldline, for infrequent access to data

- Archive, for long-term storage

These storage classes all enjoy low latency and high durability features, but their costing models differ. There are no storage limits nor minimum size object size for these Cloud Storage classes.

Standard

Standard storage is the most expensive class in Cloud Storage. There are no retrieval charges or minimum durations. Standard is ideal for transactional data that is accessed and modified frequently.

Nearline

The Nearline storage class is cheaper than the Standard class (about 50 cheaper), but it's more expensive than Coldline and Archive. Whenever an object stored on Nearline class is accessed, there is a cost associated with it, referred to as a retrieval charge. Every object that is accessed is charged a retrieval fee. Therefore, only the objects that do not require frequent access are best suited for Nearline storage.

There is a minimum of 30 days for objects stored in this class. This refers to cost and not necessarily the restrictions around deletion and modification. Google charges for objects stored for the minimum duration in a particular class, even if the objects are deleted, moved, or replaced within that duration.

Coldline

The Coldline storage class is about 25-50 percent cheaper than the Nearline class. It is inexpensive because the minimum duration is 90 days. Organizations need to determine the storage class based on the frequency of use. If an organization uses Coldline storage and accesses objects fairly frequently, they may end up paying more than for Nearline storage. Organizations need to understand the tradeoff between access and storage costs before deciding on a class.

Archive

The Archive class is the cheapest storage class in Cloud Storage. It costs about 30 percent of the Coldline storage class and about 15 percent of the Standard class. Figure 9-11 shows the costing schedules, as published by GCP at the time of writing this book.

The Archive class has a minimum of 365 days duration, which means that an object will be charged for a year of storage, regardless of when the object is deleted. As the name suggests, this class is best for storing backups that aren't likely to be accessed during their lifetime.

Regions   Dual-regions   Multi-regions

North America   South America   Europe   Middle East   Asia   Indonesia   Australia

Location	Standard storage (per GB per Month)	Nearline storage (per GB per Month)	Coldline storage (per GB per Month)	Archive storage (per GB per Month)
Iowa (us-central1)	$0.020	$0.010	$0.004	$0.0012
South Carolina (us-east1)	$0.020	$0.010	$0.004	$0.0012
Northern Virginia (us-east4)	$0.023	$0.013	$0.006	$0.0025
Columbus (us-east5)	$0.020	$0.010	$0.004	$0.0012
Oregon (us-west1)	$0.020	$0.010	$0.004	$0.0012
Los Angeles (us-west2)	$0.023	$0.016	$0.007	$0.0025
Salt Lake City (us-west3)	$0.023	$0.016	$0.007	$0.0025
Las Vegas (us-west4)	$0.023	$0.013	$0.006	$0.0025
Dallas (us-south1)	$0.020	$0.010	$0.004	$0.0012
Montréal (northamerica-northeast1)	$0.023	$0.013	$0.007	$0.0025
Toronto (northamerica-northeast2)	$0.023	$0.013	$0.007	$0.0025

Figure 9-11. *Storage classes costing model*

Figure 9-12 indicates the storage classes and its respective minimum durations.

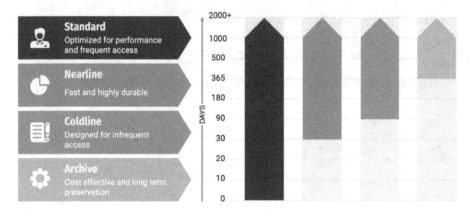

Figure 9-12. *Cloud Storage: storage classes*

Bucket Locations

Objects are stored on Cloud Storage in buckets. A *bucket* is a logical container for a storage area. Developers can create as many buckets as needed, and each bucket can be individually managed for access, class, and location. Bucket names should be unique across the Google Cloud Platform.

At the time of bucket creation, the location specifications need to be configured. A bucket can be created in a single region or across two or more regions. Each location comes with its own performance, price, and availability.

The three location considerations for Cloud Storage buckets are as follows:

- Regional

- Dual Region

- Multi-Region

Regional

If a bucket is stored with the Regional setting, the bucket will reside within the region. It will be replicated across the zones in the region. This is a good option to have if users are concentrated in a local region (like a local cable news channel), since the proximity from the data region to users ensures high latency and performance. However, if users are spread out, there will likely be performance variations with users who are situated farther away.

While performance is one aspect, redundancy is another. If a particular zone blacks out, the other zones can back it up. However, if the entire region goes down, there is a real possibility of losing access to the data. That said, in the history of GCP, this has never happened.

From a cost perspective, since the data is replicated within the zones of a region, the Regional location is the cheapest storage option. The pricing is dynamic and depends on the region. For example, São Paulo (`southamerica-east1`) is at least 50 percent more expensive than Sydney (`australia-southeast1`).

Dual Regions

In the past, redundancy was achieved by creating two storage spaces across datacenters/regions along with some replication behavior. With Cloud Storage's dual region setting, a single bucket can be created across two regions (within the same continent) and act as a single bucket, a single endpoint to interact with. The data between the two regions is replicated in real time. Most importantly, although the bucket is replicated (asynchronous for data and synchronous for metadata) across the regions, organizations have to manage just the one bucket rather than two.

Organizations can choose the regions based on business and compliance requirements. Regions can be chosen based on their workloads and on the consumption locale. For example, a United States-based organization can choose to go with US-WEST2 (Los Angeles) and US-EAST1 (South Carolina) to cover the entire country.

Replicating data across two regions provides an additional layer of redundancy. The RTO (recovery time objective) for dual-region cloud storage is 0 and the RPO (recovery point objective) is 15 minutes (for the turbo setting) and 60 minutes (for normal). This is generally mandated by certain types of industries. Typical use case for using dual regions is to provide true active-active namespaces and analytical types of workloads.

The Dual Regions option is the most expensive Cloud Storage option.

Multi-Region

Multi-Region refers to a storage setting that spreads across multiple geographic regions, providing redundancy and high availability.

Google offers multi-regional storage classes to address scenarios where data needs to be distributed across multiple locations to ensure resilience, durability, and low-latency access.

For organizations with a wide user base, the Multi-Region setting is ideal. When a bucket has the Multi-Region option, users can specify the continent where the bucket is created (see Figure 9-13).

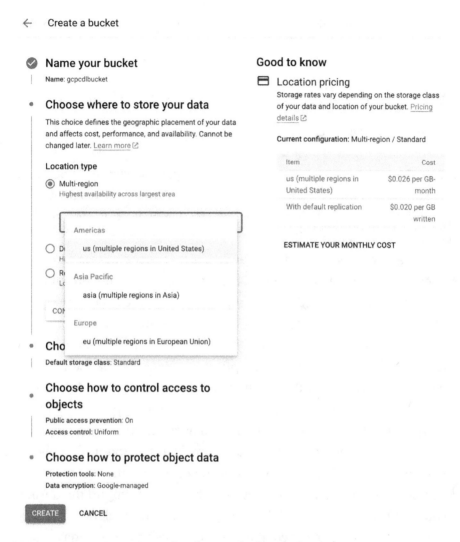

Figure 9-13. *Creating a bucket with the Multi-Region option*

There is no option to select regions within a continent. Google guarantees that the replications are done at least across two regions that are geo-diverse by at least 100 miles, which promises higher latency and availability. Note that a bucket can be created only within a continent and not across multiple continents.

The Multi-Region storage is an ideal solution for data that is accessed frequently around the world, such as video streaming and website content.

Business Intelligence and Analytics Products

This section moves ahead from data storage and handling to consumption of data: to the world of business intelligence and analytics. While storing data and guarding it is an important phase of an organization's operations, using the data is where value is delivered. Organizations leverage data scientists to read and make sense of data, read between the lines, and take action based on data intelligence.

Data analytics is the field of data science that encompasses data processing: including inspection, cleaning it up, transformation, and data modeling. The objective is simply to hear what the data is saying and discover pertinent information, then use this information to support decision making. Data analytics includes various approaches and techniques, ranging from descriptive analytics (what happened) to diagnostic analytics (why it happened), predictive analytics (what will happen), and prescriptive analytics (how to make it happen).

Business Intelligence (BI) is a subset of data analytics that deals with analysis and presentation of the data, where data is methodically collected, analyzed, and shown in a presentable format using technologies, processes, and tools. The reason for its existence is to support the business by providing actionable insights and support decision-making processes. BI encompasses a range of activities, including data gathering, data analysis, and data visualization.

The Google Cloud Platform features Looker, a product that supports data analytics and business intelligence activities. Other BI tools include Power BI and Tableau.

Looker

Looker was an independent company started in 2012; Google acquired it and brought in under the Google Cloud Platform in 2019. Just around that period, Salesforce acquired Tableau, another popular data analytics product. Since its acquisition, the tool has acquired new capabilities, including its ability to work with third-party tools and a modeler to work with other analytics platforms.

Looker is a business intelligence (BI) and data analytics platform that provides tools for exploring, analyzing, and visualizing data. The product supports organizations to make data-driven decisions by transforming raw data into intelligible insights. It is a popular tool in the market and is widely used to democratize data access, promote data-driven culture, and gain insights from data.

Key features of Looker include:

- **Reporting and dashboarding**: Looker features a user-friendly interface for writing no-code queries and building reports and attractive dashboards. This is a critical feature that helps organizations fine-tune their reporting requirements and consume the data in the least amount of time through meaningful dashboards.

- **Standardized data modeling**: We looked at data consistencies being achieved through BigQuery, a data-warehousing product. Likewise, Looker offers tools to create data models through the Looker Modeling Language (LookML). It can transform data and allows users to define and manage the data model, which enables consistent and reusable data across the organization.

- **Integration**: Looker can integrate within the Google ecosystem and outside of it. It can seamlessly integrate with BigQuery and Cloud Big Table, among others, as well as through Looker Modeler with Tableau, Amazon Redshift, and others. The ability to integrate with third-party tools eases the risks against vendor lock-in.

- **Analytics**: Looker can be integrated into applications through APIs. This allows for calling for Looker's capabilities for seamless analytics experience to end-users. For experience, Looker's integration with a banking tool can help users build and analyze balance sheets to help them understand their expenses and make decisions on where they can carve out savings.

- **Machine learning**: Looker's integration into machine learning platforms allows organizations to incorporate predictive analytics into their data-driven decision-making processes.

Summary

Data is at the heart of organization—starting from creating, storing, and using data to improve decision making. Organizations that depend on data to make decisions are bound to make more good decisions than bad ones.

To make data-driven decisions, the entire lifecycle starts with how the data is collected and stored. Earlier, all data was structured and placed into tables of rows and columns. And as we progressed into the digital age, semi-structured and unstructured data (images, videos, and other objects) became the majority of intelligible data.

Google Cloud Platform's data repertoire is healthy, with multiple products that can provide enhanced outcomes. Cloud SQL and Cloud Spanner are relational database products. Both are fully managed, with

Cloud Spanner adding a touch of serverless flavor. Storing unstructured data on NoSQL databases is done through Cloud Bigtable and Firestore.

Data unification is carried out through the data warehousing and data lake products: BigQuery and Cloud Storage, respectively. While BigQuery transforms data to bring it under a common data model, Cloud Storage is dynamic and flexible and can accommodate different data models under the same roof.

The proof in the pudding is in the eating, and Looker, the business intelligence and data analytics tool, can provide intelligence and insight from data so organizations can make good data-driven decisions.

DAY 6

Approximate Study Time: 1 hour and 35 minutes

Chapter 10 – 1 hour 1 minute

Chapter 11 - 34 minutes

DAY 6

Approximate Study Time: 1 hour and 35 minutes

    Chapter 10 – 1 hour 1 minute

    Chapter 11 - 34 minutes

CHAPTER 10

Artificial Intelligence and Machine Learning

The world needs dreamers and the world needs doers. But above all, the world needs dreamers who do.

—Sarah Ban Breathnach

For about a century, writers and filmmakers have dreamed of the machines having their own mind and thoughts. It began with the invading aliens and more recently, *I, Robot,* featuring Will Smith, where android robots serve humans. One of the robots, Sonny, is able to think on its own, have emotions, and even dream. This 2004 movie was my first encounter with artificial intelligence that did not involve aliens. Twenty years on, this science fiction movie is becoming a reality. We are in a period where the difference between the imaginary and the real world in digital media is sometimes indecipherable. Our sense of technology has moved to a different dimension, from having developed technology that responds to all situations to a technology that can learn and improvise on its own. In some ways, it is chilling to think of a future where we are not in complete control, and the reality is that we are building and improving this technology, because the true path to achieving unparalleled productivity, top notch quality, and scales of economy is through artificial intelligence and machine learning.

© Abhinav Krishna Kaiser 2024
A. K. Kaiser, *Become GCP Cloud Digital Leader Certified in 7 Days,*
https://doi.org/10.1007/979-8-8688-0438-0_10

This chapter covers artificial intelligence (AI) and machine learning (ML) basics. It explores the basic concepts of artificial intelligence, which includes machine learning, deep learning, reinforced learning, and generative AI. Further, it focuses on Google's differentiators in the world of AI/ML, through the products that are featured on the Google Cloud Platform.

What Is AI/ML?

The terms artificial intelligence and machine learning are used in conjunction or interchangeably. However, in reality, machine learning is a subset of artificial intelligence, as illustrated in Figure 10-1.

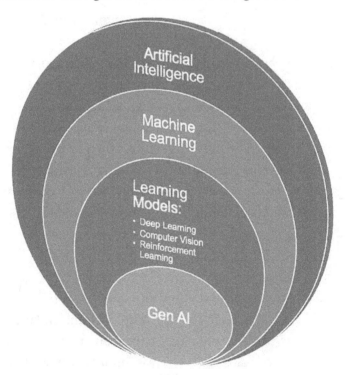

Figure 10-1. *Artificial intelligence and its components*

As you go deeper into machine learning, there are a number of learning models, such as deep learning, computer vision, and reinforcement learning, among others. Generative AI can produce content including videos, images, text, and audio.

Artificial intelligence is a field of study/technology that re-creates the human psyche in machines—understanding human language, visual perception, recognizing speech, and making decisions. Development is about teaching the machines to learn and to use that learning to generate certain outcomes.

While artificial intelligence involves learning and delivering expected outcomes, the learning phase is referred to as machine learning. Similar to how we teach children about apples and bananas by displaying pictures, we teach machines a number of topics. This learning is accelerated through spider crawlers (similar to Google crawlers), which enable the machines to learn from the information that is available on public forums apart from what is manually fed to them. ML is the driver that makes AI relevant because the knowledge is enriched by the day, and the outcomes are dynamic based on the current situation.

Big data plays a pivotal role in shaping AI and ML. The amount of clean data that is fed into these machines makes the AI smarter and strengthens its knowledgebase. These machines can identify patterns and data trends, and predict the future course of action. This is particularly useful for organizations to predict weather, demand and supply, fraud, and customers' buying behavior.

Importance of Data Quality

If you are taking care of a baby, either as a parent or as a guardian, you know that the baby is going to learn based on the information that they are exposed to. All that the baby knows about the world comes from the information. Likewise, artificial intelligence solely depends on the training data to understand, learn, and master the knowledgebase. In AI, data is the fuel that powers machine learning algorithms and enables AI systems to learn, make decisions, and perform tasks.

The machine learning algorithms are trained on the back of good data. The more diverse, relevant, and high-quality data they are exposed to, the better they can generalize and make accurate predictions and decisions. While human learning is based on conscious, images, models, and experiences, AI relies on identifying patterns and relationships in the data. If there is insufficient data or lack of clean data, AI systems may struggle to recognize patterns effectively or may return incorrect data.

We can also pin the success of an AI program on the data—both quality and the quantity of data that is used to train. Well-labeled and comprehensive datasets contribute to the accuracy and reliability of AI programs. To ensure mastery of the AI program, it needs to be trained on diverse datasets that cover a wide range of scenarios and variations.

Training AI programs is not a one-time activity. A good program will be fed with a clean source of data that the program can ingest, allowing AI programs to adapt and refine their models over time. Data may not always be available in a certain structure. Therefore, the program needs to be created to adapt in dynamic environments, and yet to churn out accurate and precise outcomes.

The majority of the data that is fed into AI programs is unstructured—with audio, images, and videos making up the bulk. Then there is the natural language processing (NLP), such as the language translators and chatbots, in which human-like data is fed into the system and the expectation is that AI responds in a meaningful, human way. While diverse data is expected, data scientists must also ensure that the data is free from biases and errors to ensure that the program considers ethics and fairness.

To summarize, data is the foundation on which AI programs are built and thoroughly trained. The quality, quantity, and diversity of the data considerably affects the performance, reliability, and ethical considerations of AI programs. As AI continues to progress, the world will use it for day-to-day operations even more, and therein lies the importance of responsible collection, management, and use of data for developing robust and effective AI systems.

Types of AI

Artificial intelligence is an emerging field and several organizations and universities across the globe are investing heavily in it. Figure 10-2 indicates the categories of AI that have been defined at this point in time. In years to come, these categories could take a different shape.

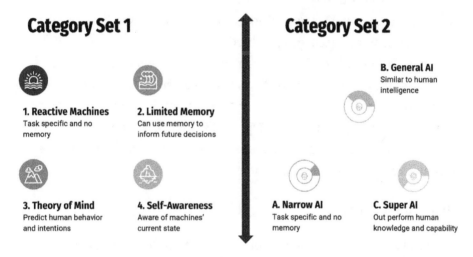

Category Set 1

1. Reactive Machines
Task specific and no memory

2. Limited Memory
Can use memory to inform future decisions

3. Theory of Mind
Predict human behavior and intentions

4. Self-Awareness
Aware of machines' current state

Category Set 2

B. General AI
Similar to human intelligence

A. Narrow AI
Task specific and no memory

C. Super AI
Out perform human knowledge and capability

Figure 10-2. *AI categories*

Reactive Machines/Narrow AI

This is the most basic form of artificial intelligence. It responds to the logic that is designed, and there is no learning and absolutely no memory embedded in this category of AI. In many ways, it is typical of logic being executed on the back of defined scenarios.

255

The famous IBM Deep Blue computer that beat Garry Kasparov in Chess in 1997 and Apple's Siri fall in this category. Based on the scenario, they can make predictions, but they do not necessarily learn from experience. In truest sense, they are not AI, but they sowed the seeds for what it is today and might become tomorrow.

Limited Memory/General AI

Limited memory or general AI refers to the capability of AI to understand, learn, and apply knowledge across a wide variety of tasks. It implies a level of cognitive ability that is close to humans.

This category of AI is not a bridge that we have crossed yet, but the technology is in research and production.

Take the example of Google's self-driving cars, which is a classic example of limited memory AI. The system can store pertinent information like the speed and distance of cars around it to make appropriate driving decisions and navigate the road. Open AI's Chat GPT is another example where unabated learning has led it to understanding natural language and responding in a meaningful manner.

Theory of Mind

Theory of mind is the art of possible using the artificial intelligence technology. The ability of AI to socialize with humans by understanding our emotions, state of mind, and circumstances is the next step in the AI evolution. There are ongoing efforts such as Fujitsu's K computer to build this capability and a supercomputer that is working toward simulating human brain's neural activities.

Self-Awareness/Super AI

This category of AI is as far as the human mind can imagine. Super AI's goal is to think and do like humans and more—surpass human knowledge and capabilities. This AI goes beyond understanding our emotions and beliefs and can evoke emotions, desires, and beliefs of its own. This sounds a lot like Skynet from the *Terminator* movie series.

The thinking behind this category of AI, which is seen as the zenith of AI systems, foresees AI having its own conscience, through which it gets its own sense of need, beliefs, emotions, and desires. This includes a sense of self-awareness.

How Does AI/ML Work?

At a macro level, AI/ML takes shape through six steps, defined in Figure 10-3.

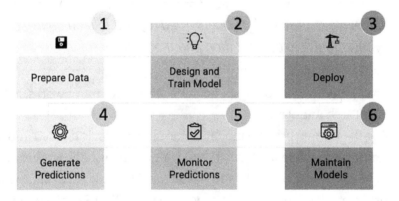

Figure 10-3. *Steps to build AI/ML*

Prepare the Data

You read about how the quality of the data is important for AI to be effective. Organizations need to ensure that the data is available, is clean from errors and biases, and is in a format that is standardized and digestible by the machines.

For example, if the AI is expected to identify car models, the data would essentially be different sets of car models. Also, the data needs to follow the most effective approach in ensuring that the car models cover the models efficiently without any clutter, duplicates, and other redundancies.

Design and Train the Model

If the prepared data is considered the foundation, then you have a good base to build the rest of the AI logic. You then design the AI model and put it through a training exercise. Python, Java, C++, and LISP are some of the programming languages used for developing AI programs. Python is the best of all, and the preferred framework is TensorFlow.

TensorFlow was created by Google in 2015, and it is an open-source library for numerical computation and machine learning.

Training neural networks can be done with other frameworks as well, such as PyTorch and Pandas.

Using the framework, the machine learning model is created and the attributes from the data are labeled and fed into the model. For example, to build AI to identify car models, you would label the images of cars with the appropriate models, such as like Chevrolet Optra, Tata Safari, and Audi A7.

After the data is fed into the system, machine learning developers and data scientists would run tests to ensure that the program identifies the car models correctly.

Deploy the Program

Upon successful testing in lower environments, the artificial intelligence program is deployed into production.

Generate Predictions

With the AI program online, a real dataset can be fed into the program. The program should be capable of carrying out what it is meant to do.

Car model images can either be fed in by exposing the APIs to sources of data or it can be batch fed. Based on the images that are fed into the program, it is expected that the AI program will identify the correct car models.

Monitor Predictions

While the data that was prepared and fed during the development and training stages was cleaned and sanitized, the same cannot be expected from live data. And yet, the AI program is expected to work accurately with the inputs so that it can recognize and maybe throw out a bad message if its outside the scope. In all the various scenarios, there must be provisions made to monitor the predictions and ensure that the program is working as expected.

Maintain Models

Monitoring serves as a feedback loop that developers use to understand any shortcomings and identify areas for improvement. With AI, there is always scope for improvement, since the inputs can come in any shape, size, or format. Developers use the feedback to fix bugs or to enhance the program.

For example, say that the existing car model that was trained to the AI program receives an upgrade in the form of body uplift. This is new data that the program needs to learn, and depending on the source of data, the developers need to ensure that the program is trained and tested before deploying the upgrade into production.

The Benefits of AI/ML

There was a time when IT was seen as a supporting character, and businesses realized that the costs had to be cut in order to remain competitive and relevant in the market. As network connectivity between continents strengthened, activities from the west were offshored toward Bangalore. For a couple of decades, this brought in cost savings. With the economies in the offshoring countries picking up along with competition to retain good talent, the cost factor between onshore and offshore became negligent. Businesses can no longer rely on offshoring services being cheaper. Plus, IT is no longer a supporting character but a partner in the business' growth and success. The solution to cutting costs lies in being more effective and efficient, and companies have gone through several cycles of optimization. Still there is a need to cut further costs and be more efficient. The path to this new efficiency lies in the success of artificial intelligence programs. This is one of the primary reasons that several organizations, research institutions, and universities have taken up the initiative to improve AI.

Apart from the obvious improvement in efficiency and productivity gains, the other benefits of AI include these:

- **Decision making**: Humans are looking at AI to make good decisions for them. With vast amounts of data being generated, humans can't digest the information in short order and make an effective decision. A well-trained AI program is much more efficient at ingesting huge amounts of data and making a good decision. For example, a stock market trader may not have sufficient people on the team to analyze the candle sticks, company records, news, and sectoral performance in a matter of minutes or hours. An AI program that is fed with all the relevant information can be a good aide in reading the data and coming up with suggestions.

- **Data analysis**: A vast amount of data is generated, and the majority of it is unstructured, such as images, videos, and audio. There are valuable insights hidden in this data, and analysis requires intelligence rather than just logic. For example, a program that scours social media for brand perception may read a post like "this burger is bad…" as negative, whereas in the natural language, the poster is referring to it as *great* colloquially. A well-trained AI program that distinguishes the context and colloquialism can differentiate and eliminate such errors.

- **Efficiency**: The market is changing at the speed of light. Therefore businesses have to pivot faster than ever before. Agile and DevOps methodologies support quick pivoting, but with the pace picking up, there needs to be a surge through AI to churn out market=ready solutions in short order. For example, a tool like GitHub Co-Pilot can help accelerate development of custom applications.

- **Customer alignment**: No two customers are the same. While the best organizations do their best to please their customers, they may end up serving 8 out of 10 customers. With AI and ML, the programs can analyze user behavior, history, and styles, among other aspects, to serve in the manner befitting the particular customers. This could help such organizations reach out to all their customers successfully.

- **Intelligent workflows**: AI can replace rule-based applications with intelligence. This capability will boost the applications to support any scenario that may come up the first time in the future. Further, AI can help automate businesses processes through the employment of Robotic Process Automation (RPA) to enhance and accelerate the processes.

Can AI Replace People?

As the science fiction movies depict, machines with intelligence end up threatening human existence. This is a perception that is shared by a certain percentage of people, and the numbers are growing steadily.

Before the industrial age, all things were handmade. As the industrial age progressed, people were replaced industrial machines. People didn't just lose their jobs. Instead of building items with their hands, they operated and maintained the machines that did the building. An example is the automobile moving assembly line, where people are still involved in assembling the car as it moves through various stages.

With advancements, industrial robots can assemble things instead of people. The people who were doing assembling earlier have either moved on to different jobs or upskilled to stay relevant. In general, automation was the first breakthrough to replace repetitive and predictive human actions. It was then said that creative work, the work that requires cognizance, will always remain with people. Not so. Artificial intelligence can learn the tricks of the trade—be it performing a surgery or writing code for a custom application. With the right set of instructions (prompts), machines are getting close to matching what humans can do. In time, there is no doubt that it can do better than people. And without fatigue, breaks, and shifts, machines can work around the clock to produce a lot faster, which will launch technological advancements.

The question remains about people. If the machines can do everything that people do, how should people be employed and what should they do?

On the outset, comparing the work that AI can do against the people it replaces can look gloomy. However, people worrying about job loss due to technological advancements isn't new. Technology has replaced what people did, and people have gone onto do more complicated work. Likewise, as AI takes shape, people should not oppose the idea and the threat it poses, but rather embrace it and work alongside AI, adding it to supplement and enhance their work. This will further advance technology.

GCP's AI/ML

Google is in the leader's category in 2023 Gartner's Magic Quadrant for Cloud AI Developers Report for the fourth consecutive time. The other notable leaders in this space are Microsoft, Amazon, and IBM. Google's ascent to leading the AI and ML spaces is due to the enormous focus and funding that has been pumped in the last decade, and this has been the period thus far with the most notable AI advancement. Google has been able to bring in their AI and ML models to seamlessly work with their GCP products. For example, auto-scaling servers and containers powered by an AI engine to determine scaling or descaling of infrastructure resources.

Google's AI products are massively trained in large language models (LLMs) with the help of huge amounts of data. Some of the more popular capabilities include image recognition, speech recognition, and translation. On GCP, the current set of products include Vertex AI, AutoML, and Vision AI, along with a repository of pretrained AI APIs. This has accelerated the building of capable AI applications in a short amount of time. Recently, Google announced the introduction of GenAI capabilities to their AI products, which is likely to take them to the top of the league.

A Large Language Model (LLM) is an AI algorithm that is capable of understanding, generating, and predicting new content.

The Google Cloud AI Platform is a suite of cloud services provided by the Google Cloud for building, training, and deploying machine learning models. It offers a comprehensive set of tools and services to streamline the end-to-end machine learning lifecycle, making it easier for developers and data scientists to work with machine learning workflows. It is fully managed and helps implement machine learning practices. Developers can use the pretrained AI models or tailor custom ones.

As I mentioned, the TensorFlow framework that is widely used on Google Cloud AI is an open-source framework that was developed by Google. It is widely used to build and train various machine learning models, particularly deep learning models. TensorFlow provides a flexible and comprehensive ecosystem of tools, libraries, and community resources, making it suitable to a wide range of applications in artificial intelligence.

Google also has AI Hub, which is a centralized repository for managing, discovering, and deploying machine learning assets. This platform allows users to store, share, and discover machine learning models, notebooks, and other ML assets. It also builds collaboration among data scientists and machine learning practitioners within and outside an organization.

Vertex AI

Vertex AI is a unified, fully managed machine learning platform in the Google Cloud Platform ecosystem. Developers can prepare data, train machine learning models, deploy, and monitor—all from the console. It has simplified the entire machine learning lifecycle and is truly an accelerator to develop capable AI applications.

Vertex AI Activities

The following activities can be carried out using Vertex AI:

- **Data preparation**: Creating datasets that contain clean data to be used for training the models. The data can include structured and unstructured data. There are tools embedded in Vertex AI that can assist in data preparation—cleaning and transforming. As discussed, cleaning data is a crucial step in ensuring AI's success.

- **Efficient development**: This is the process of creating training pipelines with pretrained models from AutoML to accelerate development or creating custom models using frameworks like TensorFlow and PyTorch.

- **Distributed training**: Vertex AI speeds up the process by carrying out distributed training. Deep learning models have large sets of data and this process has become increasingly complex.

- **API deployment**: Once thoroughly trained and tested, the ML models need to be deployed into production to make predictions. This deployment is carried out generally as API endpoints, which allow multiple applications and services to leverage the ML models, which in turn help the model learn faster.

- **Observability**: Vertex AI comes with built-in tools for monitoring the ML models to ensure that it is predicting and generating content as expected. In real time, developers can track if the ML model is serving the expected prediction/content or anomalies. This is a critical factor in getting the right feedback that will help retrain the model.

Vertex AI Feature Set

Vertex AI's feature repository includes AutoML services that allow users to build and deploy machine learning models without extensive machine learning expertise. It has prewritten applications and a simplified process for automating machine learning models. This enables developers and data analysts/scientists with limited skills to define ML models. It covers tasks such as image classification, text sentiment analysis, and tabular data prediction.

More recently, Google included Generative AI capabilities into Vertex AI. Codey is a model that helps developers write and debug code and create documentation, among other code-related tasks—similar to AWS CodeWhisperer and GitHub Copilot. Imagen is a GenAI model that creates images based on prompts—similar to DALL.E. Chirp provides the ability to converse in various languages in real-time, both in text and in speech. There have been several instances of world leaders' speeches being translated automatically—these are built on a similar technology comparable to Chirp.

Whether developers intend to use AutoML or create custom models, Vertex AI is the platform to leverage. This points to both newbies and experienced developers working on the same platform. For custom models, the product provides tools to build, deploy, and scale ML models using popular machine learning frameworks such as TensorFlow and PyTorch for all the possible scenarios.

A feature repository serves as a central repository to store all the ML models that are developed by an organization. This repository maintains consistency and accuracy in feature engineering across different stages of the ML pipeline.

Talking of pipelines, Vertex AI helps to create and manage ML pipelines, facilitating the orchestration of various steps in the ML workflow, including data preprocessing, model training, and deployment. This includes a training pipeline that consists of multiple containerized steps that can be leveraged to train an ML model.

The deployment of trained models in Vertex AI is done through RESTful APIs, which can be invoked by users for online real-time predictions. It also supports model explainability to help users understand how models make predictions.

The Vertex AI platform provides tools for monitoring model performance, tracking model drift, and ensuring the ongoing reliability of deployed models for carrying out efficient MLOps.

AutoML

The fastest way for technologies to evolve is through democratization. In AI too, the democratization (rather than proprietary) of technology has helped developers embed AI technologies into everyday gadgets. GCP's AutoML product contains several specialized AI applications for achieving different ML-related tasks. More importantly, AutoML enables users and developers with limited experience to learn hands-on with these ML tools, and those with extensive experience can customize the base product based on their respective needs.

These AutoML applications are designed to simplify the processes of building and deploying machine learning models by automating tasks such as model architecture selection, hyperparameter tuning, and training. They are part of GCP's broader effort to make machine learning more accessible to a wider audience, including those who may not have extensive expertise in machine learning or data science.

All the cloud service providers have built their respective applications/ models within the AutoML product. GCP offers the following models (also represented in Figure 10-4):

- AutoML Tabular

- AutoML Image

- AutoML Video

- AutoML Text

- AutoML Translation

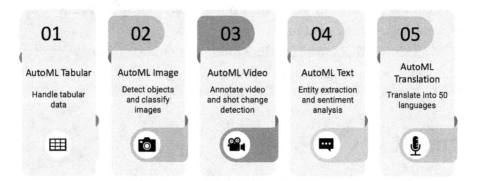

Figure 10-4. *AutoML models*

AutoML Tabular

This is a prebuilt model that supports ML tasks with structured data. Structured data comes in tables. If the dataset that you are working with is in tables, you can add columns and have AutoML Tabular's prediction capability provide forecasting data.

For example, let's say that an organization is trying to predict their revenue from their water filter business. The input dataset includes the revenue they made in the previous quarters against the items they sold, the prevailing inflation, the market reach, and some other data points. They can use AutoML Tabular to predict the revenue they are going to make if certain conditions remain the same or change based on certain intelligence.

Exam Tip   *You may be asked to identify the AutoML model that deals with structured data. Look for keywords such as tables, tabular, structured data, and AutoML to select the right answer, which is AutoML Tabular. All other models work with only unstructured data.*

AutoML Image

AutoML Image is a model in Google Cloud's AutoML designed to build custom machine learning models for image-related tasks. AutoML Image simplifies the process of creating and deploying image classification and object detection models without requiring users to have extensive machine learning expertise.

It allows users to train the model and categorize images into different classes or labels based on patterns and features it learns during the training process. Along with image classification, AutoML Image supports object detection. This involves identifying and locating multiple objects in an image and providing bounding boxes around the objects.

If you are familiar with Google's ecosystem and the Android operating system, you may have used products such as Google Photos and Google Lens. The feature that exists in Google Photos identifies and tags people in photographs and creates an album automatically based on tags. With Google Lens, you can snap a picture of anything and try to find similar objects and faces on the Internet. These are everyday applications that we use involving an ML model such as AutoML Image.

AutoML Video

While AutoML Image deals with image-related tasks, AutoML Video is tasked with building custom machine learning models for videos. It enables users to train custom models for video classification and can identify and track movement of specific objects in a video.

AutoML Video provides the capability to search for objects or people in real-time. You may have seen in movies and shows where conmen or people of interest are flagged in airports on CCTV cameras. This is not science fiction. The model can be trained by feeding videos and photographs of individuals who feature in the video. Through immersive training, the model will identify individuals based on their eyes, jawline, nose, cheek bones, and other facial features.

A not-so-premium CCTV camera that I have installed around my house sends me a notification on my phone whenever people are identified through its lens. The notification reads: human detected. It is simply awe-inspiring to see how AI has been integrated into inexpensive gadgets. And I must also mention that the accuracy of human detection is close to 100 percent, although the notifications get to be annoying.

AutoML Text

AutoML text helps classify documents, allowing users to build models that can categorize text documents into different classes or labels based on their content. For example, if a law firm has loosely thrown in their files including deposition transcripts, evidence, and statements, among others in a drive, the model can be trained to classify and label them meaningfully based on the content and the title.

This can be used for recognizing specific entities—such as identifying and extracting entities like names of people, locations, and organizations mentioned in the text. For example, a world leader's speech can be analyzed to see where the focus was: with finance, politics, the environment, and so on.

Further, the AutoML Text model can support sentiment analysis, which is the process of determining the sentiment expressed in a piece of text, such as positive, negative, or neutral. For example, a consumer may have rated a product as 1/5 because the delivery experience was terrible, and they may have qualified with a text review. The model has the capability to understand the sentiment behind the review and does not categorize it with the rest of the negative feedback that may have resulted directly from using the product.

AutoML Translation

AutoML Translation is one of the first AI tools to have come out the Google stable. It focuses on the task of language translation, allowing users to create custom models that can translate text from one language to another.

It can translate over 100 languages, it is known to understand the different contexts when certain phrases are used, and it is able to identify the majority of accents.

The difference between a tool like a normal translation program and AutoML Translation is profound. Translation programs generally run on rules. AutoML Translation and the majority of the translation tools that are offered understand the natural language, the context, and the sentiment.

It is also worth noting that organizations have started replacing human translators with AI translators, and the feedback is that the AI tools are quite natural and accurate.

Pretrained AI APIs

Similar to AutoML, additional models are available on Google Cloud that can be directly leveraged—these are pretrained AI APIs. If the organization has the right set of data and the muscle to train AI models, then the best option is AutoML. If the organization does not have one or the other or both, pretrained AI APIs come in handy. These AI models have been trained by Google's data engineers. It is like buying a puppy that has undergone toilet training rather than training it yourself (AutoML). This is illustrated in Figure 10-5.

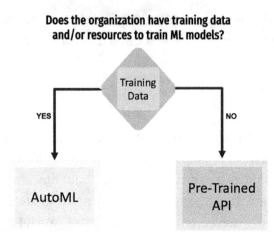

Figure 10-5. *Decision tree for choosing AutoML or pretrained API*

The pretrained AI models that are available as APIs on Google Cloud are shown in Figure 10-6.

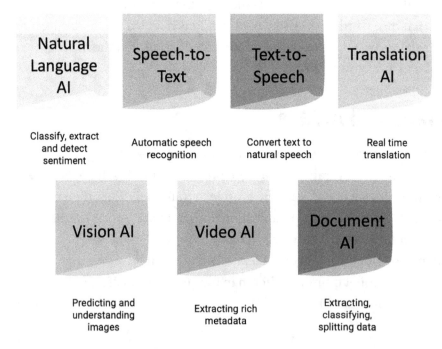

Figure 10-6. *Pretrained AI APIs*

Natural Language AI

Natural language AI can understand human speech. Classic examples are in digital assistants like Google Assistant and Alexa, which can understand different accents and responding with an appropriate answer. This technology has existed for a few decades now, but earlier it was rule-based. So, people had to speak in a particular fashion/accent for the machines to understand the speech. Now with AI, it has evolved and is attuned to different speech patterns.

Google Cloud has a well-trained Natural Language AI that can be leveraged without any further training.

The use cases include text classification, where natural speech is analyzed to understand the emotion behind it, which is useful in sentiment analysis. Text extraction is another important use case where the most critical parts of a text are pulled out and analyzed. This data can be particularly useful in search engine optimization (SEO). This feature is also helpful in the healthcare industry, where health-related insights can be pulled out from medical documents, provided they are in a readable format.

Speech-to-Text

This trained AI is an extension of the Natural Language AI and is capable of understanding human speech and converting it to text. The most common use case is visible on YouTube, where videos are automatically captioned.

On the Google Cloud, there are multiple models available based on the type of conversation—phone calls, long speeches, short blurbs, medical dictations, among others. At the time of this writing, Google supports speech-to-text for 125 languages and their variants.

Text-to-Speech

The reverse of transcribing speech to text is also possible through the Text-to-Speech AI. This AI provides an alternate method for organizations to engage with their employees and customers. For example, a number of trainings that organizations develop can be created as an audiovisual feature through the Text-to-Speech AI, with realistic voices that don't sound robotic. Audio books can be developed by using this model.

There are multiple voice variants available, and users have the flexibility to change the pitch, speed, and the voice on demand. It is also possible to train the model using a custom voice.

Translation AI

Google Cloud's Translation AI aids in translating documents, websites, applications, audio files, and videos. It supports more than 100 pairs of languages.

Google Translate (`https://translate.google.co.in/`) is a popular tool in the Google ecosystem that is used for translating text, OCR, and website content. It is the same neural machine translation that powers Translation AI as well. However, with Translation AI, it is offered as an API to allow developers to plug the feature into their own applications and websites. Plus, there are advanced features on Translation AI that preserve formats after translating documents, PDF files, and Google Workspace.

Vision AI

Vision AI is a model that can analyze images to extract pertinent information. The model can read text embedded in the images, including handwritten ones, classify and label images, and detect objects.

Video AI

With Video AI, you can analyze videos to identify and tag 20,000+ objects. For example, if I wanted to identify all the Chevrolet cars that have passed through a tollgate, AI can automatically do it without further training.

The Video AI API can be integrated into other applications and IoT devices to gain real-time insights from the streamed video, annotate objects, and create triggers based on criteria.

Other use cases include content moderation, content recommendation, creating and tagging media archives, and identifying locations in video to place contextual ads.

Document AI

Document AI can help analyze documents and extract pertinent information. The AI model has leveraged GenAI capability to classify, split, and extract structured data from documents. It can read handwritten documents in 50+ languages and 200+ languages for typewritten documents using the OCR feature.

Summary

Whether we know it or not, we are interacting with artificial intelligence in our daily lives. Advancements in the next five years will be on artificial intelligence and GenAI.

The critical success factor for AI is extensive training, which is determined by the quality of data. Leveraging clean and rich data will ensure that the AI models are successful. AI works primarily through the diligence of its developers, which includes preparing the right data, training the machines through proper testing, and using the data in production to generate predictions. Constant monitoring is necessary to ensure that the model behaves as it should, and anomalies are considered feedback to retrain the model.

On the Google Cloud Platform, Vertex AI is the unified AI platform that can host custom AI models along with AutoML models. It is a fully managed service that can create and manage AI models. There are trained AI models called AutoML which can accelerate AI adoption into organizational streams. Tabular, Image, Video, Text, and Translation are the AutoML models that are trained and available for use. Apart from AutoML, Google has exposed AI APIs for the models to be leveraged on application, IoT devices, and websites. The models are pretrained by Google engineers and can instantly perform a variety of actions. The APIs include Natural Language, Speech-to-Text, Text-to-Speech, Translation, Vision, Video, and Document.

CHAPTER 11

Financial Governance on the Cloud

The cloud is exciting because it paves way for new ways of working, and with the affluence of new technology and innovation, it is almost impossible not to get immersed in it. Financial governance of the cloud is important, although often overlooked. Leveraging the cloud does reduce costs over on-premises options, and organizations need to be able to forecast and control costs.

This chapter is non-technical. It covers finances, and the best practices to manage costs in a cloud environment, specifically from the Google Cloud Platform perspective.

Introduction

The cloud is a new beast and governing financial aspects of it requires a different approach than what was used in the past. The entire discipline of financial management—including budgeting, accounting, tracking, and monitoring spends—needs to be carried out in a dynamic manner rather than in a yearly or quarterly planning cycle.

© Abhinav Krishna Kaiser 2024
A. K. Kaiser, *Become GCP Cloud Digital Leader Certified in 7 Days*,
https://doi.org/10.1007/979-8-8688-0438-0_11

The cloud does not offer anything for free. Everything that an organization uses is charged unlike the days when organizations owned the infrastructure and usage was considered part of the planned financial model. Therefore, with the cloud, real-time monitoring needs to be factored into the financial governance model.

Startups and smaller organizations are a lot more dynamic and can pivot at any time, because they generally have a single person or a small group managing the budgeting, accounting, optimization, and monitoring of the cloud costs. And given their size, they are in a good position to keep their fingers on the pulse. Large enterprises work in a different manner, where the engineering/development teams often have the access/liberty to spin up their own resources, and they do not necessarily consider costs when carrying out their activities. A separate finance team is responsible for controlling cloud costs and keeping them within the prescribed budget. This chapter later explains how this can work.

Challenges with Managing Cloud Costs

With on-premises solutions, organizations owned the infrastructure, the application licenses, and the other IT components. There was the capital expenditure, which was huge, and then a small portion of operational expenditure included charges for leased lines, Internet use, and other charges, which were outsourced. The costs were managed based on the IT resources used by the business units, including those that were shared between multiple service lines. The depreciation cost of the infrastructure was added to track the asset costs until its end of life. This method was set in its ways and organizations and business units had a great deal of understanding of the IT costs that can be expected from these quarters.

Everything on the cloud is rented/leased. There is no capital expenditure and a relatively big operational expenditure. The pay-as-you-go model is great, but organizations must control it and get a handle on how much to spend every year. If a particular business unit spins up high-end servers or if they are unleashed with a big load, there is no telling how high cost can spike.

Controlling costs is a real challenge on the cloud. The financial governance ways used during the on-premises period do not cut it anymore. There were server teams, procurement teams, and the engineering/development teams. While the engineering/development requested IT resources, it went to the right set of channels for approvals, cost considerations, and then the records were keyed in before spinning up new IT resources. In the current scenario, every engineering/development team can start spinning up servers and getting their share of cloud products. Who is there to question or restrict them? This can be a real problem. There is a need to bring in structure, and to do it in a manner that does not restrict creativity and freedom, and at the same time, does not throw the company financials into a tizzy.

Managing Cloud Costs

There is no prescription for managing cloud costs. Depending on the organization and the dynamics, organizations choose to manage their costs differently. However, there are some broad recommendations that can be made to curtail costs and to introduce accountability.

If you are familiar with DevOps, you know that its foundational parts are people, process, and technology. Since DevOps is a culture, the change should start with people aligning to the new ways of working, and to bring in shared responsibility between team members. Then developers groom for cohesiveness, set up an atmosphere of experimentation, and ensure that the product teams are not distracted by unwanted aspects that should ideally not bother them, such as managing build and test tool implementation. Once the process is firmed up, the technology is there to assist, to automate aspects of the product development and operations that are set forth by the process, to implement the workflows that will accelerate product development, and to ensure transparency between the team members. This is a powerful combination if it's done right, which can propel the product development and maintenance to greater heights.

Developers can leverage the same concept to manage cloud costs as well—people, process, and technology—since what works in making DevOps work also encourages accountability and transparency when managing cloud costs. This is further illustrated in Figure 11-1.

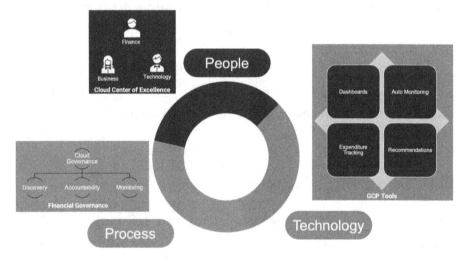

Figure 11-1. *Managing cloud costs through people, process, and technology*

People

The engineering/development (technology) team should be able to spin up IT resources depending on their needs. This work should not be outsourced in the name of governance, or it will be counterproductive. The costs for the IT resources utilized from the cloud are borne by the business. The finance teams are tasked with monitoring costs to ensure that they remain under budget. Given the varied responsibilities of the three teams in the realm of the cloud, it is prudent to include representatives from each of the teams to create the cloud center of excellence (CCoE).

The primary objective of the CCoE is to ensure that the best practices are exercised in determining cloud cost management. The group should understand the business' priorities to begin with and start formulating what is good spending and what isn't based on these priorities. To deliver a product feature in the one week might require additional resources (and costs), but if the group agrees it's necessary, even if it exceeds the budget, they should account for those costs. There will be certain tradeoffs needed to ensure that costs are not out of control, and these decisions are made by the CCoE. At the center of it all is the clean data, which acts as a source for making data-driven decisions.

Process

Having a CCoE in place is not enough. You also need a process that binds each of the stakeholders to their responsibilities. A robust process needs to be developed and implemented to ensure that there is transparency in terms of what is being used, what is really required, what is being traded-off, and whether the agreed route is taking the organization toward the business strategy or against it.

The incumbent process of planning and accounting on a quarterly or yearly basis does not cut it anymore. It needs to be more dynamic. The finance stakeholders should be in a position to monitor cloud usage on a regular basis, such as weekly or bi-weekly, coinciding with the sprint length perhaps. There needs to be an objective view on what is being utilized against what is created on the cloud. The technical team must have their fingers on the cloud costs every day, to ensure that a server isn't created and then forgotten. A process for discovery to understand cloud resources and to monitor them against set parameters is required.

Each of the stakeholders on the CCoE must be accountable for their areas of responsibility. The technical team must be in a position to provide optimization options to ensure that only what is absolutely needed is being used.

Technology

Putting a robust process in place is good, but if the process to manage cloud costs ends up requiring significant effort, it is a failure. The technology should back the process by reducing or eliminating manual work. This can done through smart dashboarding, automated monitoring, and notifications when the costs exceeds the budget, as well as tracking expenditure and obtaining recommendations from AI tools.

Google Cloud Platform has a set of native tools that manage and optimize costs. They are discussed later in this chapter. The tools help developers have visibility, control costs and overspending, and provide data-driven recommendations to optimize costs.

Total Cost of Ownership

Total Cost of Ownership (TCO) is a financial estimate intended to help organizations assess direct and indirect costs associated with the cost of IT. This includes the cost of infrastructure, applications, real estate costs, people costs, and others, over its entire lifecycle.

Let's say you are considering whether to buy and maintain a car or just use a taxi as and when you need a ride. For the purpose of this example, you plan to keep the car for a period of five years. If you opt to buy the car, the capital expenditure to pay for the car is significant. There are also associated taxes and insurance that you have to pay periodically. Fuel and maintenance costs over the period of five years are also expenditures. Suppose you decide not to buy the car, but just hail a taxi every time you need a ride. You pay for the taxi based on the distance and the surge fee every time. The cost of the taxi over the period of five years depends on how many times you used it at the prevailing rate. There is no way to tell which one will be cheaper with the limited information that I have shared. If you traveled perhaps once or twice a week consistently for five years, the taxi option may be more economical. And if you travel every day, with multiple hops, then owning a car makes more sense.

In this example, figuring out the better TCO is possible. But there is something more to consider. By paying for the car upfront, you are deprived of that capital that you could have, for example, invested in the stock market to potentially get juicy returns (called opportunity cost). Likewise, coming back to the on-premises versus cloud example, the total cost of ownership costs may swing from one extreme to the other, depending on the context, but the capital expenditure that organizations save when choosing the cloud is pure gold. This is money that they could potentially invest in various innovations and programs, such as proof of concepts and acquisition of smaller entities.

Dealing with Complexity Over TCO

Calculating TCO is not straight forward. There are a number of direct and indirect costs associated with any product or service. Look at it as different layers, beginning with direct costs such as real estate costs, followed by infrastructure acquisition costs, applications and licenses, engineers who maintain the infrastructure, applications, databases, and networks. Indirect costs, like the project management office, human resources, and taxes, also play a role. All these feature when you consider an on-premises arrangement. Although the list is quite long, there is a sense of predictability—it's straightforward and most importantly not done frequently.

Moving to the cloud, where only operational expenditure exists, might sound straightforward but it isn't. It is more complicated than on-premises because predicting the costs often (every week or fortnight) is challenging. Figure 11-2 shows the increasing level of complexity in computing total cost of ownership.

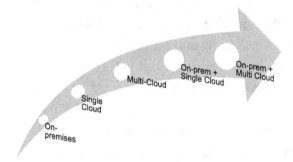

Figure 11-2. *Complexity in computing total cost of ownership (TCO)*

Likewise, an organization that has a presence in two or more clouds (multi-cloud) has to consider a number of parameters to predict their total costs, which are a combination of all the clouds they use. This is bound to be more complex than a single cloud.

Moving up the ladder, organizations that have opted for a hybrid setup—hosting a few of their product in-house and others on the cloud—will find it quite difficult to get the TCO computation right.

Financial Governance in GCP

Earlier, you read about the foundational aspects of people, process, and technology that will bring some semblance of financial management to the Google Cloud Platform. Putting these into action is a journey onto itself. Through steps and missteps, organizations have learned what works and what doesn't. This section does not talk about what hasn't worked but rather focuses on general principles and good practices that organizations have successfully used to add rigor to their cloud spending and accounting.

Principles of Financial Governance

The four principles of financial governance are shown in Figure 11-3.

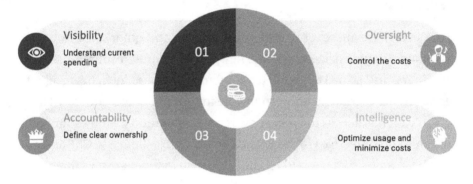

Figure 11-3. *Principles of financial governance*

Visibility

The first step before starting any engagement is to assess the current state. To get a handle on financial governance on the cloud, organizations must first undertake a similar exercise to understand the current state and understand the IT resources being used. A map such as a configuration management database (CMDB) could be a great way to achieve this.

The next step is to check for historical trends, which show the pathway to forecasting cloud spends for the upcoming period. At this step, you are not trying to fix anything, but just get a feel for how things are looking. There may be other ways to identify forecasts—looking at upcoming growth, seasonal trends, and gut feelings by subject matter experts.

GCP aids in gaining visibility over cloud spending and forecasting. The Pricing Calculator tool allows users to estimate the cost of using GCP services based on their usage patterns and requirements. It helps users understand the potential costs associated with deploying and running applications, services, and resources. Built-in reporting tools and custom dashboards can also be designed to provide pertinent information.

Oversight

In projects there are several developers, testers, and other roles. You should not provide access to create new Google Cloud resources (servers, containers, and so on) to all the team members. There must be designated people on the team who are responsible for adding new resources. The person who has access to create new resources should be fully aligned to the goals and objectives of the Cloud Center of Excellence (CCoE), and must be in a position to conduct due diligence before agreeing to new the resource request.

The power of oversight is not only over the control or restriction of new IT resources but also across the budget. It is possible to create projects on Google Cloud and stack the IT resources under the project. Each of the projects should be allocated a budget based on the forecasting exercise. Alerts can be set at different thresholds to ensure that the stakeholders can take necessary corrective or preventive action if there is a possibility of an overspend. Through budgeting and alerting, the involved stakeholders will be in a position to put limits on what can be spent. If the costs are exceeded, stakeholders can take necessary actions to curtail them or work toward getting additional budget.

Accountability

As mentioned earlier, in the Google Cloud, you can create projects and assign a budget to a project individually. Typically, the project would identify a particular team member, such as the product owner who is accountable for the project spends, including cloud expenditure. The product owner in this instance is the budget owner, and this person is accountable for ensuring that the project adheres to budget constraints.

Tagging accountability to a person or maybe a group of people (such as CCoE) is important, because they will focus on the objective of managing cloud costs and not leave it to fate.

Intelligence

With a budget, a budget owner, and the processes for oversight, companies now can determine what they think they will spend. But how do they determine any are opportunities for saving on costs? Any costs that could be potentially saved could be spent in areas concerning innovation and dousing fires.

There was a time when developers used to conduct optimization exercises, whereby a team would be asked to review the utilization and architecture and come up with optimization recommendations. This exercise carried on for several weeks before developers were able to act on it. On GCP, intelligent tools such as Recommender can provide a recommendation at the snap of a finger. For example, if certain files on a Cloud storage system are not accessed in the last quarter, the tool can provide a recommendation to move them from standard storage to cold line storage, which saves on costs.

Good Practices for GCP Financial Governance

There are several ways to manage finances on Google Cloud. This section covers some of the good practices that lead to proper management of finances.

Point of Accountability

It is best to have somebody who is responsible for the budget; somebody accountable for the GCP finances of a project. A product owner may be the best option for this role, as the product owner sets the tone and the focus of development, and the development route has a bearing on cloud costs. Secondly, the product owner generally comes from the business, and since the business foots the bills, it makes sense to make them the owner.

Invoice vs. Cost Management Tools

An invoice is generated and shows the cloud costs for that particular period. These are merely numbers. Stakeholders who are accountable for the budget and other concerned parties (CCoE) should start with the invoice, but also start exploring the cost management tools on GCP. The cost management tools are part of the GCP console and they reveal more details on the utilization, per unit costs, and how the numbers stack up. These details are pertinent for carrying out optimization and due diligence exercises.

Budget Alerts

Budget alerts are critical to effective financial governance. Budget thresholds and corresponding alerts need to be set up. On the back of the alerts, follow-up actions need to be defined as well. For example, when an alert for 90 percent budget consumption is received, the budget owner should seek for additional budget, depending on when the alert was received.

Leverage Recommender

Recommender is a tool that helps users optimize and improve the performance, reliability, and cost-effectiveness of their cloud resources. It leverages machine learning algorithms to analyze the usage patterns and configurations of GCP resources and provides actionable, data-driven recommendations for optimization. The tool supports a wide range of GCP products, and the preferred approach is to identify a schedule and an owner who uses the tool properly.

Apply Labels

Realizing IT budgets for projects may not always be straightforward. In bigger organizations, some IT resources are bound to be shared between multiple business units. In such a scenario, a best practice is to label these IT assets with appropriate labels to help split the costs.

Summary

Governing finances on the cloud is not straightforward, for one, because the cost predictions are not simple. To effectively manage a cloud budget—accounting for the spends and monitoring and charging back—there needs to be a disciplined effort to bring in visibility to the cloud spends, an oversight committee (Cloud Center of Excellence), and an accountability party, The company needs to leverage the recommendations provided natively from GCP. There are certain good practices, like analyzing cloud spends and splitting costs between projects, that must be diligently carried out.

DAY 7

Approximate Study Time: 1 hour and 54 minutes

    Chapter 12 - 44 minutes

    Chapter 13 - 70 minutes

CHAPTER 12

Cloud Security

When the cloud first came onto the scene and a pitch was made to migrate from on-premises to the cloud, one of the key objections that was raised was around the security of organizational data, which had been previously tucked away within the organizations' confines—the datacenters they managed. Since then, a lot of water has passed under the bridge, and security on the cloud is considered to be very safe.

This chapter covers the security aspects of the Google Cloud Platform (GCP), starting with the fundamental security terminology. The chapter also discusses the prevailing security threats to data privacy, followed by deep diving into the GCP specific aspects of security features, including Identity and Access Management (IAM). Finally, it covers resource hierarchy.

Fundamental Security Terminology

Before moving further into cloud security, this section explains some of the terms used in cybersecurity. These terms are used repeatedly in the rest of the chapter, so it's important to know what they mean.

Privacy

Definition: Privacy is about the data that an individual or an organization has access to and who they can share it with.

© Abhinav Krishna Kaiser 2024
A. K. Kaiser, *Become GCP Cloud Digital Leader Certified in 7 Days*,
https://doi.org/10.1007/979-8-8688-0438-0_12

It refers to the protection of digital information and includes safeguarding the data from unauthorized access and providing individuals or organizations with control over the collection, use, and sharing of the data.

Say that you maintain a personal journal, where you record your personal thoughts and experiences. This diary is meant to be for your eyes only, or at some point in time, you may choose to share it with someone you trust. If a colleague who visits your home happens to find your journal lying around and starts to read your entries without your knowledge or consent, this is a violation of your privacy. The journal entries that were meant for your consumption only have been accessed by an unauthorized person.

Unauthorized access and data breaches can compromise digital information. Protecting privacy ensures that only the people who are allowed to access the data have access to it. In an on-premises scenario, the owner of the data is responsible for building strong security measures to ensure that their data does not get into the wrong hands. Whereas with the cloud, the data is entrusted with the Google Cloud Platform. GCP boasts of the best-in-class security to ensure that the data remains safe from unauthorized access. Even the administrators working with GCP cannot get their hands on the data. The privacy is protected to the letter.

Security

Definition: Security in the cloud refers to the set of practices, technologies, policies, and controls implemented to protect data, applications, and infrastructure in cloud computing environments.

It is a shared responsibility between the cloud service provider and the stakeholders who own or have access to the data.

Going back to the journal example, it is your responsible to keep your journal in a secured location (such as a locked drawer) to ensure that anybody in your room cannot access your journal.

Likewise, GCP has a responsibility to keep customer's data safe from external threats. They have a responsibility to utilize strong security measures like placing firewalls and implementing intrusion detection and prevention measures to ensure that their customer's data is safe at all times. They also have to provide controls so businesses can decide who has access to the data. Data can be leaked due to business negligence (providing access to unintended recipients) as well—hence the shared responsibility of both GCP and the business.

Compliance

Definition: Compliance refers to the act of conforming to rules, regulations, standards, laws, or guidelines set forth by external authorities or governing bodies, such as the International Standards Organization (ISO).

The act of compliance is not uniform across the board. Some sectors (like banking and healthcare) are more stringent than others because of the sensitivity of the data involved.

Availability

Definition: Availability refers to the guaranteed time that the data and services are available to users. The crux is that the data should be available as and when individuals and organizations need to access it.

GCP makes this guarantee and it can vary for different services. It is generally noted as a percentage per year: 99 percent available in a year means that organizations can expect a downtime of 3.65 days in a year. The downtime could be in a single stretch or in a series of outages across the year. With multiple outages, a related term—reliability—comes into play, and it goes hand in hand with availability.

Prevailing Cybersecurity Risks

Organizations have to be vigilant against security threats. Before the computer age, security was mostly in the form of physical security, where the threats were against thieves breaking into offices, stores, and banks and stealing money, assets, and other secrets. Today, with the emergence of digital age, these threats have moved to the cyberworld.

The use of the word cyber *in the context of computers and technology dates back to the mid-20th century. The term became popular by the cybernetics movement, which emerged in the late 1940s and 1950s. Cybernetics is the study of communication and control in living organisms, machines, and organizations.*

A cybersecurity threat refers to malicious activity or event with the intent of stealing data or digital assets or causing disruption to individuals or organizations. In other words, a cybersecurity threat compromises the security, confidentiality, integrity, or availability of information systems, networks, and data.

As technology has evolved, so has the ability of cybercrooks to target individuals, organizations, or even entire nations. These threats are often intentional and are carried out by cybercriminals, hackers, state-sponsored actors, or other malicious entities.

If you have watched *Money Heist* on Netflix, you know the amount of planning that went into the heist at the Royal Mint of Spain. The professor and his team planned to breach the physical security of the mint. Contrast that with the 2007 movie *Live Free or Die Hard,* where a single hacker was able to bring a country to its knees by disabling essential infrastructure. While it is a movie, the possibility of something like this happening is very real, several times more probable than a group of terrorists storming into the Royal Mint of Spain. The reason is simple—information security resides on the network. Everything is connected to the network, including our phones, Internet of Things (IoT) devices, bank accounts, health records, and more. You name an aspect of our lives or an organization's focus area, and it is accessible through the Internet. The threat of a cybersecurity attack is very real. Therefore, organizations need to remain vigilant and stay at least a couple of steps ahead of the cybercrooks.

The possibility of cyberattacks is more probable with an on-premise infrastructure than on clouds because cloud service providers hire the best IT security consultants and architects to prevent cyberattacks. On-premises infrastructure may not get the same level of focus because the business' focus areas will generally be on their core. The next sections look at some of the common cyberthreats that exist today.

Phishing Attacks

A phishing attack is a type of cyberattack in which hackers use devious tactics to trick people into providing sensitive information, such as financial credentials, logins, passwords, or other sensitive information. These generally originate from fraudulent emails, WhatsApp/text messages, or websites that mimic legitimate entities. Figure 12-1 shows a phishing email pretending to be from LinkedIn.

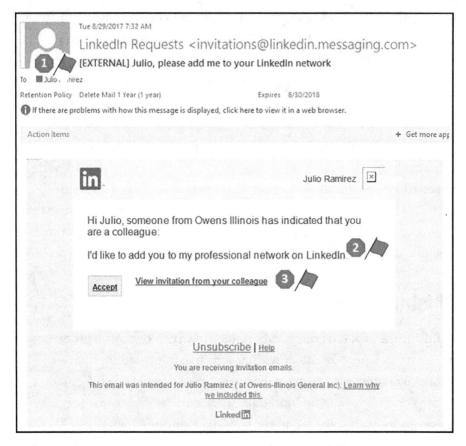

Figure 12-1. Phishing email example (Credit: Wikimedia Commons)

If you observe closely, you can see that the email did not originate from LinkedIn but from an email registered with a different domain. The hyperlinks to see the invitation will take you to a link that is designed to trick you rather than to the LinkedIn website.

Organizations try to sensitize their employees by sending fake phishing messages and educate those who fall into traps with specific examples. Here are some things that can be done to avoid getting phished.

- Set distrust as the default option: Verify the legitimacy of unexpected communications, especially those requesting sensitive information.

- Check the hyperlinks: Hover over links to inspect their actual destinations before clicking.

- When in doubt, don't click: Be cautious about clicking links and especially downloading attachments from unknown or unexpected sources.

Malware Attacks

Malware stands for malicious software. Its intent is to harm or exploit computer systems, networks, or users. The main objective of this software is to gain access to computers and sensitive data, and disrupt, damage, or find ways to gain information from the stolen data.

Malware is a generic term. There is also a dangerous type of malware called *ransomware*. It gets into your computer and encrypts your entire filesystem. Users can't gain access or delete files since the attackers take control of the master boot record (MBR). Unless users pay a ransom to the attacker, the data and the computer (the hard drive specifically) will be lost forever, or worse, it will be leaked over the Internet.

Viruses and trojan horses are also types of malware that get into the filesystem and disrupt the normal workings of a computer; they can transmit data to the hacker.

Spyware is dangerous as well. It is attached to a computer and does not cause any harm and generally goes undetected. But it captures sensitive information like logins, passwords, credit card information, and other personally identifiable information (PII).

Cybersecurity measures—such as antivirus software, firewalls, and regular software updates—are crucial for preventing and mitigating the impact of malware infections. Additionally, user education and awareness play a vital role in recognizing and avoiding potential threats.

Physical Damage

While the threats from cyberattackers is real, so are the threats to information security from physical damage: destruction to physical infrastructure, hardware, and equipment that can compromise the security, availability, and integrity of data.

The threat could come from natural disasters or human disasters like flooding, earthquakes, and attacks, or through poor design of real estate and infrastructure, leading to water leaks and power outages. There is a possibility of a sabotage, vandalism, or even a terrorist attack that can compromise security. Ensuring hot backups at remote sites can help mitigate these risks.

A common security threat that is quite prevalent is the loss of the endpoint infrastructure, such as when employees misplace laptops or thieves physically taking them. This can result in loss of sensitive data, but organizations have mostly mitigated against this threat by encrypting the data and enabling remote wipe mechanisms.

Misconfiguration

Misconfiguring computer systems, networks, or software applications is a security risk, because it creates vulnerabilities that can potentially invite cyberattackers to access the data. It can inadvertently introduce security weaknesses, expose sensitive information, or create openings for unauthorized access, leading to potential security breaches.

Misconfiguration can result from improper access management, poorly configured databases, misconfigured network routers, and failure to enforce security policies.

The threat from misconfiguration is quite common with custom-built software, especially if it is released in a hurry. Therefore, DevOps pipelines must be built with static and dynamic code-analysis tools like SonarQube, as well as application security scans, to ensure such vulnerabilities do not exist in the code and binary.

Unsecured Third-Party Systems

If you integrate with a third-party system that is poorly designed or configured, you run the risk of security lapses, even if your data was initially well secured. The third-party application's inherent security weaknesses will act as a window to your data, and the threat is as real as the threat of misconfiguration discussed earlier.

The threat from third-party systems happens if it is inadequately equipped to comply with the security policies of your organization. Weak authentication or providing access to unintended recipients can add to the threat. It's also possible that these third-party systems come under the influence of malware, spyware, ransomware, viruses, trojan horses, or other worms that might end up harming the security of your organization's sensitive data.

Any third-party systems that can be integrated into organizational assets must meet the same set of security policies intended for the software owned and managed by the organization. Also, planning and executing regular software security audits will help catch these issues as they arise.

GCP's Security Features and Products

Google has committed to keeping the cloud safe from cyberattackers. It has, over time, implemented a number of security controls and features to keep hackers at bay and to ensure that organizations have complete access over how they want to control the data.

In the list of responsibilities discussed earlier, the shared responsibility model dictates that GCP act as the data processor while the organization/customer is the data controller. All the levels of data handling are given over to organizations and they can choose to do as they want with it. For example, if a company wants to keep their data on a public network, or have it accessed through private networks, they can make either choice.

GCP provides the controls to make it happen one way or the other. Also, from an access management standpoint, organizations have the liberty to provide access to individuals or other third-party organizations. GCP defines the different levels of access, and the keys to the access management system are handed over to organizations to operate.

Google's Security Commitment to its Customers

There are a few commitments that Google has made from an information security perspective:

1. Google has made it clear that it does not own the data, and it is just a data processor. Organizations own the data, and they have the liberty to provide access, share, edit, and delete it, among other data-related actions.

2. You may have observed contextual ads on Gmail and on other Google products. This does not happen with GCP, as Google has committed to not use the data for advertising purposes. Further, they do not sell data to other third-party organizations.

3. When data is uploaded to any of the Google products, it is encrypted. The encryption remains at rest and in transit. In transit refers to when data moves through a network (private or public).

4. Google Cloud Platform staff with the highest level access cannot access customer's data. The systems are designed such that the encryption allows only for the data owners and their designates to be able to access the data.

5. In 2020, the FBI wanted to access the data on locked iPhones belong to certain terrorists, but Apple refused on the grounds that the encryption is designed to be only decrypted in conjunction with the device password. Google has also committed to not giving local and federal governments backdoor access to organization's data. This is not in the same league as the Apple's case, as Google has to comply and share data with the government if the government produces a relevant court order.

6. There are security-related certifications administered by the International Standards Organization (ISO). Google Cloud is certified as ISO 27001, ISO 27017, and ISO 27018, which means that they comply with the controls that are mentioned in these standards. Every six months, there are audits conducted by ISO auditors, who check the compliance against the controls.

ISO 27001 outlines and provides the requirements for an information security management system (ISMS), specifies a set of best practices, and details the security controls that can help manage information risks.

ISO 27017 provides guidelines for information security controls applicable to the provision and use of cloud services.

ISO 27018 relates to one of the most critical components of cloud privacy: the protection of personally identifiable information (PII).

Identity and Access Management

One of the security features discussed earlier in GCP is the provision for organizations to control the level of access that can be assigned to individuals and teams playing different roles. Identity and Access Management (IAM) is the product that cuts across all the other GCP products to manage these respective access lists.

Permission to access various Google Cloud products is controlled through IAM. Developers can go as granular as they need to when providing permissions to users/groups. There are predefined roles and an organization can create custom roles as well. Users are mapped to their respective roles and the permissions that are allowed for each of the roles are mapped to users. These roles are discussed more later in this section.

An IAM policy works on three basic parts: "who" "can do what" "on which resource." This is illustrated in Figure 12-2.

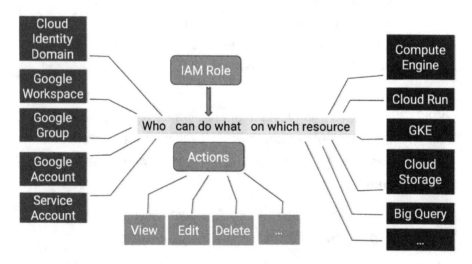

Figure 12-2. *Identity and Access Management (IAM) policy*

The "who" part of the IAM policy (referred to as the principal) identifies who needs access to certain GCP resources. The entity can be an individual with a GCP account, or the individual can be a part of a Google group. The other recognized entities are service accounts, Google workspace accounts, and cloud identity domains.

A service account is a special type of account that is used by applications, services, or VMs to authenticate and interact with other resources within a cloud environment.

The second part of the policy looks at what actions can be completed, or what permissions need to be provided. This is done through various roles that are predefined on IAM or through custom roles. Every identified individual/group is mapped to one of the roles, and each role has a certain level of access.

The last bit of the policy pinpoints the cloud resources where access/ permission is provided. So, for example, if an individual has the role of server administrator, that does not mean that they can administer all the servers under the organization's ambit. In IAM, you can provide permission to a group of servers or to individual servers.

Roles and Access

The principle followed by an IAM product is referred to as the least-privilege model, and it advocates providing individuals or systems with the minimum level of access or permission necessary to perform their tasks, and no more. This approach helps reduce the risk of unauthorized access, data breaches, and other security incidents by limiting the scope of permissions to what is essential to that role or function.

IAM roles can be assigned in three variations: basic, predefined, and custom.

A basic role has three traditional roles—owner, editor, and viewer. An owner has super access, and has permission to access all products and services, as well as perform any activity. An editor is one rung below the owner. They can perform all the activities that an owner can do, other than delete existing resources and provide access to others. A viewer has the least privileges and has access to view the resources but not make any changes to them. Auditors are generally provided this type of access to carry out their audit activities where they check for configurations but don't make any changes. There is another basic role in beta called a browser, where the permission is specifically to browse through the GCP products but not view the cloud resources. Figure 12-3 shows the entry screen for IAM.

Figure 12-3. *IAM entry screen*

At the time of this writing, 1,515 predefined roles existed on IAM. Depending on the role of the individual or the team, an appropriate predefined role can be provided. For example, the compute viewer role is described as: "Read-only access to get and list information about all Compute Engine resources, including instances, disks, and firewalls. Allows getting and listing information about disks, images, and snapshots, but does not allow reading the data stored on them."

This role provides 294 permissions, and Figure 12-4 shows some of the permissions provided through this role.

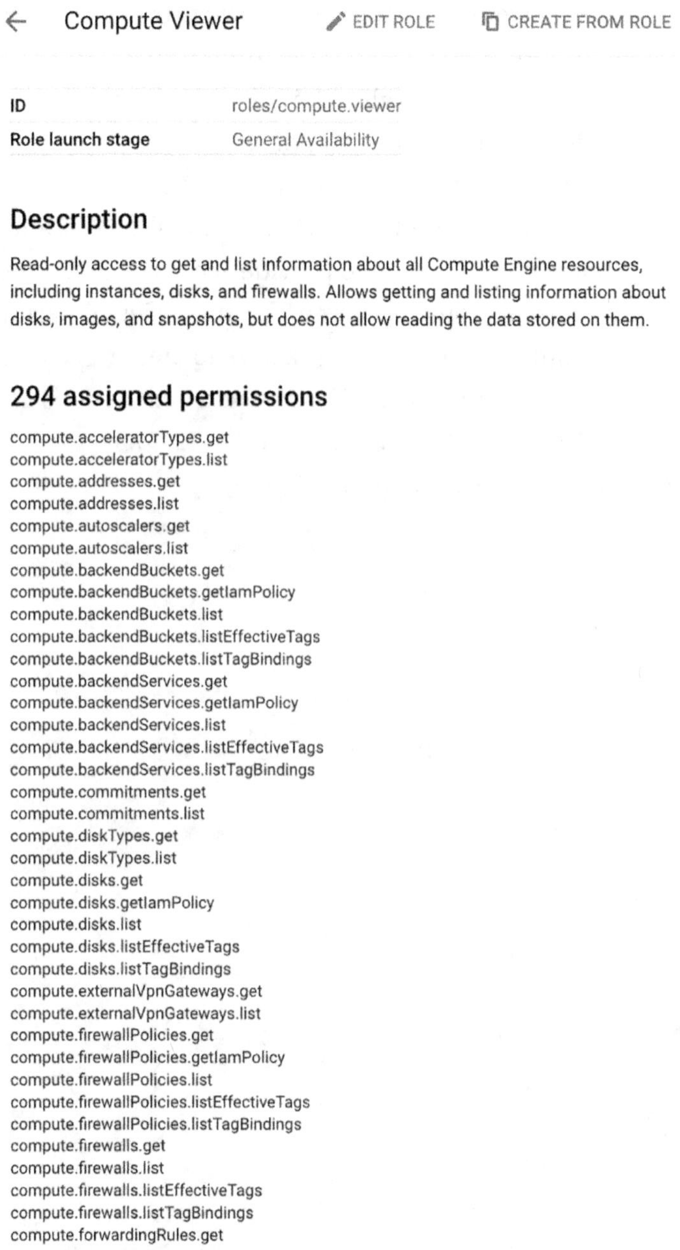

←   Compute Viewer   ✏ EDIT ROLE   ⧉ CREATE FROM ROLE

ID   roles/compute.viewer
Role launch stage   General Availability

Description

Read-only access to get and list information about all Compute Engine resources, including instances, disks, and firewalls. Allows getting and listing information about disks, images, and snapshots, but does not allow reading the data stored on them.

294 assigned permissions

compute.acceleratorTypes.get
compute.acceleratorTypes.list
compute.addresses.get
compute.addresses.list
compute.autoscalers.get
compute.autoscalers.list
compute.backendBuckets.get
compute.backendBuckets.getIamPolicy
compute.backendBuckets.list
compute.backendBuckets.listEffectiveTags
compute.backendBuckets.listTagBindings
compute.backendServices.get
compute.backendServices.getIamPolicy
compute.backendServices.list
compute.backendServices.listEffectiveTags
compute.backendServices.listTagBindings
compute.commitments.get
compute.commitments.list
compute.diskTypes.get
compute.diskTypes.list
compute.disks.get
compute.disks.getIamPolicy
compute.disks.list
compute.disks.listEffectiveTags
compute.disks.listTagBindings
compute.externalVpnGateways.get
compute.externalVpnGateways.list
compute.firewallPolicies.get
compute.firewallPolicies.getIamPolicy
compute.firewallPolicies.list
compute.firewallPolicies.listEffectiveTags
compute.firewallPolicies.listTagBindings
compute.firewalls.get
compute.firewalls.list
compute.firewalls.listEffectiveTags
compute.firewalls.listTagBindings
compute.forwardingRules.get

Figure 12-4. *Compute viewer role permissions*

The compute viewer must have access to view the servers created in Compute Engine,. They must also be able to view the network settings for the servers and various firewalls. They also need VPC access, which is included in the list of provided permissions.

If the predefined roles do not suffice, organizations can create custom roles to provide specific types of access to individuals, roles, and teams. For example, say that you do not want to provide access to the compute viewer role to view the firewalls, which is part of the 294 assigned permissions. You can use the compute viewer role as a base to create a custom role and remove the unwanted permissions. You can add permissions as well. To do this, you click CREATE FROM ROLE (see Figure 12-4). Figure 12-5 shows the screen for creating custom roles.

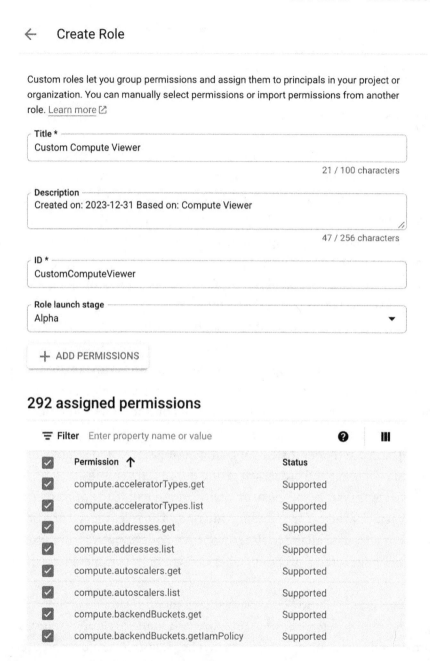

Figure 12-5. *Creating custom roles on IAM*

Note that while basic and predefined roles and their permissions change over time with updates from Google, custom roles need to be managed by organizations only.

Resource Hierarchy

An indicator that an organization is surviving is through its growth. An organization that gets smaller might soon wither away and die. An organization that grows will add new people, which requires reorganization into multiple business units and service lines to manage work, people, and everything in between. The hierarchy of an organization dictates that the person on the top is the leader of all the people in their hierarchy. It does not depend how high in the chain they sit, the people beneath will always be part of their hierarchy.

Google has re-created the organization structure on GCP to ensure that a fairly close mirror copy will aid in managing permissions and access and reduce the strain on keeping this going. Organizations can create groups that mirror the organization's teams. For example, consider a team that manages customer Y and another team that conducts ISO audits across the organization. The group will be given certain permissions to carry out their work activities instead of giving permissions to individual team members—making the process of giving permissions more efficient.

Consider several projects in an organization where the objective of the project is based on an intended outcome. The roles tagged at a project level need access to all the project resources. For example, an architect, project manager, and a product owner need to have complete view of the project.

In the Google Cloud Platform, resource hierarchy refers to the organizational structure used to organize and manage cloud resources. It provides a hierarchical framework that helps administrators and users organize, control, and apply policies to resources in a structured manner.

Resource hierarchy consists of several levels, allowing for the organization of resources based on different criteria. Figure 12-6 shows the resource hierarchy in GCP.

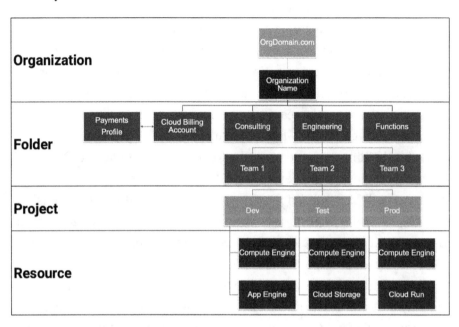

Figure 12-6. *Resource hierarchy in GCP*

Organizations

The top-most level of the structure is the domain name of the organization. The domain name sits outside of the Google Cloud Platform and is handled through cloud identity. At the time of building the hierarchy, the organization is asked by Google to prove their ownership credentials. The domain is followed by the organization, which is typically the name of the organization. Individuals or team members with permissions at this level will have access to all the resources in GCP registered under that organization.

Folders

The next level in the structure is the folder. This is an optional level that organizations can choose to skip. But, if they want to be smart in managing access efficiently, they should re-create their organization structure within folders. Folders help organize resources based on business units, teams, projects, or any other organizational criteria. In the example in Figure 12-6, consulting, engineering, and functions are three business units and underneath them are the teams. In this example, I have shown only the teams under engineering—team 1, 2, and 3.

A cloud billing account sits in the folder directly under the organization hierarchy. They track all the charges coming through the resources and their utilization. This watches the cloud spends, aligns charges to specific projects, is in charge of budgets. It's the single point of contact for all billing issues. Google recommends organizations have a single billing account.

The payment profile is similar to the Google accounts that we use. The payment profile is common across all Google services. Likewise, the payment profile for GCP sits outside of it and is responsible for payments.

Projects

A project is the basis for enabling and using Google Cloud capabilities. It is a fundamental GCP resource that encapsulates various cloud resources, such as virtual machines, storage buckets, databases, and others. All GCP resources belong to a project, and projects are used to organize and isolate resources. A good rule of thumb is to create a new project for every environment, such as for dev, test, and prod.

Resources

Virtual machines, cloud storage buckets, databases, AutoML models, BigQuery datasets, and so on, are the resources that appear under projects. These resource types represent the specific services and features available in GCP.

Resource Hierarchy Features

Inheritance: Policies applied at higher levels (organizations and folders) are inherited by the lower levels (projects and resources). This helps ensure consistency in policy application throughout the hierarchy.

Isolation: Projects provide a level of isolation, allowing organizations to manage resources independently. Each project has its own set of IAM policies, billing, and configurations.

Flexibility: The resource hierarchy provides flexibility for organizations to structure their cloud environment based on their specific needs. For example, it could be by service line, business unit, or project.

Summary

Having good security is critical to keeping data safe and cyberattackers away. Moving to the cloud helps organizations tighten up IT security, as cloud service providers focus on bringing excellent security, with large investments. They implement security procedures that are highly secured.

Some cyberattacks that organizations can expect are phishing attacks, malware attacks, ransomware attacks, and security threats from physical damage, misconfigurations, and onboarding of unsecured third-party systems.

Google is fully committed to keeping customer data safe. However, control over customer data is the responsibility of the organizations. Therefore, it is a shared responsibility between Google and the organizations to keep the data safe.

The identity and access management (IAM) product cuts across all the GCP resources and is responsible for processing permissions and access. IAM has identified several roles that are combined under traditional roles, predefined roles, and custom roles. The GCP resource hierarchy ensures that a mirror of the organization can be created, which starts with the domain on the top followed by organizations, folders, projects, and resources.

CHAPTER 13

Operations and Monitoring

Innovating and developing new features can catapult an organization's growth. But this is just half of the story. For organizations to sustain that growth, to continue earning their customer's trust, to keep the lights on, more is needed. That *more* is operations. This is the most critical cog in the wheel, because it helps organizations grow.

Operations runs hand in hand with observability—monitoring, to state it simply. Operations becomes effective through proper monitoring of the critical paths of an organization's delivery to the customer, their critical development engines, and all other bits and pieces that keep it all together.

This chapter focuses on operations and monitoring. In the process, the chapter delves into the challenges that developers face during the operations phase, especially due to conflicts with simultaneous development. Further, the DevOps and SRE methodologies are touched upon briefly as vehicles to meet these challenges. The GCP tools for monitoring and operations are also briefly discussed.

© Abhinav Krishna Kaiser 2024
A. K. Kaiser, *Become GCP Cloud Digital Leader Certified in 7 Days*,
https://doi.org/10.1007/979-8-8688-0438-0_13

The Operations Quagmire

Operations is a broad topic. Every area of study has its own set of operations that needs to be managed. For example, a business needs to be managed through business operations, a store needs its own set of operations, and IT operations has its own set of processes and guidelines. A store's operation will involve supply chain processes, ensuring that the aisles are stocked with designated products, the products are accurately represented on the billing software, and the billing matches the sales and stock. Likewise, the business operations for a bank revolve around banking disciplines. Every operational discipline needs to looked at independently because its scope and expertise vary vastly. However, the common thread that stitches all operational disciplines together is that they keep the business running and ensure that there is foundational support for growth. The customers' point of contact is generally the operational teams. The performance of the operations will reflect on the organization. Therefore, it is even more critical that operational processes be tightened and given due focus. This chapter refers to IT operations as just operations.

Operations is challenging. You never how things might start going south. You never know if a new government policy will affect the operational process. You never know if a knock-on effect will paralyze operations, which will then require a major reboot. Operations has a lot of dependencies, and these dependencies tend to play out at the most unexpected times. This is an opportunity to build an operations system that's flexible, that can pivot on a moment's notice, and that can reach the goals started by the business. Operations is therefore fun, in-the-spotlight, and challenging—all at the same time.

When an organization finds itself in financial trouble, the first casualty is operations. The rationale is that operations must maintain status quo and, if done effectively, can be done with fewer resources and lower costs.

Whereas innovation and development require dedicated people, so there are no cuts in those areas unless and until they run out of options after cutting operation costs.

Finding the right talent for operations is also a difficult task. With people to troubleshoot, maintain, and fix problems, it is not the most sought-after role in the job market. So the chances of finding the best are remote.

With remote working and increased threats from cyberattackers, work environments have been hardened. Accessing environments has become a circuitous process, with multi-factor authentication and plenty of checks and balances to ensure proper access. All this adds to the complications and hinders efficient operations.

Operations is viewed as a reactive process, where teams react to incidents, fix problems, and try to put out the fires. Although this is mostly the case, there is more to it than meets the eye. Operations can be proactive by performing good problem management—identifying and implementing preventive fixes and building automation and self-healing measures. When there are innovative ideas, operations can be as interesting as the developmental process.

DevOps

There are multiple perceptions about DevOps in the core. In fact, if you search the Internet, you will be surprised to find multiple definitions for DevOps and that no two original definitions converge on common aspects and elements.

I have trained thousands in the area of DevOps, and the best answer I have is that DevOps brings together the development and operations teams, and that's about it. Why does bringing two teams together create such a strong buzz across the globe? In fact, if it actually was just the culmination of two teams, DevOps probably would have been talked of in the human resources ecosphere, and it would have remained a semi-complex HR management process.

At the beginning of the DevOps era, to amuse my curiosity, I spoke to a number of people to understand what DevOps is. Most bent toward automation, some spoke of that thing they do in startups, and there were very few who spoke of it as a cultural change. Interesting! A particular example made me sit up and start joining the DevOps dots, and it all made sense eventually.

DevOps Example

Say that you are a project manager for an Internet banking product. The past weekend you deployed a change to update a critical component of the system after weeks of development and testing. The change was deployed successfully; however, during the post-implementation review, it threw an error that forced you to roll back the change.

The rollback was successful, and all the artifacts pertaining to the release were brought to the table to examine and identify the root cause the following Monday. Now what happens? The root cause is identified, a developer is pressed into action to fix the bug, and the code goes through the scrutiny of various tests, including the tests that were not originally included that could have caught the bug in the functional testing stage rather than in production. All the tests run okay, a new change is planned, it is approved by the change advisory board, and the change is implemented, tested, and given the green light.

These are the typical activities taken when a deployment fails and has to be replanned. However, the moment things go south, what is the first thing that comes to your mind as the project manager? Is it what objective action you should take next, or do you start thinking of the developer who worked in this area, the person responsible for the bug in the first place? Or do you think about the tester who identified the scenarios, wrote the scripts, and performed exploratory testing? It is true that you might start to think about the people responsible for the mess. Why? Because of our culture. We live in a culture that blames people and tries to pass the buck.

I mentioned earlier about some respondents telling me that DevOps is about culture. So, what culture am I talking about in the context of this example? The example depicts a blameful culture, where the project manager is trying to pin the blame on the people on the team directly responsible for the failure. They could be factually right in pinning the blame on the people directly responsible, but I am focusing on the *practice* of blaming individuals.

How is this practice different from a DevOps culture? In DevOps, the responsibility of completing a task is not considered an individual responsibility but rather a shared responsibility. Although an individual works on a task, if the person fails or succeeds, the entire team gets the carrot or the stick. Individuals are not responsible when we look at the overall DevOps scheme of things, and we don't blame individuals. We follow a blameless culture. This culture of blamelessness culminates from the fact that we all make mistakes because we are humans after all and far from perfect. We make mistakes. So, what's the point in blaming people? In fact, we should expect that people will make mistakes, not based on negligence but from adopting an experimentation mindset. This acceptance (of developers making mistakes) has led us to develop a system where mistakes are identified and rectified in the developmental stages, much before they reach production.

A blameless culture does not mean that individuals who make repeated mistakes go scot-free. Individuals will be appraised justly and appropriately but in a constructive manner.

How is this system (to catch mistakes) built? To make it happen, the development and operations teams are brought together (to avoid disconnect). Processes are developed that are far more effective and efficient than what is out there (discussed in the rest of the book), and finally automation efficiently provides feedback (as speed is one of the main objectives).

DevOps is a common phrase, and with its spread reaching far and wide, there are multiple definitions from various quarters. No two definitions are alike, but they have a common theme: culture. So, for me, DevOps is a cultural transformation that brings people together from across disciplines to work under a single umbrella. They collaborate and work as one unit with an open mind to remove inefficiencies.

Objectives of DevOps

DevOps exists for a reason, and the reason is simple enough—to deliver software rapidly. The end goal seems easy enough, but the means to the end is quite complex, mainly due to existing organizational constructs. This can be explained through a metaphor, called the wall of confusion, as shown in Figure 13-1.

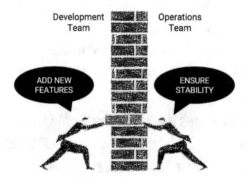

Figure 13-1. *The wall of confusion*

On the left side of the wall, the development team consists of developers and testers. On the right side are the operations teams.

In organizations that are not aligned to DevOps, the development and operation teams sit in different silos, which is nothing but a wall in between the two parties, similar to what you see in Figure 13-1.

Consider the development and operations teams based on what their jobs entail. The development team develops new features and products. The operations team ensures that the environments are maintained and stable. In other words, the operations teams want to maintain the status quo.

The development team's objectives of developing new features involves changes to the existing environment. So, it necessarily means that changes are pushed into the environment. So, in effect, a potentially stable environment can become destabilized due to the development team's changes, which is in direct conflict with the objective of the operations team.

This conflict is represented as the confusion in the wall of confusion metaphor. There is a direct conflict in what the development and operation teams want to do. One wants change, and the other doesn't because it risks stability.

If you have ever been in a change advisory board (CAB) meeting, you will often hear the operations team pushing back on the changes by questioning the changes, asking about various test cases and tests that have been performed. In other words, they try to put a wrench into the works. I am not saying that they are wrong to do so. Think at it from their perspective. If the testing is incomplete or is not done satisfactorily, this could result in a failed change implementation or incidents in the production environment. This would undermine the stability of the system.

In DevOps, teams are not situated in silos. The development and operations teams support a product. The development and operations teams are part of the same team. They do not have different objectives.

The entire team has a single set of objectives that apply to everybody on the team. This is in stark contrast to non-DevOps teams, where development team's objectives are to introduce new features and operations teams' objective is to maintain stability.

The objective of a DevOps team is to rapidly develop new features and to introduce them to production as quickly as possible. Most importantly, while changes happen to the product, the environment needs to remain stable. They are not compromising on the stability of the system in order to push these changes. They want the yin and the yang.

How does it work on the ground? How do they maintain stability while introducing rapid changes?

Continuous testing is embedded into the development process, and this is one of the drivers that ensures quality. But in this context, the key is to consider where the operations team handshake takes place.

The operations personnel are a part of the development team. So, they are aware of the various features and changes to the product being developed. They have first-hand information about the various tests that have been performed and the outcome of each of these tests. The results are out there for all team members to see.

If the operations teams have any questions about the changes or new features, they ask these questions during the development and testing stages, not during the release stage, which is generally the case with non-DevOps organizations. And definitely not during CAB meetings! It is important that the operations teams constructively question the developers to ensure that any chinks that may have been in the armor are addressed. This will make the product stable and address the issues in lower environments rather than in production. Developers would rather have a thousand bugs in the development environment than one bug in the production environment, generally speaking.

As for the operations teams, since they are part of the entire setup from the onset, there will be no such thing as transitioning to support. The operations teams is ready to start supporting from day one without a formal handover. They have been as intimate with the changes as the development team.

This is a classic example of a win-win situation where the DevOps methodology not only breaks down the wall but makes the entire process of development and support look seamless.

To summarize, the following points are the core objectives of DevOps:

- Reduce silos between teams

- Accept failure as normal

- Improve product quality

- Implement gradual changes

- Leverage tooling and operations

- Measure everything

Site Reliability Engineering

DevOps is development + operations, and yet, the focus is mostly on the development side of the activities. If you observe the processes closely, the operation in DevOps is through the lens of development. The developers either double up to perform operations or there are dedicated operational people who address incidents and perform maintenance fixes.

Now flip the switch and shift the focus toward operations. Look at development through the lens of operations. The focus is on operational tasks as the center while developing new features. Enter Site Reliability Engineering (SRE). SRE is a methodology that focuses on attaining stabilization of production to begin with, before embarking on developing and rolling out new features.

SRE is the brainchild of Google. It dates back to 2003 when their senior vice president Ben Treynor, who was leading technical operations, was tasked with creating integrated teams. The main objectives at the time of conception were to use engineering with a software development background to perform operations work and to automate everything through these smart engineers. According to Ben, SRE is what happens when you ask a software engineer to design an operations team.

SRE is a methodology that focuses on creating scalable and highly reliable software systems. It blends principles from software engineering and applies them to infrastructure and operations problems. Like DevOps, the primary goal of SRE is to bridge the gap between development and operations, ensuring that software systems are not only functional but also reliable, available, and efficient in a production environment.

Pitting SRE against DevOps, the question isn't about which one to choose but rather how to integrate the two to bring the best of both worlds. While DevOps is strong on the development processes focusing on rapid development and faster releases, SRE focuses on operations, stabilization, and scalability of the production systems. Underlying them is the common objective of automating whatever is possible and ensuring that the customer objectives become the north star for the rest of the activities to follow. The cultures behind DevOps and SRE are very similar—with both methodologies insisting on building a blameless culture that looks at problems objectively, learns from failures, and encourages collaboration, transparency, and continuous improvement.

How SRE Works

DevOps embeds Agile processes and the roles that it carries become an inherent part of DevOps—such as product owner, scrum master, and Agile team members. Apart from this, DevOps engineers and architects are responsible for putting together the solution and implementation of DevOps architecture—continuous integration, continuous delivery, and continuous deployment. Likewise, on the SRE end, a site reliability engineer is a developer who performs operations. So, the expectation is that they keep the product stable, reliable, and scalable. In comparison, the DevOps engineer's and site reliability engineer's roles are similar, but the latter comes with a background of software development, which is an advantage to stabilize the product. Both roles are expected to be adept at tool configuration, integration, and building automation.

Focusing on the work areas, SRE relies on doing the operations on the back of principles, as shown in Figure 13-2.

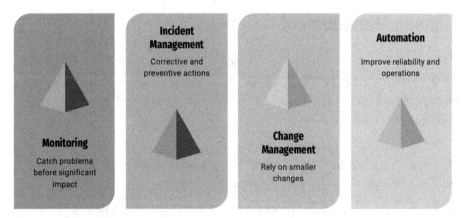

Figure 13-2. *SRE principles*

Monitoring

SRE establishes robust monitoring systems to track the performance and health of services in real-time. Alerts are set up to notify teams when the system is deviating from expected behavior, allowing for proactive intervention.

The monitoring systems are configured with the thresholds based on the service level objectives, which act as a basis for triggering events. For example, if the thresholds are breached, there could be automated actions such as self-healing or notifying teams of the threshold breach.

Incident Management

Incident management is a practice in the Information Technology Infrastructure Library (ITIL) service management framework. Its core objective is to restore the broken service as quickly as possible.

In SRE, incident management refers to fixing the problems as soon as they occur, even if the customer community has not been identified yet. More importantly, it involves enacting preventive actions to ensure that the incident does not occur again.

Change Management

The principle behind Agile and DevOps is to build in small increments and roll them into production regularly. This will ensure that failures are identified faster, and fixes (if needed) can be applied as soon as they are identified. Since the changes are small, the impact of failure is not expected to impact the customer greatly.

In the SRE world, a similar principle is used to release changes frequently and maintain system reliability. These small changes are expected to increase the efficiencies in the process, and the feedback loops measure system performance in real-time to alert teams if their intervention is required.

Automation

Automation is a fundamental aspect of SRE. Routine operational tasks are automated to reduce manual intervention and minimize the risk of human error. This includes the deployment, monitoring, and incident response processes.

At every step, starting from development to the production systems, where the SLOs are identified, there is constant monitoring and automated self-healing.

SRE Metrics and Terminology

There are a few concepts/terms that are commonly accepted in SRE and used in the operational processes. This section briefly touches on them.

Service Level Agreement

A service level agreement (SLA) is a formal understanding between a service provider/cloud service provider and a customer. It defines the customer's expectations in terms of service levels. The document is drafted, agreed on, and signed by signatories from both sides of the table. Typically, the expectations around service uptime, resolution times, performance, and responsibilities of each party become part of the SLA document.

For instance, before I signed up with my Internet Service Provider, the service provider set up the following expectations:

> Internet speed: 300Mbps at the point of termination at my home
>
> Monthly uptime: 99.9%
>
> Resolution response: 2 business hours
>
> Issue resolution for Internet breakdown: 24 hours
>
> Issue resolution for non-major issues: 48 hours

My Internet Service Provider was basically setting the expectations, by stating that I would get a minimum of 300Mbps when I connect my laptop directly to their fiber line. If I report an issue, such as loss of Internet connection or slow speeds, they need a maximum of two business hours to respond to my request and a maximum of 24 hours to resolve the issue. These expectations are published on their app and their website, and are shared via email when I signed up. When I log an incident, the ticket computes the timeline for when the issue is due to be resolved, which is based on the SLA expectations.

The operational level agreement (OLA) defines the interdependent relationships between the different groups in an organization that support the delivery of a particular service. It is an agreement to ensure that it is constructed within the boundaries of the SLA, and ensures that the service providers do not pass the buck and inconvenience the customers. In principle, OLAs provide a clear understanding of the parties' roles, responsibilities, and dependencies.

While the service provider and the customer are free to add their respective expectations in the SLA document, there are certain components found in any SLA.

The Google Cloud Platform's SLAs can be accessed from the following URL (see Figure 13-3): `https://cloud.google.com/terms/sla`.

Google Cloud Platform Service Level Agreements

The following are the Service Level Agreements for the following Google Cloud Platform services.

AI Platform Training and Prediction	AlloyDB
Apigee	App Engine
Application Integration	AutoML Translation
Bare Metal Solution	BigQuery
Blockchain Node Engine	Cloud Bigtable
Cloud CDN	Cloud Build
Cloud Data Fusion	Cloud Composer
Cloud DNS	Cloud DLP
Cloud Filestore	Cloud External Key Manager
Cloud Healthcare	Cloud Functions
Cloud Identity Services	Cloud HSM
Cloud Key Management Service	Cloud Interconnect
Cloud Natural Language API	Cloud NAT
Cloud Scheduler	Cloud Run
Cloud SQL	Cloud Spanner
Cloud Storage for Firebase	Cloud Storage
Cloud Translation	Cloud Tasks
Cloud VPN	Cloud Vision
Compute Engine and Load Balancing	Cloud Workstations
Dataplex	Dataflow
Datastore	Dataproc
Dataproc Metastore	Data Catalog
Document AI	Dialogflow
Duet AI in Google Cloud	Google Cloud Armor
Firestore	Google Cloud VMware Engine
Google Cloud NetApp Volumes	Google Kubernetes Engine
Google Earth Engine	IoT Core
Identity Platform	Managed Service for Microsoft Active Directory
Looker Studio Pro	Network Connectivity Center
Memorystore	Operations
Payment Gateway	Pub/Sub
reCAPTCHA Enterprise	Secret Manager
Security Command Center	Speech-to-Text
Spectrum Access System	Talent Solution
Text-to-Speech	Vertex AI Platform
Vertex AI Vision	Video Intelligence API
Workflows	

Figure 13-3. *GCP SLAs*

The associated SLAs of the GCP products are listed in their respective pages, as shown in Figure 13-3. For example, take a closer look at the SLA document for Cloud Functions shown in Figure 13-4. It's an SLO that guarantees a monthly uptime of 99.95 percent. If Google fails to achieve said SLO, customers can expect a financial credit.

Cloud Functions Service Level Agreement (SLA)

During the Term of the agreement under which Google has agreed to provide Google Cloud Platform to Customer (as applicable, the "Agreement"), the Covered Service will provide a Monthly Uptime Percentage to Customer as follows (the "Service Level Objective" or "SLO"):

Covered Service	Monthly Uptime Percentage
Cloud Functions	>= 99.95%

If Google does not meet the SLO, and if Customer meets its obligations under this SLA, Customer will be eligible to receive the Financial Credits described below. Monthly Uptime Percentage and Financial Credit are determined on a calendar month basis per Project. This SLA states Customer's sole and exclusive remedy for any failure by Google to meet the SLO. Capitalized terms used in this SLA, but not defined in this SLA, have the meaning stated in the Agreement. If the Agreement authorizes the resale or supply of Google Cloud Platform under a Google Cloud partner or reseller program, then all references to Customer in this SLA mean Partner or Reseller (as applicable), and any Financial Credit(s) will only apply for impacted Partner or Reseller order(s) under the Agreement.

Definitions

The following definitions apply to the SLA:

- **"Covered Service"** means an individual Cloud Function within a Project and in the "active" state.
- **"Downtime"** means more than a ten percent Error Rate.
- **"Downtime Period"** means a period of one or more consecutive minutes of Downtime. Partial minutes or intermittent Downtime for a period of less than one minute will not be counted towards any Downtime Periods.
- **"Error Rate"** for the Covered Service is defined as the number of errors divided by the total number of attempted function executions, subject to a minimum of 100 attempted executions in the measurement period. An error is defined as a result of SYSTEM_ERROR in response to a valid invocation event.
- **"Financial Credit"** means the following:

Monthly Uptime Percentage	Percentage of monthly bill for the respective Covered Service that does not meet SLO that will be credited to Customer's future monthly bills
99% to < 99.95%	10%
95% to < 99%	25%
< 95%	50%

- **"Monthly Uptime Percentage"** means total number of minutes in a month, minus the number of minutes of Downtime suffered from all Downtime Periods in a month, divided by the total number of minutes in a month.

Customer Must Request Financial Credit

In order to receive any of the Financial Credits described above, Customer must notify Google technical support within 30 days from the time Customer becomes eligible to receive a Financial Credit. Customer must also provide Google with log files showing Downtime Periods and the date and time they occurred. If Customer does not comply with these requirements, Customer will forfeit its right to receive a Financial Credit. If a dispute arises with respect to this SLA, Google will make a determination in good faith based on its system logs, monitoring reports, configuration records, and other available information.

Maximum Financial Credit

The maximum aggregate number of Financial Credits issued by Google to Customer for all Downtime Periods in a single billing month will not exceed 50% of the amount due from Customer for the Covered Service for the applicable month. Financial Credits will be in the form of a monetary credit applied to future use of the Covered Service and will be applied within 60 days after the Financial Credit was requested

SLA Exclusions

The SLA does not apply to any (a) features or services designated pre-general availability (unless otherwise set forth in the associated Documentation); (b) features or services excluded from the SLA (in the associated Documentation); or (c) errors (i) caused by factors outside of Google's reasonable control; (ii) that resulted from Customer's software or hardware or third party software or hardware, or both; (iii) that resulted from abuses or other behaviors that violate the Agreement; or (iv) that resulted from quotas applied by the system or listed in the Admin Console.

Figure 13-4. *SLA for Cloud Functions*

Service Scope

This section draws the boundaries of the services that come under the confines of the agreement. A good scope definition will spell out every last bit of detail to remove ambiguity to the fullest extent.

A well-documented SLA will also include service exclusions to remove any ambiguity and keep the scoped areas crystal clear.

Roles and Responsibilities

To ensure continuous availability of cloud services, it is important that both the cloud service provider and the customer play their respective roles in harmony. This includes tasks such as maintenance, support, reporting, and communication channels. Therefore, the respective roles and their responsibilities need to be well understood. These roles are formalized in the SLA document.

Service Levels

The various aspects of the service levels are clearly spelled out. Uptime, resolution time, and performance benchmarks are some of the service metrics defined in this document. These are referred to as service level objectives (SLO), and are discussed in detail in the next section.

Information Security

Clauses pertaining to handling and protecting customer data within the cloud service provider's environments is key here. This also addresses the compliance, governmental, and legal regulation parameters and how the issues pertaining to them will be handled.

Penalties and Remedies

This component specifies the consequences if the service provider fails to meet the agreed-upon service levels. This may include financial penalties, service credits, or other remedies.

Termination Clause

An exit clause is agreed upon beforehand. Either of the parties have the freedom to terminate the contract, and the conditions of such a termination are planned, documented, and agreed upon in this section.

Service Level Objective

I briefly talked about Service Level Objectives (SLO) in the previous section. SLOs are specific, measurable targets within an SLA, such as 99.999 percent up time. The SLO defines a particular aspect of the service's performance, such as uptime, response time, or availability. SLOs are more granular and focus on quantifying the quality of service for specific metrics.

To comply with the SLA, service providers need to meet the defined targets, which is the SLO. According to Google, SLOs are the lowest level of reliability that the service provider can get away with for each service.

When defining the SLOs, the stakeholders must be prudent and identify the right set of SLOs that matter to them. Over-engineering this will lead to wasted effort, additional expenses, and more importantly, value that is disproportional to the costs incurred. For example, since the technology provides the provision to measure the percentage of CPU, memory, and other components on individual servers, adding thresholds as SLO in a SLA document may in fact be a fruitless exercise. The effort needed to track the actual performance (which is referred to as service level indicator and is discussed in the next section) is more than the actual value derived from measuring and tracking it. If there is value to doing it, for example a server's component level performance has a direct bearing on an application's performance, then it's a good SLO to have. But, if it isn't, the stakeholders must ensure that judiciousness plays a significant role in identifying SLOs.

To summarize, defining the right set of SLOs is the need of the hour for both cloud service providers and customers, as SLOs provide a clear understanding of performance expectations. They help measure and monitor the effectiveness of services, allowing organizations to identify areas for improvement or address issues before they impact users. When creating SLAs, defining realistic and achievable SLOs is crucial to maintaining a healthy service provider relationship and ensuring that services align with business objectives.

Service Level Indicator

You are probably familiar with the term Key Performance Indicator (KPI). Service Level Indicator (SLI) is similar to KPI in the sense that the SLIs indicate the performance of a service against the SLOs, which are documented in the SLAs. For example, against an SLO of 99.999 percent uptime, a cloud service provider achieves 99.998 percent uptime (SLI). This SLI is a specific number measured over time, which is agreed upon when the SLA is written, and this SLI indicates that the service uptime did not quite meet the agreed upon expectations.

To identify SLIs, monitoring tools are leveraged. The tools are configured to read particular service levels against the set parameters. For example, if the agreed uptime is 99 percent during business hours of 8AM-6PM, the monitoring tools are configured to measure the service only during the service window and not outside of it. Even if the service was down during non-business hours, the monitoring tools, and hence the SLIs, would not pick up the readings.

Error Budget

A glass can be either half full or half empty. It's a question of perception on how you want to see the glass. Error budgets are half empty glasses.

An error budget is the permissible amount of errors or deviations from the desired service level that a service can tolerate within a specified timeframe without violating the agreed-upon service level commitments. For example, if the uptime SLO is 99.99 percent, then the associated error budget is 0.01 percent, which corresponds to around 52 minutes downtime in a year. So, instead of asking the cloud service provider to meet 99.99 percent uptime, the error budget indicates the amount of time they can have a downtime without impacting the customer contracts.

Error budgets came into being through service reliability engineering (SRE), which is discussed in the next section. Error budgets are used as a foundation to take further risks. For example, if a particular service is running on 100 percent uptime with one month left for the SLI measurement, the service provider has the freedom to bring the services down for 52 minutes in the next 30 days. This means that the service provider can take more risks, release more, experiment more, and be more innovative because they still have significant error budgets left. Conversely, if the service provider has exhausted their error budgets or is looking at the prospect of breaching the SLOs, it is not a good time to do further releases and take risks.

The error budget approach balances customer commitment against innovation. It takes a pragmatic view of reducing the number of incidents while increasing the risk exposure. In a DevOps setup (discussed in the next section), a service or product is managed by a DevOps team that consists of the development and operational responsibilities within a single team. In this setup, the team sifts through the balance of maintaining stability while developing new features with the error budget acting as a frame of reference. With increased downtimes leading to exhausted error budget, the DevOps team will play it safe with more focus on maintaining stability. With more error budget, they have the room to introduce new features and be more daring with their releases.

GCP Products for Operations

To support cloud operations, Google Cloud Platform has developed products that cut across all other GCP products in supporting operational tasks, such as monitoring, event management, and logging.

This section briefly looks at the following products:

- Cloud Monitoring
- Cloud Logging
- Error Reporting

Cloud Monitoring

The Cloud Monitoring product helps realize service reliability engineering principles and objectives. It provides insights into the availability, performance, and health of cloud-hosted applications and infrastructure. This is achieved through active monitoring of various GCP resources, followed by event management actions such as identifying and setting up alerts/notifications. The tool also enables developers to create dashboards to visualize and analyze key metrics.

Some of its key features are covered in the following sections.

Dashboards

The Cloud Monitoring product hosts several predefined dashboards that can be leveraged readily, and it also provides the ability to create custom dashboards. Dashboards can be used to visualize important metrics and KPIs through charts, graphs, and widgets that display real-time data.

These predefined dashboards cover most aspects of the GCP products, making it easy to get started with monitoring. Figure 13-5 shows a predefined dashboard from Google Compute Engine.

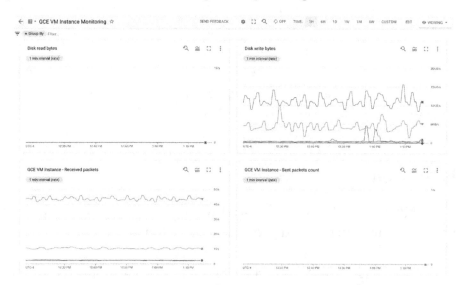

Figure 13-5. *Predefined dashboard for Google Compute Engine*

When a need arises to combine the resources from multiple products, the custom dashboard option will come in handy.

Metrics

Cloud Monitoring supports a wide range of metric types that cover aspects such as resource utilization, system health, and application performance. Examples include CPU usage, disk I/O, network traffic, and custom application metrics.

Developers can define and monitor custom metrics relevant to their specific applications and services.

Alerts and Notifications

Cloud Monitoring provides robust support for managing alerts and events. Developers can create custom alerts (referred to as *policies*) to define conditions that trigger alerts when certain thresholds are breached. For example, when a website becomes unavailable, Cloud Monitoring can detect the event and, based on the alert policy, can initiate a set of actions.

It also supports various notification channels, including email, SMS, and integrations with third-party tools like Slack, Google Chat, and PagerDuty.

Integration

Cloud Monitoring integrates seamlessly with other GCP products, allowing users to monitor metrics and performance data from various resources, including Compute Engine, App Engine, Cloud Storage, and others. It can additionally integrate with Cloud Logging, allowing users to correlate monitoring data with logs for deeper insights and troubleshooting.

The integration is not limited to GCP alone but can be extended to monitor on-premise applications and infrastructure, along with resources hosted on other cloud service providers.

SLO Monitoring

The cloud monitoring product includes SLO monitoring that monitors, alerts, and notifies the defined channels based on the performance of the SLOs.

APIs

Cloud Monitoring includes a Monitoring API, which allows developers to programmatically access and retrieve monitoring data. This is useful for automation, custom reporting, and integration with other systems.

Cloud Logging

In the world of IT and data, logs are like gold dust. They reveal insights into the health and performance of IT resources. The Cloud Logging product works across all GCP products and plays a crucial role in providing observability into the behavior and performance of applications, as well as facilitating troubleshooting, debugging, and compliance efforts.

The product enables users to store, search, analyze, and monitor log data generated by applications and services running on GCP.

Some of its key features are covered in the following sections.

Aggregation

Cloud Logging aggregates log entries from various GCP products and applications, consolidating them into a centralized storage system. This is particularly helpful in its management analysis activities.

Users can define retention policies to control how long log data is retained to meet regulations and to cut costs.

Analysis

There is an built-in query language that allows users to search and filter log entries based on various criteria. Further, the log data can be used to perform real-time analysis and gain insights into system behavior, identify issues, and troubleshoot problems.

Log Sink

Logs are stored on the Cloud Logging log bucket by default. However, the Log Sink feature allows users to route or forward log entries to multiple destinations, including Cloud Storage and Big Query, or onto other cloud storage buckets and on-premises storage solutions.

Integration

Like Cloud Monitoring, the Cloud Logging product is natively integrated into various GCP products, which means it can capture logs from products like Compute Engine, Cloud Functions, App Engine, Kubernetes Engine, Cloud Storage, and others.

Further, APIs can integrate the log data with custom applications and other products outside of the Google ecosystem.

Error Reporting

Error reporting is a prescriptive way of viewing errors in the cloud system. It aggregates all the errors that occur across GCP products when running cloud services. In a single view, organizations can see all the errors, and the product helps analyze them based on their recurrence, impact, and new errors, among other factors.

The data used to report errors comes from Cloud Logging, by tagging the errors as such, and these are automatically picked up by the Error Reporting API, which and analyzes and displays them centrally.

Some of its key features are described in the following sections.

Collection

Error Reporting is integrated with various GCP products to capture errors and exceptions generated by applications that are deployed on various products such as Compute Engine, GKE, and App Engine, among others.

Developers can use client libraries and SDKs to integrate Error Reporting into their applications, enabling the automatic reporting of errors.

Analysis

The Error Reporting product has the ability to aggregate similar errors into groups, making it easier to understand the frequency and impact of specific issues. For example, all the DNS issues are grouped together into a single bucket while memory issues are grouped into another.

The product leverages artificial intelligence-based grouping algorithms to group similar errors together, reducing noise and helping teams focus on root causes.

Details and Context

The product provides detailed stack traces that let developers identify the exact location and sequence of code that led to the error. For applications hosted on the web, the products capture relevant request context information, such as HTTP request details, therefore making it easier to diagnose issues.

Tracking

Errors can be tracked centrally using Error Reporting, and developers can mark errors as resolved when a fix has been applied. This provides a full lifecycle of an error from logging through resolution to closure.

Not all errors can be resolved, and these are referred to as known errors. Such errors can be muted on the product to ensure that the focus remains on the errors that are new, recurring, and need resolving.

Products for Performance

To manage the performance of applications hosted on the cloud, the Google Cloud Platform has developed products that optimize and improve performance through debugging and analyzing resource use.

This section briefly looks at the following products:

- Cloud Trace
- Cloud Profiler

Cloud Trace

Cloud Trace traverses through an application and gathers performance-related statistics. It allows developers to capture, analyze, and visualize distributed traces of requests as they traverse through various components of an application—such as the cache, database, or external integration points.

The product measures the application's end-to-end latency and performance of requests, making it easier to identify bottlenecks, optimize performance, and enhance the overall user experience.

Some of the key features are described in the following subsections.

Tracing

Every application, depending on its complexity, has multiple hops of data exchange. Delays in any of these hops could lead to performance issues. Cloud Trace can capture traces of requests as they move through different components and services of a distributed application. This helps developers identify the root cause of any performance issues.

Further, as the traces traverse, they enables end-to-end visibility into the flow of requests and hence the performance measure of the application. This helps developers understand the sequence of interactions across microservices or different parts of the application.

Trace Viewer

Trace Viewer is available on the GCP Console within Cloud Trace. It allows users to visualize and analyze traces interactively. It displays the sequence of spans, their duration, and their relationships. This analysis isn't AI based, so the information provided and visualized is based on the information gathered.

The associated performance metrics, such as response time, error rates, and other pertinent information, can be used to improve the application performance or fix performance related issues.

Integration

The Cloud Trace product is natively integrated with various GCP products, to provide an end-to-end view of the applications and infrastructure from products like Compute Engine, Cloud Functions, App Engine, Kubernetes Engine, Cloud Storage, and others.

Annotations and Attributes

Developers can insert custom annotations and attributes in the application to enrich trace data. These markers provide additional information that can help developers troubleshoot more quickly and more effectively. Examples include user IDs, geographical locations, and custom context information. Cloud Trace can read the metadata and visualize the trace on the Trace Viewer along with the annotations and attributes.

Cloud Profiler

Another product that can improve application performance is the Cloud Profiler. It is a great tool for dealing with poor coding, which has the potential to increase latency and the cost of applications.

The product helps developers by continuously analyzing real-time performance of the CPU and other aspects of the application. It enables continuous profiling of applications running in production environments, capturing detailed information about function execution, CPU use, memory allocation, and other performance-related metrics. The product basically helps identify performance bottlenecks in the applications by presenting the call hierarchy and resource consumption in an interactive manner. This helps developers understand the latencies and performance measures of the resources in the path.

With the ability to profile data and conduct further analysis, developers can optimize their code, improve application performance, and enhance the overall efficiency of their applications.

Some of its key features are covered in the following subsections.

Continuous Profiling

Cloud Profiler captures of observability data through automatic instrumentation. It creates this observability data from applications written in various languages, including Java, Python, Node.js, Go, and Ruby. This can be done either with minimal or no manual intervention.

The agent in the profile can automatically instrument applications without requiring code modifications. And the profiling is designed to have minimal impact on application performance, allowing continuous profiling in production environments without significant resource overhead.

Detailed Profiling

If you are a fan of psychological thrillers, you have seen FBI profilers determine criminal characteristics based on their antecedents. When more data is available to these investigators, they can create more accurate profiles, which will lead to the identification and capture of criminals.

Likewise with Cloud Profiler, the level and depth of details that can be expected is quite ingrained and the details go into the depth of functions, allowing developers to determine which functions consume the most resources. Cloud Profiler also provides insight into CPU use and pinpoints the functions that contribute to the CPU usage numbers. The memory allocation patterns are also included in the profiling data, enabling developers to optimize memory usage.

Integration

Cloud Profiler is natively integrated with various GCP products, which provides an end-to-end view of application performance from products like Compute Engine, Cloud Functions, App Engine, Kubernetes Engine, Cloud Storage, and others.

Its ability to integrate with other GCP observability tools provides a holistic approach to application performance monitoring. The obtained profiling data can further be correlated/triangulated with logs and monitoring data from Cloud Logging and Cloud Monitoring for a more comprehensive understanding of application behavior.

Summary

Development and operations are two different beasts. While development focuses on rapid development and introduction of new features, operations is about continuity of services and stability. To this end, the DevOps and SRE methodologies are framed to integrate the development side of the organization with operations. The move is to bring together the best practices from both sides and to foster an environment of collaboration, cost savings, and increased productivity.

The SRE methodology plays a significant role in providing guidance to monitoring and operational activities. It works on the pillars of monitoring the critical aspects of an application/service, including the best practices of incident management, releasing changes gradually to production, and automating whatever is possible.

To support monitoring and operations, GCP has a fleet of products that includes Cloud Monitoring, Cloud Logging, and Error Reporting for running operations, and Cloud Trace and Cloud Profiler for managing application performance.

Index

A

Accountability, 42, 279, 280, 286–288

Advanced Research Projects Agency Network (ARPANET), 7

Agile
and DevOps, 326
processes, 324
team members, 324

AI Platform, 95, 264, 267, 276

Amazon S3, 235

Amazon Web Services (AWS), 9, 18, 19, 23, 198

Anthos
AWS and Azure Kubernetes installations, 126
Cloud Services Platform, 122
clusters creation, 125
container orchestration, 122
enterprises, 123
features, 123, 124
GCP, 125
GKE installation/ configuration, 126
Google, 122
Kubernetes installations, 127
organizations, 122

API-first design, 180, 194

Apigee
Google Cloud Platform, 195
key features, 196–198
Sonoa Systems, 195

App Engine, 20, 145, 338, 340, 343, 345

Application layer, 11

Application modernization, 79, 81, 173
APIs role, 194, 195
benefits, 183–184
business alignment, 182
cloud-native architecture, 180, 181
definition, 179
five Rs, 185
rebuild, 187
refactor, 185, 186
replatforming, 186
retain, 187
retire, 187, 188
leave legacy applications behind, 174–177
modernization program, 179
patterns
brownfield modernization, 192

© Abhinav Krishna Kaiser 2024
A. K. Kaiser, *Become GCP Cloud Digital Leader Certified in 7 Days*,
https://doi.org/10.1007/979-8-8688-0438-0

E

F

GPSR Compliance
The European Union's (EU) General Product Safety Regulation (GPSR) is a set
of rules that requires consumer products to be safe and our obligations to
ensure this.

If you have any concerns about our products, you can contact us on

ProductSafety@springernature.com

In case Publisher is established outside the EU, the EU authorized
representative is:

Springer Nature Customer Service Center GmbH
Europaplatz 3
69115 Heidelberg, Germany